Data Lakes

D1127646

for
dummies®
A Wiley Brand

Data Lakes

by Alan Simon

A Wiley Brand

Data Lakes For Dummies®

Published by: **John Wiley & Sons, Inc.**, 111 River Street, Hoboken, NJ 07030-5774, www.wiley.com

Copyright © 2021 by John Wiley & Sons, Inc., Hoboken, New Jersey

Published simultaneously in Canada

For general information on our other products and services, please contact our Customer Care Department within the U.S. at 877-762-2974, outside the U.S. at 317-572-3993, or fax 317-572-4002. For technical support, please visit https://hub.wiley.com/community/support/dummies.

Wiley publishes in a variety of print and electronic formats and by print-on-demand. Some material included with standard print versions of this book may not be included in e-books or in print-on-demand. If this book refers to media such as a CD or DVD that is not included in the version you purchased, you may download this material at http://booksupport.wiley.com. For more information about Wiley products, visit www.wiley.com.

Library of Congress Control Number: 2021939570

ISBN 978-1-119-78616-0 (pbk); ISBN 978-1-119-78617-7 (ebk); ISBN 978-1-119-78618-4 (ebk)

Manufactured in the United States of America

SKY10027491 061121

Contents at a Glance

Table of Contents

Introduction

In December 1995, I wrote an article for *Database Programming & Design* magazine entitled "I Want a Data Warehouse, So What Is It Again?" A few months later, I began writing *Data Warehousing For Dummies* (Wiley), building on the article's content to help readers make sense of first-generation data warehousing.

Fast-forward a quarter of a century, and I could very easily write an article entitled "I Want a Data Lake, So What Is It Again?" This time, I'm cutting right to the chase with *Data Lakes For Dummies*. To quote a famous former baseball player named Yogi Berra, it's déjà vu all over again!

Nearly every large and upper-midsize company and governmental agency is building a data lake or at least has an initiative on the drawing board. That's the good news.

The not-so-good news, though, is that you'll find a disturbing lack of agreement about data lake architecture, best practices for data lake development, data lake internal data flows, even what a data lake actually *is!* In fact, many first-generation data lakes have fallen short of original expectations and need to be rearchitected and rebuilt.

As with data warehousing in the mid-'90s, the data lake concept today is still a relatively new one. Consequently, almost everything about data lakes — from its very definition to alternatives for integration with or migration from existing data warehouses — is still very much a moving target. Software product vendors, cloud service providers, consulting firms, industry analysts, and academics often have varying — and sometimes conflicting — perspectives on data lakes. So, how do you navigate your way across a data lake when the waters are especially choppy and you're being tossed from side to side?

That's where *Data Lakes For Dummies* comes in.

About This Book

Data Lakes For Dummies helps you make sense of the ABCs — acronym anarchy, buzzword bingo, and consulting confusion — of today's and tomorrow's data lakes.

This book is not only a tutorial about data lakes; it also serves as a reference that you may find yourself consulting on a regular basis. So, you don't need to memorize large blocks of content (there's no final exam!) because you can always go back to take a second or third or fourth look at any particular point during your own data lake efforts.

Right from the start, you find out what your organization should expect from all the time, effort, and money you'll put into your data lake initiative, as well as see what challenges are lurking. You'll dig deep into data lake architecture and leading cloud platforms and get your arms around the big picture of how all the pieces fit together.

One of the disadvantages of being an early adopter of any new technology is that you sometimes make mistakes or at least have a few false starts. Plenty of early data lake efforts have turned into more of a data dump, with tons of data that just isn't very accessible or well organized. If you find yourself in this situation, fear not: You'll see how to turn that data dump into the data lake you originally envisioned.

I don't use many special conventions in this book, but you should be aware that sidebars (the gray boxes you see throughout the book) and anything marked with the Technical Stuff icon are all skippable. So, if you're short on time, you can pass over these pieces without losing anything essential. On the other hand, if you have the time, you're sure to find fascinating information here!

Within this book, you may note that some web addresses break across two lines of text. If you're reading this book in print and want to visit one of these web pages, simply key in the web address exactly as it's noted in the text, pretending as though the line break doesn't exist. If you're reading this as an e-book, you've got it easy — just click the web address to be taken directly to the web page.

Foolish Assumptions

The most relevant assumption I've made is that if you're reading this book, you either are or will soon be working on a data lake initiative.

Maybe you're a data strategist and architect, and what's most important to you is sifting through mountains of sometimes conflicting — and often incomplete — information about data lakes. Your organization already makes use of earlier-generation data warehouses and data marts, and now it's time to take that all-important next step to a data lake. If that's the case, you're definitely in the right place.

If you're a developer or data architect who is working on a small subset of the overall data lake, your primary focus is how a particular software package or service works. Still, you're curious about where your daily work fits into your organization's overall data lake efforts. That's where this book comes in: to provide context and that "aha!" factor to the big picture that surrounds your day-to-day tasks.

Or maybe you're on the business and operational side of a company or governmental agency, working side by side with the technology team as they work to build an enterprise-scale data environment that will finally support the entire spectrum of your organization's analytical needs. You don't necessarily need to know too much about the techie side of data lakes, but you absolutely care about building an environment that meets today's and tomorrow's needs for data-driven insights.

The common thread is that data lakes are part of your organization's present and future, and you're seeking an unvarnished, hype-free, grounded-in-reality view of data lakes today and where they're headed.

In any event, you don't need to be a technical whiz with databases, programming languages such as Python, or specific cloud platforms such as Amazon Web Services (AWS) or Microsoft Azure. I cover many different technical topics in this book, but you'll find clear explanations and diagrams that don't presume any prerequisite knowledge on your part.

Icons Used in This Book

As you read this book, you encounter icons in the margins that indicate material of particular interest. Here's what the icons mean:

TIP

These are the tricks of the data lake trade. You can save yourself a great deal of time and avoid more than a few false starts by following specific tips collected from the best practices (and learned from painful experiences) of those who preceded you on the path to the data lake.

WARNING

Data lakes are often filled with dangerous icebergs. (Okay, bad analogy, but you hopefully get the idea.) When you're working on your organization's data lake efforts, pay particular attention to situations that are called out with this icon.

TECHNICAL STUFF

If you're more interested in the conceptual and architectural aspects of data lakes than the nitty-gritty implementation details, you can skim or even skip material that is accompanied by this icon.

REMEMBER

Some points are so critically important that you'll be well served by committing them to memory. You'll even see some of these points repeated later in the book because they tie in with other material. This icon calls out this crucial content.

Beyond the Book

In addition to the material in the print or e-book you're reading right now, this product comes with a free Cheat Sheet for the three types of data for your data lake, four zones inside your data lake, five phases to building your data lake, and more. To access the Cheat Sheet, go to www.dummies.com and type **Data Lakes For Dummies Cheat Sheet** in the Search box.

Where to Go from Here

Now it's time to head off to the lake — the data lake, that is! If you're totally new to the subject, you don't want to skip the chapters in Part 1 because they'll provide the foundation for the rest of the book. If you already have some exposure to data lakes, I still recommend that you at least skim Part 1 to get a sense of how to get beyond all the hype, buzzwords, and generalities related to data lakes.

You can then read the book sequentially from front to back or jump around as needed. Whatever path works best for you is the one you should take.

1
Getting Started with Data Lakes

Chapter **1**

Jumping into the Data Lake

T he lake is the place to be this season — the data lake, that is!

Just like the newest and hottest vacation destination, everyone is booking reservations for a trip to the data lake. Unlike a vacation, though, you won't just be spending a long weekend or a week or even the entire summer at the data lake. If you and your work colleagues do a good job, your data lake will be your go-to place for a whole *decade* or even longer.

What Is a Data Lake?

Ask a friend this question: "What's a lake?" Your friend thinks for a moment, and then gives you this answer: "Well, it's a big hole in the ground that's filled with water."

Technically, your friend is correct, but that answer also is far from detailed enough to really tell you what a lake actually is. You need more specifics, such as:

>> How big, dimension-wise (how long and how wide)

>> How deep that "big hole in the ground" goes

>> How much variability there is from one lake to another in terms of those length, width, and depth dimensions (the Great Lakes, anyone?)

>> How much water you'll find in the lake and how much that amount of water may vary among different lakes

>> Whether a lake contains freshwater or saltwater

Some follow-up questions may pop into your mind as well:

>> A pond is also a big hole in the ground that's filled with water, so is a lake the same as a pond?

>> What distinguishes a lake from an ocean or a sea?

>> Can a lake be physically connected to another lake?

>> Can the dividing line between two states or two countries be in the middle of a lake?

>> If a lake is empty, is it still considered a lake?

>> If one lake leaves Chicago, heading east and travels at 100 miles per hour, and another lake heads west from New York . . . oh wait, wrong kind of word problem, never mind. . . .

So many missing pieces of the puzzle, all arising from one simple question!

You'll find the exact same situation if you ask someone this question: "What's a data lake?" In fact, go ahead and ask your favorite search engine that question. You'll find dozens of high-level definitions that will almost certainly spur plenty of follow-up questions as you try to get your arms around the idea of a data lake.

TIP

Here's a better idea: Instead of filtering through all that varying — and even conflicting — terminology and then trying to consolidate all of it into a single comprehensive definition, just think of a data lake as the following:

A solidly architected, logically centralized, highly scalable environment filled with different types of analytic data that are sourced from both inside and outside your enterprise with varying latency, and which will be the primary go-to destination for your organization's data-driven insights

Wow, that's a mouthful! No worries: Just as if you were eating a gourmet fireside meal while camping at your favorite lake, you can break up that definition into bite-size pieces.

Rock-solid water

A data lake should remain viable and useful for a long time after it becomes operational. Also, you'll be continually expanding and enhancing your data lake with new types and forms of data, new underlying technologies, and support for new analytical uses.

REMEMBER

Building a data lake is more than just loading massive amounts of data into some storage location.

To support this near-constant expansion and growth, you need to ensure that your data lake is well architected and solidly engineered, which means that the data lake

>> Enforces standards and best practices for data ingestion, data storage, data transmission, and interchange among its components and data delivery to end users

>> Minimizes workarounds and temporary interfaces that have a tendency to stick around longer than planned and weaken your overall environment

>> Continues to meet your predetermined metrics and thresholds for overall technical performance, such as data loading and interchange, as well as user response time

Think about a resort that builds docks, a couple of lakeside restaurants, and other structures at various locations alongside a large lake. You wouldn't just hand out lumber, hammers, and nails to a bunch of visitors and tell them to start building without detailed blueprints and engineering diagrams. The same is true with a data lake. From the first piece of data that arrives, you need as solid a foundation as possible to help keep your data lake viable for a long time.

A really great lake

You'll come across definitions and descriptions that tell you a data lake is a centralized store of data, but that definition is only partially correct.

A data lake is *logically* centralized. You can certainly think of a data lake as a single place for your data, instead of having your data scattered among different databases. But in reality, even though your data lake is logically centralized, its data is *physically* decentralized and distributed among many different underlying servers.

TECHNICAL STUFF

The data services that you use for your data lake, such as the Amazon Simple Storage Service (S3), the Microsoft Azure Data Lake Storage (ADLS), or the Hadoop Distributed File System (HDFS) manage the distribution of data among potentially numerous servers where your data is actually stored. These services hide the physical distribution from almost everyone other than those who need to manage the data at the server storage level. Instead, they present the data as being logically part of a single data lake. Figure 1-1 illustrates how logical centralization accompanies physical decentralization.

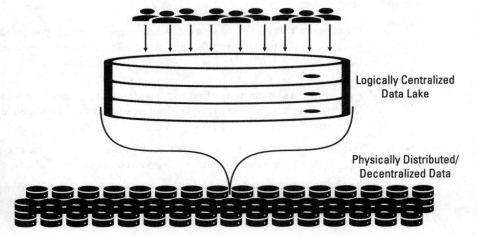

Logically Centralized Data Lake

Physically Distributed/ Decentralized Data

FIGURE 1-1: A logically centralized data lake with underlying physical decentralization.

Expanding the data lake

How big can your data lake get? To quote the old saying (and to answer a question with a question), how many angels can dance on the head of a pin?

Scalability is best thought of as "the ability to expand capacity, workload, and missions without having to go back to the drawing board and start all over." Your data lake will almost always be a cloud-based solution (see Figure 1-2). Cloud-based platforms give you, in theory, infinite scalability for your data lake. New servers and storage devices (discs, solid state devices, and so on) can be incorporated into your data lake on demand, and the software services manage and control these new resources along with those that you're already using. Your data lake contents can then expand from hundreds of terabytes to petabytes, and then to exabytes, and then zettabytes, and even into the ginormousbyte range. (Just kidding about that last one.)

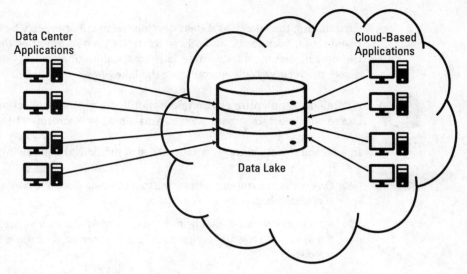

FIGURE 1-2:
Cloud-based data
lake solutions.

Data Center Applications

Cloud-Based Applications

Data Lake

TIP

Cloud providers give you pricing for data storage and access that increases as your needs grow or decreases if you cut back on your functionality. Basically, your data lake will be priced on a pay-as-you-go basis.

Some of the very first data lakes that were built in the Hadoop environment may reside in your corporate data center and be categorized as *on-prem* (short for *on-premises,* meaning "on your premises") solutions. But most of today's data lakes are built in the Amazon Web Services (AWS) or Microsoft Azure cloud environments. Given the ever-increasing popularity of cloud computing, it's highly unlikely that this trend of cloud-based data lakes will reverse for a long time, if ever.

As long as Amazon, Microsoft, and other cloud platform providers can keep expanding their existing data centers and building new ones, as well as enhancing the capabilities of their data management services, then your data lake should be able to avoid scalability issues.

TECHNICAL STUFF

A multiple-component data lake architecture (see Chapter 4) further helps overcome performance and capacity constraints as your data lake grows in size and complexity, providing even greater scalability.

More than just the water

Think of a data lake as being closer to a lake resort rather than just the lake — the body of water — in its natural state. If you were a real estate developer, you might buy the property that includes the lake itself, along with plenty of acreage surrounding the lake. You'd then develop the overall property by building cabins, restaurants, boat docks, and other facilities. The lake might be the centerpiece of the overall resort, but its value is dramatically enhanced by all the additional assets that you've built surrounding the lake.

REMEMBER

A data lake is an entire environment, not just a gigantic collection of data that is stored within a data service such as Amazon S3 or Microsoft ADLS.

In addition to data storage, a data lake also includes the following:

» One or (usually) more mechanisms to move data from one part of the data lake to another.

» A catalog or directory that helps keep track of what data is where, as well as the associated rules that apply to different groups of data; this is known as *metadata.*

» Capabilities that help unify meanings and business rules for key data subjects that may come into the data lake from different applications and systems; this is known as *master data management.*

» Monitoring services to track data quality and accuracy, response time when users access data, billing services to charge different organizations for their usage of the data lake, and plenty more.

Different types of data

If your data lake had a motto, it might be "All data are created equal."

In a data lake, data is data is data. In other words, you don't need to make special accommodations for more complex types of data than you would for simpler forms of data.

Your data lake will contain structured data, unstructured data, and semi-structured data (see Figure 1-3). The following sections cover these types of data in more detail.

Structured data: Staying in your own lane

You're probably most familiar with *structured data,* which is made up of numbers, shorter-length character strings, and dates. Traditionally, most of the applications you've worked with have been based on structured data. Structured data is commonly stored in a relational database such as Microsoft SQL Server, MySQL, or Oracle Database.

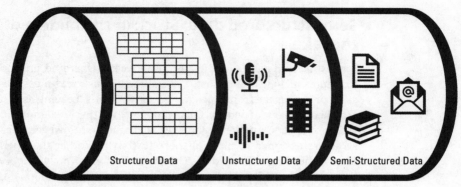

FIGURE 1-3:
Different types
of data in your
data lake.

In a database, you define columns (basically, fields) for each of your pieces of structured data, and each column is rigidly and precisely defined with the following:

>> **A data type,** such as INTEGER, DECIMAL, CHARACTER, DATE, DATETIME, or something similar

>> **The size of the field,** either explicitly declared (for example, how many characters a CHARACTER column will contain) or implicitly declared (the system-defined maximum number for an INTEGER or how a DATE column is structured)

>> **Any specific rules that apply to a data column or field,** such as the permissible range of values (for example, a customer's age must be between 18 and 130) or a list of allowable values (for example, an employee's current status can only be FULL-TIME, PART-TIME, TERMINATED, or RETIRED)

>> **Any additional constraints,** such as primary and foreign key designations, or *referential integrity* (rules that specify consistency for certain columns across multiple database tables)

Unstructured data: A picture may be worth ten million words

Unstructured data is, by definition, data that lacks a formally defined structure. Images (such as JPEGs), audio (such as MP3s), and videos (such as MP4s or MOVs) are common forms of unstructured data.

Semi-structured data: Stuck in the middle of the lake

Semi-structured data sort of falls in between structured and unstructured data. Examples include a blog post, a social media post, text messages, an email message, or a message from Slack or Microsoft Teams. Leaving aside any embedded or attached images or videos for a moment, all these examples consist of a long string of letters, numbers, and special characters. However, there's no particular structure assigned to most of these text strings other than perhaps a couple of lines of heading information. The body of an email may be very short — only a line or two — while another email can go on for many long paragraphs.

In your data lake, you need to have all these types of data sitting side by side. Why? Because you'll be running analytics against the data lake that may need more than one form of data. For example, you receive and then analyze a detailed report of sales by department in a large department store during the past month.

Then, after noticing a few anomalies in the sales numbers, you pull up in-store surveillance video to analyze traffic versus sales to better understand how many customers may be looking at merchandise but deciding not to make a purchase. You can even combine structured data from scanners with your unstructured video data as part of your analysis.

If you had to go to different data storage environments for your sales results (structured data) and then the video surveillance (unstructured data), your overall analysis is dramatically slowed down, especially if you need to integrate and cross-reference different types of data. With a data lake, all this data is sitting side by side, ready to be delivered for analysis and decision-making.

TECHNICAL STUFF

In their earliest days, relational databases only stored structured data. Later, they were extended with capabilities to store structured and unstructured data. Binary large objects (BLOBs) were a common way to store images and even video in a relational database. However, even an *object-extended* relational database doesn't make a good platform for a data lake when compared with modern data services such as Amazon S3 or Microsoft ADLS.

Different water, different data

A common misconception is that you store "all your data" in your data lake. Actually, you store all or most of your *analytic* data in a data lake. Analytic data is, as you may suspect from the name, data that you're using for analytics. In contrast, you use *operational* data to run your business.

What's the difference? From one perspective, operational and analytic data are one and the same. Suppose you work for a large retailer. A customer comes into one of your stores and makes some purchases. Another customer goes onto your company's website and buys some items there. The records of those sales — which customers made the purchases, which products they bought, how many of each product, the dates of the sales, whether the sales were online or in a store, and so on — are all stored away as official records of those transactions, which are necessary for running your company's operations.

But you also want to analyze that data, right? You want to understand which products are selling the best and where. You want to understand which customers are spending the most. You have dozens or even hundreds of questions you want to ask about your customers and their purchasing activity.

REMEMBER

Here's the catch: You need to make copies of your operational data for the deep analysis that you need to undertake; and the copies of that operational data are what goes into the data lake (see Figure 1-4).

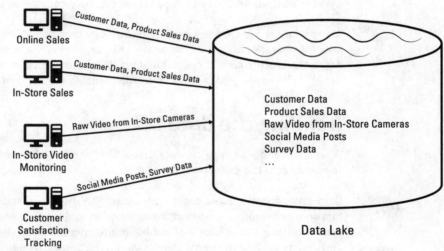

FIGURE 1-4:
Source applications feeding data into your data lake.

Wait a minute! Why in the world do you need to copy data into your data lake? Why can't you just analyze the data right where it is, in the source applications and their databases?

Data lakes, at least as you need to build them today and for the foreseeable future, are a continuation of the same model that has been used for data warehousing since the early 1990s. For many technical reasons related to performance, deep analysis involving large data volumes and significant cross-referencing directly in your source applications isn't a workable solution for the bulk of your analytics.

Consequently, you need to make copies of the operational data that you want for analytical purposes and store that data in your data lake. Think of the data inside your data lake as (in used-car terminology) previously owned data that has been refurbished and is now ready for a brand-new owner.

But if you can't adequately do complex analytics directly from source applications and their databases, what about this idea: Run your applications off your data lake instead! This way, you can avoid having to copy your data, right? Unfortunately, that idea won't work, at least with today's technology.

TECHNICAL STUFF

Operational applications almost always use a relational database, which manages *concurrency control* among their users and applications. In simple terms, hundreds or even thousands of users can add new data and make changes to a relational database without interfering with each other's work and corrupting the database. A data lake, however, is built on storage technology that is optimized for retrieving data for analysis and doesn't support concurrency control for update operations.

Many vendors are working on new technology that will allow you to build a data lake for operational, as well as analytical purposes. This technology is still a bit down the road from full operational viability. For the time being, you'll build a data lake by copying data from many different source applications.

Refilling the data lake

What exactly does "copying data" look like, and how frequently do you need to copy data into the data lake?

REMEMBER

Data lakes mostly use a technique called ELT, which stands for either *extract, transform, and load* or *extraction, transformation, and loading.* With ELT, you "blast" your data into a data lake without having to spend a great deal of time profiling and understanding the particulars of your data. You extract data (the *E* part of *ELT*) from its original home in a source application, and then, after that data has been transmitted to the data lake, you load the data (the *L*) into its initial storage location. Eventually, when it's time for you to use the data for analytical purposes, you'll need to transform the data (the *T*) into whatever format is needed for a specific type of analysis.

TECHNICAL STUFF

For data warehousing — the predecessor to data lakes that you're almost certainly still also using — data is copied from source applications to the data warehouse using a technique called ETL, rather than ELT. With ETL, you need to thoroughly understand the particulars of your data on its way into the data warehouse, which requires the transformation *(T)* to occur before the data is loaded *(L)* into its usable form.

With ELT, you can control the *latency,* or "freshness," of data that is brought into the data lake. Some data needed for critical, real-time analysis can be *streamed* into the data lake, which means that a copy is sent to the data lake immediately after data is created or updated within a source application. (This is referred to as a *low-latency data feed.*) You essentially push data into your data lake piece by piece immediately upon the creation of that data.

Other data may be less time-critical and can be "batched up" in a source application and then periodically transmitted in bulk to the data lake.

You can specify the latency requirements for every single data feed from every single source application.

REMEMBER

The ELT model also allows you to identify a new source of data for your data lake and then very quickly bring in the data that you need. You don't need to spend days or weeks dissecting the ins and outs of the new data source to understand its structure and business rules. You "blast" the data into your data lake in the natural form of the data: database tables, MP4 files, or however the data is stored. Then, when it's time to use that data for analysis, you can proceed to dig into the particulars and get the data ready for reports, machine learning, or however you're going to be using and analyzing the data.

Everyone visits the data lake

Take a look around your organization today. Chances are, you have dozens or even hundreds of different places to go for reports and analytics. At one time, your company probably had the idea of building an *enterprise data warehouse* that would provide data for almost all the analytical needs across the entire company. Alas, for many reasons, you instead wound up with numerous *data marts* and other environments, very few of which work together. Even enterprise data warehouses are often accompanied by an entire portfolio of data marts in the typical organization.

Great news! The data lake will finally be that one-stop shopping place for the data to meet almost all the analytical needs across your entire enterprise.

Enterprise-scale data warehousing fell short for many different reasons, including the underlying technology platforms. Data lakes overcome those shortfalls and provide the foundation for an entirely new generation of integrated, enterprise-wide analytics.

WARNING

Even with a data lake, you'll almost certainly still have other data environments outside the data lake that support analytics. Your data lake objective should be to satisfy *almost* all your organization's analytical needs and be the go-to place for data. If a few other environments pop up here and there, that's okay. Just be careful about the overall proliferation of systems outside your data lake; otherwise, you'll wind up right back in the same highly fragmented data mess that you have today before beginning work on your data lake.

The Data Lake Olympics

Suppose you head off for a weeklong vacation to your favorite lake resort. The people who run the resort have divided the lake into different zones, each for a different recreational purpose. One zone is set aside for water-skiing; a second zone is for speedboats, but no water-skiing is permitted in that zone; a third zone is only for boats without motors; and a fourth zone allows only swimming but no water vessels at all.

The operators of the resort could've said, "What the heck, let's just have a free-for-all out on the lake and hope for the best." Instead, they wisely established different zones for different purposes, resulting in orderly, peaceful vacations (hopefully!) rather than chaos.

A data lake is also divided into different zones. The exact number of zones may vary from one organization's data lake to another's, but you'll always find at least three zones in use — bronze, silver, and gold — and sometimes a fourth zone, the sandbox.

Bronze, silver, and gold aren't "official" standardized names, but they are catchy and easy to remember. Other names that you may find are shown in Table 1-1.

TABLE 1-1

Data Lake Zones

Recommended Zone Name	Other Names
Bronze zone	Raw zone, landing zone
Silver zone	Cleansed zone, refined zone
Gold zone	Performance zone, curated zone, data model zone
Sandbox	Experimental zone, short-term analytics zone

All the data lake zones, including the sandbox, are discussed in more detail in Part 2, but the following sections provide a brief overview.

WARNING

The boundaries and borders between your data lake zones can be fluid (Fluid? Get it?), especially with streaming data, as I explain in Part 2.

The bronze zone

You load your data into the bronze zone when the data first enters the data lake. First, you extract the data from a source application (the *E* part of ELT), and then the data is transmitted into the bronze zone in raw form (thus, one of the alternative names for this zone). You don't correct any errors or otherwise transform or modify the data at all. The original operational data should look identical to the copy of that data now in the bronze zone.

TIP

Your catchphrase for loading data into the bronze zone is "the need for speed." You may be trickling one piece of data at a time or bulk-loading hundreds of gigabytes or even terabytes of data. Your objective is to transmit the data into the data lake environment as quickly as possible. You'll worry about checking out and refining that data later.

The silver zone

The silver zone consists of data that has been error-checked and cleansed but still remains in its original format. Data may be copied from a source application in JavaScript Object Notation (JSON) format and land in the bronze zone in raw form, looking exactly as the data was in the source system itself — errors and all.

You'll patch up any known errors, handle missing data, and otherwise cleanse the data. Then you'll store the cleansed data in the silver zone, still in JSON format.

REMEMBER

Not all data from your bronze zone will be cleansed and copied into your silver zone. The data lake model calls for loading massive amounts of data into the bronze zone without having to do upfront analysis to determine which data is definitely or likely needed for analysis. When you decide what data you need, you do the necessary data cleansing and move only the cleansed data into the silver zone.

The gold zone

The gold zone is the final home for your most valuable analytical data. You'll *curate* data coming from the silver zone, meaning that you'll group and restructure data into "packages" dedicated to your organization's high-value analytical needs.

LINKING THE DATA LAKE ZONES TOGETHER

The following figure shows the progressive pipelines of data among the various zones, including the sandbox. Notice how not every piece or group of data is cleansed and then sent from the bronze zone to the silver zone. You'll spend time refurbishing, refining, and transmitting data to the silver zone that you definitely or likely need for analytics.

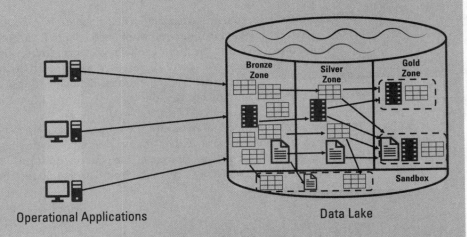

Operational Applications   Data Lake

Likewise, select data sets are sent from the silver zone to the gold zone. Remember that another name for the gold zone is the curated zone, meaning that you've especially selected certain data to be consolidated and then placed in "packages" within the gold zone.

You might transmit raw, uncleansed data from the bronze zone into the sandbox along with data from the silver zone, depending on the specifics of your experimental or short-term analytical needs.

TECHNICAL STUFF

You will almost certainly replicate data across the various gold zone packages, but that's not a problem at all. As long as you carefully control the data flows and the replicated data, you're unlikely to run into problems with uncontrolled data proliferation.

The sandbox

Your bronze, silver, and gold zones combine to form a *data pipeline*. In your gold zone, you create data packages that are closely aligned with high-value, pervasive analytical needs and that will provide data-driven insights to your organization for a long time.

But what about shorter-term analytical needs or experiments that you want to run with your data? You may be building new machine learning models to predict customer behavior, optimize your supply chain, or determine new treatment plans for a hospital system's patients. You need to experiment with different machine learning techniques, and you need actual data for your work.

Head over to the sandbox and start playing. You'll load whatever data you need for your short-term or experimental work and do your thing. The data lake isolates the sandbox from the data pipeline, so you can do whatever you need without interfering with your organization's primary analytical work.

Data Lakes and Big Data

Turn the clock back to the early 2010s when big data burst onto the scene. Almost every organization was exploring how this new generation of data management technology can overcome many of the barriers and constraints of relational databases, particularly for analytical storage.

Big data promised — and delivered — significantly greater capacity than was possible with relational databases. With big data, you can store unstructured and semi-structured data alongside your structured data. You can also bring new data into a big data environment with lower latency than with relational databases.

Wait a minute! That sounds just like the description of a data lake! So, is a data lake just another name for big data?

Well, sort of . . . possibly . . . or maybe not. . . .

The best way to think of the two disciplines in relation to one another is as follows:

>> Big data is the underlying core technology used to build a data lake.

>> A data lake is an environment that includes big data but also potentially other data management technologies along with services for data transmission and data governance.

THE THREE (OR FOUR OR FIVE OR MORE) VS OF BIG DATA AND DATA LAKES

Quick quiz: Name all the Vs of big data and data lakes. You can start with the original three: volume, variety, and velocity. But you'll also find blog posts and online articles that mention value, *veracity* (a formal term for accuracy), visualization, and many others. In fact, don't be surprised if one day you read an article or blog post that also includes Valentine's Day!

The original three Vs of big data came from a Gartner Group analyst named Doug Laney, way back in 2001. Volume, variety, and velocity were primarily aspirational characteristics of data environments, describing next-generational characteristics beyond what the relational databases of the time were capable of supporting.

Over the years, other industry analysts, bloggers, consultants, and product vendors added to the list with their own Vs. The difference between the original three Vs and those that followed, though, is that value, veracity, visualization, and others all apply to tried-and-true relational technology just as much as to big data.

Don't get confused trying to decide how many Vs apply to big data and to data lakes. Just focus on the original three — volume, variety, and velocity — as the must-have characteristics of your data lake.

WARNING

You'll find varying perspectives on the relationship between big data and data lakes, which certainly confuses the issue. Some technologists reverse the relationship between big data and data lakes; they consider a data lake to be the core technology and big data to be the overall environment. So, if you run across a blog post or another description that differs from the one I use, don't worry. As with almost everything about data lakes and much of the technology world, you'll find all sorts of opinions and perspectives, especially when you don't have any official standards to govern a discipline.

The Hadoop open source environment, particularly the HDFS, is one of the first and most popular examples of big data. Some of the earliest data lakes were built, or at least begun, using HDFS as the foundation.

TECHNICAL STUFF

For purposes of establishing a data lake foundation, Amazon's S3 and Microsoft's ADLS both qualify as big data. Why? Both S3 and ADLS support the three Vs of big data, which are as follows:

>> Storing extremely large *volumes* of data

>> Supporting a *variety* of data, including structured, unstructured, and semi-structured data

>> Allowing very high *velocity* for incoming data into the data lake rather than requiring or at least encouraging periodic batches of data

TIP

Think of big data as a core technology foundation that supports the three Vs of next-generation data management. Big data by itself, however, is just a platform. It's the natural body of water — the lake itself — at a popular lakeside resort. When you divide your big data into multiple zones, add capabilities to transmit data across those zones, and then govern the whole environment, you've built a data lake surrounding that big data foundation. You've done the analytical data equivalent of building the docks, the restaurants, and the boat slips surrounding the lake itself.

The Data Lake Water Gets Murky

In addition to data lakes, you may come across references to data ponds, data puddles, data rivers, data oceans, and data hot tubs. (Just kidding about the last one.) What's going on here?

WARNING

Your job when planning, architecting, building, and using a data lake is complicated by the fact that you don't have an official definition published by some sort of standards body, such as the American National Standards Institute (ANSI) or the International Organization for Standardization (ISO). That means that you or anyone else can define, use, and even publish your own terminology. You can call a smaller portion of a data lake a "data pond" if you want, or refer to a collection of data lakes as a "data ocean."

Don't panic! Of all the "data plus a body of water" terms you'll run across, *data lake* is by far the most commonly used. All the characteristics of a data lake — solid architecture, support for multiple forms of data, a support ecosystem surrounding the data — apply to what you can call a data pond or any other term.

If William Shakespeare were still around and plied his trade as an enterprise data architect rather than as a writer, he would put it this way: "A data lake by any other name would still be worth the time and effort to build."

BACK TO THE FUTURE WITH NAME CHANGES

In the early 1990s, data warehousing was the newest and most popular game in town for analytical data management. By the mid-'90s, the concept of a data warehouse was adapted to a *data mart* — essentially, a smaller-scale data warehouse. The original idea behind a data mart called for the data warehouse feeding a subset of its data into one or more data marts — sort of a "wholesaler-retailer" model.

The first generation of data warehouse projects, especially very large ones, was hallmarked by a high failure rate. By the late '90s, data warehouses were viewed as large, complex, and expensive efforts that were also very risky. A data mart, on the other hand, was smaller, less complex, and less expensive, and, thus, considered to be less risky.

The need for integrated analytical data was stronger than ever by the end of the '90s. But just try to get funding for a data warehousing project! Good luck!

Time for plan B.

Data warehouses went out of style for a while. Instead, data marts became the go-to solution for analytic data. No matter how big and complex an environment was, chances are, you'd refer to it as a data mart rather than a data warehouse. In fact, the idea of an *independent* data mart sprung up, and the original architecture for a data mart — receiving data from a data warehouse rather than directly from source systems — became known as a *dependent* data mart.

Fast-forward a couple of decades, and it's back to the future. First, big data sort of evolved into data lakes. Now you have analysts, consultants, and vendors complicating the picture with their own terminology. This won't be the last time you'll see shifting names and terminology in the world of analytic data, so stay tuned!

Chapter 2

Planning Your Day (and the Next Decade) at the Data Lake

Suppose that you and about 15 other family members or friends all head to your favorite lake for a weeklong summer vacation.

You love going to the lake because you jump into your sailboat every day and spend hours out on the water. Others in your group, though, have their own favorite pastimes. Some prefer a boat with a little more "oomph" and spend their days in speedboats, zooming up and down the length of the lake. Others prefer leisurely canoeing. Some are into waterskiing, so they take turns latching onto one of those speedboats and zipping along the water. Others in your group are into fishing, and that's how they spend most of their time at the lake. Still others aren't all that interested in even going out on the water at all — they plop down on the beach to read, soak up some rays, and even grab a snooze every afternoon.

A data lake is very much like that weeklong trip to your favorite lake. Because a data lake is an enterprise-scale effort, spanning numerous organizations and departments, as well as many different business functions, you and your coworkers will likely seek a variety of varying benefits and outcomes from all that hard work.

The best data lakes are those that satisfy the needs of a broad range of constituencies — basically, something for everyone to make the results well worth the effort.

Carpe Diem: Seizing the Day with Big Data

Maybe your organization has been dabbling in the world of big data for a while, going back to when Hadoop was one of the hottest new technologies. You've built some pretty nifty predictive analytics models, and now you're fairly adept at discovering important patterns buried in mountains of data.

So far, though, your AAA — adventures in advanced analytics — have been highly fragmented. In fact, your analytical data is all over the place. You don't have consistent approaches to cleansing and refining raw data to get the data ready for analytics; different groups do their own thing. It's like the Wild West out there!

The concept of a data lake helps you harness the power of big data technology to the benefit of your entire organization. By following emerging best practices, avoiding traps and pitfalls, and building a solidly architected data lake, you can seize the day and help take your organization to new heights when it comes to analytics and data-driven insights.

REMEMBER

You'll achieve *economies of scale* for the data side of analytics throughout your organization, which means that you'll get "more bang for your buck" when it comes to acquiring, consolidating, preparing, and storing your analytical data on behalf of your enterprise as a whole rather than repetitively doing so for numerous smaller groups.

Managing Equal Opportunity Data

Your data lake's big data foundation presents you with an opportunity that, not too long ago, was out of reach for most organizations. You can store, manage, and analyze all three types of data — structured, unstructured, and semi-structured — within a single environment, and without having to jump through hoops to do so!

Many of the business questions you ask of your data will only require structured data. Suppose you work in the supply chain organization within your company. You'll definitely want your data lake to provide insight into the following:

>> Who among your strategic suppliers has the best combination of on-time component production and also very low problem rates?

>> Which third-party logistics firms have the best — or worst — on-time shipping performance?

>> What's the percentage of product spoilage among all internal and third-party warehouses during the past six months?

Other critical business analytics may involve unstructured or semi-structured data. You'll want to know the following:

>> What percentage of tweets from your customers represent a positive sentiment about your product quality? Negative sentiment? What "hot spots" are showing up in blogs, tweets, and other social media posts, as well as YouTube videos, that can mean profitability and market share problems for you down the road?

>> Your reports show a dramatic increase in breakage in Warehouse #2. You have surveillance cameras in all your facilities. Is there anything that shows up on video that could indicate one or more root causes for this breakage that you can address through procedural changes?

REMEMBER

Your data lake gives you *one-stop shopping* for structured, unstructured, and semi-structured data in a logically centralized, cohesive environment.

Building Today's — and Tomorrow's — Enterprise Analytical Data Environment

Building an all-new analytical data environment around big data technology sounds like a great idea, right? You may be worried, though, that your organization can invest a ton of money over the next couple of years, only to find that your data lake is obsolete because of an entirely new generation of technology.

In other words, can your data lake be not just today's but also tomorrow's go-to platform for more and more analytical data and data-driven insights? Absolutely!

Constructing a bionic data environment

Maybe you've heard of a B-52. No, not a member of the American new wave music group (so don't start singing "Love Shack") but rather the U.S. Air Force plane.

The B-52 first became operational in 1952. The normal life span for an Air Force plane is around 28 years before it's shuffled off to retirement, which means that B-52s should've gone out of service around 1980. Instead, the B-52 will eventually be retired sometime in the 2050s. That's a hundred years — an entire century!

However, a B-52 today bears only a slight resemblance to one made in the '50s or '60s. Sure, if you were to put one of the original B-52s side by side with one of today's planes, the two aircraft would look nearly identical. But the engines, the avionics, the flight controls . . . pretty much every major subsystem has been significantly upgraded and replaced in each operational B-52 at least a couple times over the years.

Better yet, a B-52 isn't just some old plane that you may see flying at an airshow but that otherwise doesn't have much purpose due to the passage of time. Not only is the B-52 still a viable, operational plane, but its mission has continually expanded over the years thanks to new technologies and capabilities.

In fact, you can think of a B-52 as sort of a bionic airplane. Its components and subsystems have been — and will continue to be — swapped out and substantially upgraded on a regular basis, giving the plane a planned life span of almost *four times* the normal longevity of the typical Air Force plane. Talk about an awe-inspiring feat of engineering!

However, all those enhancements and modifications to the B-52 happened gradually over time, not all at once. Plus, the changes were all carefully planned and implemented with longevity and continued viability top of mind.

Your data lake should follow the same model: a "bionic" enterprise-scale analytical data environment that regularly incorporates new and improved technologies to replace older ones, as well as enhancing overall function. You almost certainly won't get an entire century's usage out of a data lake that you build today, but if you do a good job with your planning and implementation, 10 or even 20 years of value from your data lake is certainly achievable.

More important, your data lake won't be just another aging system hanging around long past when it should've been retired. You almost certainly have plenty of those antiquated systems stashed in your company's overall IT portfolio. That's why the B-52 is the perfect analogy for the data lake, with a "bionic" approach to regularly replacing major subsystems helping to keep your data lake viable for years to come.

Strengthening the analytics relationship between IT and the business

If a tree falls in a forest, but nobody is around to hear it fall, does it make a sound?

Or how about this one: If you build a system to support analytics across your organization and load it with tons of data, but nobody really uses it, does your organization really have analytical data?

Don't worry, you didn't go back in time to a college philosophy class — you won't be graded on your responses to either of these questions.

REMEMBER

You can think of a *data warehouse* as a direct ancestor of a data lake. Data warehousing came onto the scene around 1990, and it has been the primary go-to approach for enterprise analytics in the decades since.

Far too many of today's data warehouses are like that tree falling in a forest. The IT side of your company originally set out to build an enterprise-wide home for analytical data that will support reporting, business intelligence, data visualization, and other analytical needs from every corner of your organization.

Alas, that data warehouse, like so many others, came up short. Maybe the data warehouse doesn't contain certain sets of data that are needed for critical analytics. Perhaps the data warehouse contents aren't properly organized and structured and are difficult to access with the business intelligence tools available. Whatever the reason may be, your organization's business users finally said, "To heck with it!" and built their own smaller-scale *data marts* to satisfy their own departmental or functional analytical needs.

Along the way, a sense of distrust built up — at least when it came to analytics and data — between your IT organization and the business users who are supposed to be their customers. Not good!

The data lake presents your organization with an opportunity for a fresh start. You can apply many of the best practices and also the painful lessons from 30-plus years of data warehousing to your data lake efforts and avoid repeating the mistakes and shortcomings of the past. As your data lake gets built, no matter if you're on the IT side or the business side of your company, you can help rebuild that essential trust, especially when it comes to all-important analytics and the resulting data-driven insights.

Reducing Existing Stand-Alone Data Marts

You really can't argue with the original concept of an enterprise data warehouse! Figure 2-1 illustrates the basic idea of a single home for most or all of the data needed to support a broad range of analytics across the entire enterprise.

Sounds like a great idea, right?

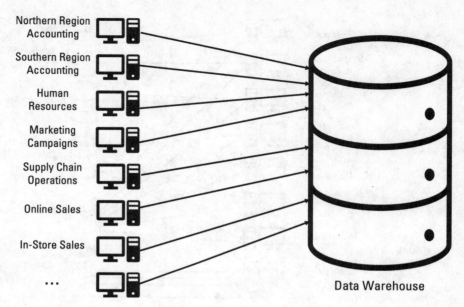

Northern Region
Accounting

Southern Region
Accounting

Human
Resources

Marketing
Campaigns

Supply Chain
Operations

Online Sales

In-Store Sales

...

Data Warehouse

FIGURE 2-1:
The vision of an
enterprise data
warehouse.

Dealing with the data fragmentation problem

A lofty vision is one thing; reality is often something else. Figure 2-2 illustrates how almost every organization's idea of centralized, enterprise-scale data warehousing eventually surrendered to a landscape littered with numerous stand-alone, nonintegrated data marts.

Okay, so maybe the idea of "Do your own thing, and build your own data mart" got out of control. Now that you can see what a mess that approach created, why not just retire those data marts and fold them into your enterprise data warehouse that's probably underutilized?

**TECHNICAL
STUFF**

A collection of independent data marts is almost always hampered by a lack of common master data (for example, to sales, a "customer" may be something different than a "customer" is to your marketing team), different software packages and technologies across the data marts, and other challenges. Taken together, these challenges make it almost impossible to consolidate separate, independent data marts back into a single data warehouse. Most organizations instead throw their hands up in the air and say that they're following a *federated data warehouse* approach. You "create" a federated data warehouse by simply declaring that some or all of your data marts are part of a "federation" that, when considered together, are sort of like a data warehouse. "Um . . . yeah, that's our story, and we're sticking to it. It's magic!" (Not really . . . and not all that valuable from an enterprise-wide perspective.)

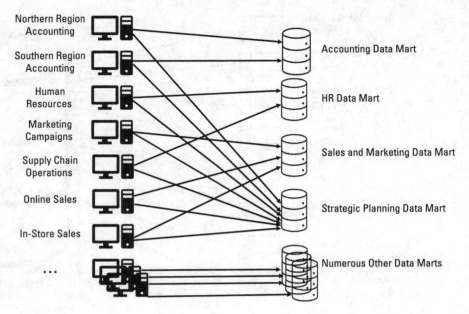

FIGURE 2-2: The reality of numerous stand-alone data marts.

Labels in figure (left to right):

Northern Region Accounting
Southern Region Accounting
Human Resources
Marketing Campaigns
Supply Chain Operations
Online Sales
In-Store Sales

Accounting Data Mart
HR Data Mart
Sales and Marketing Data Mart
Strategic Planning Data Mart
Numerous Other Data Marts

Decision point: Retire, isolate, or incorporate?

What should you do about your proliferation of data marts now that your organization is building a data lake? The short answer: Get rid of the data marts . . . or at least most of them!

You have three main options for how to deal with your proliferation of independent data marts as part of your data lake initiative:

>> Retire some or all of the data marts, and replace them with data lake functionality.

>> Isolate some of the data marts, and leave them in place alongside your new data lake.

>> Incorporate some of your data marts as components of your data lake.

Data mart retirement

If your existing data marts are creaking and groaning and are now coming up short even for the analytical needs of their respective users, here's a great idea: Get rid of them!

Figure 2-3 shows how your new data lake gives you the perfect opportunity to not only get your data mart proliferation under control, but also upgrade your overall analytics.

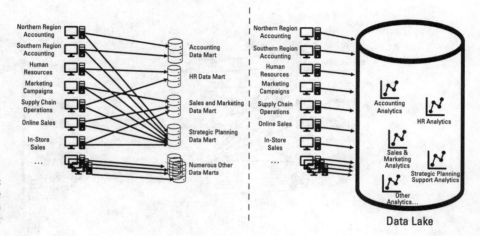

FIGURE 2-3:
Using a data lake to retire data marts.

TECHNICAL STUFF

Chances are, most of your data marts, especially those that have been around for a while, support *descriptive analytics* (basic business intelligence functions such as drilling deeper into summarized data to gain additional insights from lower levels of your data). But what about advanced analytical needs such as machine learning or other data mining and artificial intelligence–enabled analytical needs? Probably not so much!

So, why keep those aging data marts around? Redirect the data feeds from your source systems into your new data lake, and rebuild your analytics for accounting, your human resources (HR) organization, sales and marketing, and other parts of your enterprise within the data lake environment.

Data mart isolation

What if one of your existing data marts is an absolute work of genius? Suppose that three or four years ago, your company built a data mart to support your annual strategic planning cycle. Your strategic planning data mart has data feeds from numerous applications and systems around your enterprise. Do you really want to reinvent the wheel just because you're now building a data lake?

Great news: You don't have to throw away your data mart baby along with the data lake water! (Okay, maybe not the best metaphor, but you get the idea.)

Figure 2-4 shows how you can leave that strategic planning data mart in place alongside the new data lake. You're essentially isolating that data mart from the new epicenter of your enterprise analytics. True, some data feeds will be duplicated between the strategic planning data mart and the data lake. But that's okay! And over time, maybe you'll decide to incorporate the strategic planning data mart into the data lake itself.

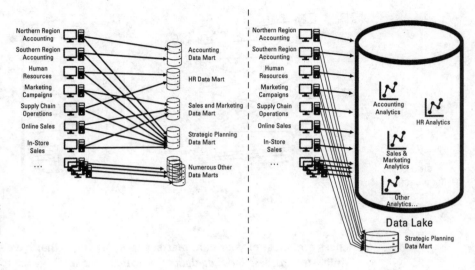

FIGURE 2-4:
Leaving a data mart intact and alongside your data lake.

Data mart incorporation

The primary difference between isolating an existing data mart (refer to Figure 2-4) and incorporating that data mart into the data lake (see Figure 2-5) is that you eliminate the duplicate data feeds between the two.

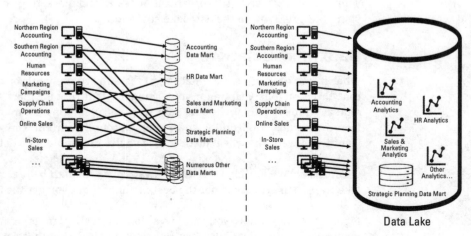

FIGURE 2-5:
Incorporating a data mart into your data lake.

Suppose your data feeds for your strategic planning data mart are exceptionally well architected. Why not move them over to bring data into the data lake? Chances are, other analytical needs for accounting, finance, HR, marketing, and other organizations and functions within your enterprise can also leverage that data. At the same time, all the great work that your organization did to consolidate and organize data for your annual strategic planning can become part of your overall data lake.

Eliminating Future Stand-Alone Data Marts

WARNING

Even after getting your data mart proliferation under control as part of your data lake efforts, beware: History can easily repeat itself!

Make no mistake about it: Just because you're now in the data lake era rather than the earlier data warehouse era, business organizations will still likely want to create their own smaller-scale data marts for their specific analytics needs.

Your data lake gives you a carrot-and-stick, one-two punch to help prevent the proliferation of future data marts.

First the stick, and then the carrot.

Establishing a blockade

Your company's top leadership needs to help you establish a blockade against new data marts springing into existence. Your chief information officer (CIO) needs to make this policy crystal clear, in concert with their counterparts on the business side: the chief operating officer (COO), chief financial officer (CFO), and others in your company's executive ranks.

TIP

Ideally, even your chief executive officer (CEO) should sign a declaration that another round of data mart proliferation won't be tolerated.

Should a "no proliferation" edict be written in stone? Probably not. Some departments within your company will inevitably come up with some unique, time-is-of-the-essence analytical need that is better met through a stand-alone data mart than through the data lake.

However, the proponents of a new data mart should be required to prove their case and have their data mart project approved as an exception to the "no proliferation" rule. They need to declare the following:

>> What the business imperative is for building a new stand-alone data mart (for example, to address some sort of business crisis or to take advantage of a market opportunity that must be addressed immediately)

>> Why their analytical needs can't be met using the data lake in the same time frame that it would take to build their new data mart

>> Whether their planned data mart will be used only for a short period of time and be retired or if it will subsequently be incorporated into the data lake

Providing a path of least resistance

Business users around your organization build new stand-alone data marts because that's what they've done for a long, long time. They realize that the best way to bring data-driven insights into the way they do business is to take charge of their own fate and build an end-to-end solution. Old habits are extremely difficult to break!

Beyond a blockade on new data mart development, your data lake can give these business users a path of least resistance. Make it easier for them to go to the data lake for the data they need instead of doing everything on their own.

Suppose that a new chief people officer (CPO) is hired to lead your company's HR organization. Jan, the new CPO, is a big believer in applying super-advanced analytics, such as machine learning and artificial intelligence, to numerous HR functions: employee evaluations, salary adjustments and promotions, succession planning, and more.

Jan appoints an analytics team within HR and tells them that, within the next three months, they need to have some initial machine learning models built in time for the semiannual employee evaluation cycle. Raul, the analytics teamleader, has been with your company for 15 years and has built several HR-specific data marts in the past for similar needs.

Raul assigns two of the team members, Julia and Dhiraj, to analyze the HR data in Workday (a cloud-based HR and financial management system) to figure out what data needs to be brought into the machine learning model. Raul also assigns another team member, Tamara, to start designing an Amazon Redshift database to store the HR data and support the machine learning algorithms.

Not so fast, Raul!

Raul submits his budget request for the new HR employee incentive evaluation and involvement operations (EIEIO) data mart and is surprised to learn that he needs to present his business case to the company's new data mart exception board. Raul starts preparing his PowerPoint slides, and comes across item number 2: "State why your analytical needs cannot be met through existing data lake content."

"Hmm . . . a data lake," Raul thinks. "I wonder if the data we need is already in there?"

Sure enough, Raul goes browsing through the data lake catalog and finds that the data lake already has a ton of HR data from Workday that is regularly refreshed. He asks Julia and Dhiraj to match up the work that they've done so far with what the data lake catalog shows. Within two hours, they report back with the fantastic news: "Everything we need is in the data lake already!"

A well-constructed data lake offers business users a path of least resistance when it comes to gathering the data they need for their analytical needs. Raul's team will still need to build the machine learning models to produce the analytics that Jan, your CPO, wants to apply to the next evaluation cycle. But they no longer need to proceed with analytics on a business-as-usual basis, constantly acquiring and storing the same data over and over in different data marts.

Over time, as familiarity with the data lake spreads throughout your organization, fewer unnecessary data mart requests such as Raul's will need to be redirected back to the data lake. Raul wasn't deliberately trying to do everything on his own; he just wasn't familiar enough with what the data lake provided, not only to HR but to your company as a whole.

Establishing a Migration Path for Your Data Warehouses

Data warehousing has been on the scene since around 1990, which means that thousands of enterprise-wide data warehouses have been built and deployed over the years. In fact, looking back at the B-52 analogy earlier in this chapter, you can think of a data warehouse as the equivalent of a propeller-driven airplane that preceded the jet aircraft era, which, of course, makes the data lake the equivalent of that technology-leaping jet.

TECHNICAL STUFF

Some ultramodern, large-scale enterprise data warehouses have been built in the past several years, using relatively new technologies such as the SAP HANA in-memory database management system. Many others, however, were built on older relational databases and are still chugging along. They still work okay, for the most part. But in this new era of data lakes, it's time to decide what to do about the old-timers.

Sending a faithful data warehouse off to a well-deserved retirement

If your data warehouse is really showing its age, your best bet is to hold a nice retirement party in the company cafeteria with cake and ice cream for everyone and with a few speeches about how wonderful the data warehouse has served the company's enterprise-wide reporting and business intelligence mission over the years. (Okay, you can probably skip the cake and ice cream, as well as the cafeteria party itself.)

Then you can do the same thing for your data warehouse that you do for any of your creaky, brittle data marts. Build a new set of data feeds from your source applications and systems into the data lake. Then within your data lake, rebuild the data models that your data warehouse used to support business intelligence and reporting alongside machine learning and other advanced analytics (see Figure 2-6).

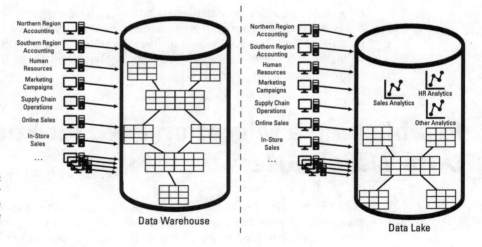

FIGURE 2-6: Migrating your data warehouse into your new data lake.

TECHNICAL STUFF

Your old data warehouse contents were likely stored in a dimensional model such as a *star schema* or a *snowflake schema*. Inside a data lake, the equivalent models might also be dimensional. Alternatively, you could be using a *columnar database* such as Amazon Redshift. You can still use a visualization tool such as Tableau or a classic business intelligence tool such as MicroStrategy, but your database design will differ from your old data warehouse.

Resettling a data warehouse into your data lake environment

Suppose you and your team actually did a fantastic job architecting and building your data warehouse. You did your work and deployed the data warehouse only a few years ago, using fairly modern technology. To put it simply, your data warehouse just isn't ready for retirement. But you still want to build a data lake to take advantage of modern big data technology. What should you do in this case?

Just as with a solidly built data mart, you can sort of "forklift" a well-architected data warehouse into your data lake environment. You'll still have to do some rewiring of data feeds, and you'll be adding complexity to your overall analytical data architecture. But there's no sense in exiling a solidly built data warehouse into oblivion if it can still deliver value for you for a while to come.

Aligning Data with Decision Making

REMEMBER

You don't set out to build a data lake just to stuff tons of data into a modern big data environment. You build a data lake to support analytics throughout your enterprise. And the reason for your organization's analytics is to deliver *data-driven insights*, with the emphasis on the term *data-driven*.

For better or for worse, the term *analytics* means different things to different people. As you set out to build your data lake, you need to understand what *analytics* means to your organization.

Deciding what your organization wants out of analytics

You should think of *analytics* as a continuum of questions that you ask about some particular function or business process within your organization, with the answers coming from your data:

>> What happened?

>> Why did it happen?

>> What's happening right now?

>> What's likely to happen?

>> What's something interesting and important out of this mountain of data?

>> What are our options?

>> What should we do?

REMEMBER

Your data lake needs to support the entire analytics continuum in all corners of your organization.

Suppose that Jan, your company's CPO, is incredibly pleased with the work that Raul's team did to have your data lake support machine learning models for the evaluation cycle. So, she asks Raul to expand the HR organization's usage of analytics that are enabled by the data lake. Raul sits down with his analysts, Julia and Dhiraj, to create a master list of analytical questions that should be considered for implementation.

Raul's team has the easiest time with "What happened?" types of questions, because these are what your company's data warehouse and data marts have been producing for years. Now, though, your data marts and data warehouse will either be retired or incorporated into the data lake environment, so your data lake can take over this mission and serve up the data to answer questions along the lines of:

>> Which employees have consistently been rated in the top quintile in each department during the past three years?

>> Which employees have received the largest percentage salary increases during all evaluation periods during the past five years?

>> How many new employees were hired in each of the past three years?

>> How many employees left during each of the past years? How many of those resigned? How many were involuntarily terminated? How many retired?

Because your company's executives are somewhat on the formal side, your list of "What happened?" questions will be categorized under the label *descriptive analytics*. In other words, your data lake will be producing analytics that describe something that happened in the past (which might be the very recent past, several years ago, or perhaps even farther back). But just like your existing data warehouse and data marts mostly do, your data lake will now be producing descriptive analytics.

You also need the data lake to help you dig into the reasons something happened. For example, your descriptive analytics tell you that the number of employees who voluntarily resigned from the company last year was 25 percent above the yearly average for the previous five years. Inquiring minds want to know why!

Diagnostic analytics help you dig into the "why" factor for what your descriptive analytics tell you, and — congratulations! — your data lake will take on another assignment. In this case, you can be sure that Jan, your CPO, will be digging for answers now that she's clued in to the increase in employee turnover.

Raul is well aware that, although insight into past results is an important part of your company's analytics continuum, Jan and the other executives — as well as many others at all levels of your organization — also need deep insights into what's happening right now. Before working in HR, Raul used to be in the supply chain organization. His specialty there was providing up-to-the-minute, near-real-time reports and visualizations for logistics and transportation throughout the entire supply chain.

This special variation of descriptive analytics — basically, factually describing what's happening right now — may have some applicability to HR, though probably less so than over in the supply chain organization. Still, Raul makes a note to dive into these types of questions.

Jan, Raul, Julia, Dhiraj, Tamara, and most everyone else in HR knows with absolute certainty that *predictive analytics* need to be a critical capability when the data lake functionality is built out. Even though predictive analytics aren't exactly a crystal ball with guaranteed predictions, the sophisticated models can ingest data and tell the HR team and others what's likely to happen. This way, the data lake can help provide insights such as the following:

>> Which employees are most at risk of resigning in the next year?

>> Which employees with less than three years of experience are most likely to become top performers in their next jobs?

>> Which employees with between 10 and 15 years of experience are most likely to underperform during the rest of this fiscal year?

>> Who are the top 50 nonmanagerial employees most likely to succeed as managers?

Predictive analytics generally falls under the category of *data mining.* Another form of data mining is digging into mountains of data, seeking interesting and important patterns and other insights that otherwise may remain hidden. *Discovery analytics* helps you mine your data to see the following:

>> Have any of your employees exhibited behavior that may indicate inappropriate or illegal activities, such as expense account fraud?

>> Is there anything going on in the company that can legally expose the company?

>> Overall, are employees happy working here?

Descriptive, diagnostic, predictive, and discovery analytics all help you gain valuable insights into different aspects of your organization, its performance, possible risks, and much more. However, you need more than insights! You need to drive those insights into decisions and actions.

Prescriptive analytics is a relative newcomer into the overall analytics continuum. "Wait a minute!" you may be thinking. "I've been making decisions and taking actions for a long time!" The "secret sauce" of prescriptive analytics, however, is making those decisions and taking those actions with a healthy assist from your organization's data being fed into increasingly sophisticated analytics. And yes, you guessed it: Your data lake will play a starring role in driving prescriptive analytics. So, your data lake will help you with the following scenarios:

>> Based on market forecasts and the overall economy, you need to cut approximately 10 percent of your headcount. What are your options? How do you get the work done? Can you shift some of the work to lower-cost contractors? Should you try a voluntary early retirement program to reduce the number of involuntary terminations? Name four or five scenarios with all the data and all the trimmings!

>> Then, out of those four or five scenarios, which one is "best" and why? Are there any downside surprise risks you should be aware of?

Table 2-1 shows you the relationship between the easy-to-understand questions and the more formal names you'll use as you plan your data lake.

TABLE 2-1 ## Matching Analytics and Business Questions

Question	Type of Analytics
What happened?	Descriptive analytics
Why did it happen?	Diagnostic analytics
What's happening right now?	Descriptive analytics
What's likely to happen?	Predictive analytics
What's something interesting and important out of this mountain of data?	Discovery analytics
What are our options?	Prescriptive analytics
What should we do?	Prescriptive analytics

Mapping your analytics needs to your data lake road map

Jan, your CPO, is thrilled with the work that Raul and his team have done compiling the HR analytics continuum. They've produced an exhaustive list of more than 500 analytical functions that will be supported by the data lake, covering the broad continuum from simple "What happened?" descriptive analytics through more than a dozen complex prescriptive analytics scenarios.

Now what?

As you might guess, that 500-plus master list of HR analytics isn't going to be available the first day your data lake goes operational. A data lake is built in a phased, incremental manner, probably over several years.

But where to start?

In Chapter 17, I show you how to build your road map that will take you from your first ideas about your data lake all the way through multiple phases of implementation.

REMEMBER

Your data lake road map should be driven by your organization's analytical needs rather than by available data. You should address your highest-impact, highest-value analytics needs first, for two reasons:

>> **You need the *initial operating capability* (IOC) of your data lake to come with some "oomph."** In other words, you want people across your organization to sit up and take notice that the data lake is, from its first days, providing some really great analytics.

>> **You want to build your data lake using a "pipeline" approach that not only loads your data lake with lots of data but carries that data all the way through to critical business insights.**

Building the best data pipelines inside your data lake

A *data pipeline* is an end-to-end flow of data from the original sources all the way to the end users of analytics. Figure 2-7 shows a data pipeline overlaying the journey from source systems, through the data lake's bronze zone (the home of raw data), through the cleansing of that data into the silver zone, into the gold zone that consists of curated "packages" of data, and then finally to the users who consume the data-driven insights.

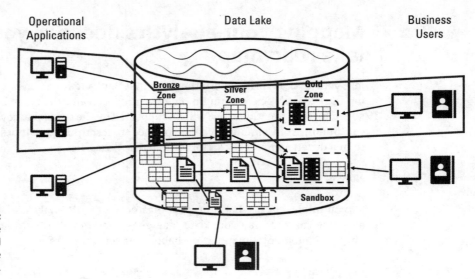

FIGURE 2-7:
A data pipeline into, through, and then out of the data lake.

TIP

You can think of a data pipeline in the same context that you may think of shopping. Suppliers sell and ship their products to wholesalers, who then resell and ship some of those products to a wholesaler. The wholesaler then resells and ships the products yet again to a retailer, which is where you come to buy whatever it is that you're looking for. Figure 2-8 shows how this paradigm can apply to data pipelines within a data lake.

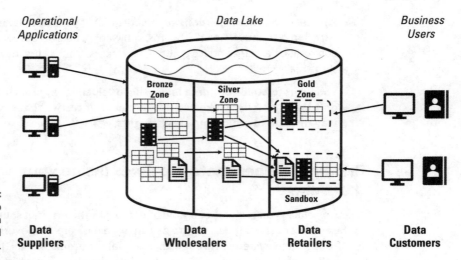

FIGURE 2-8:
An easy way to understand data pipelines and data lakes.

Addressing future gaps and shortfalls

Your road map is only the beginning of your data lake journey. You may think you have a pretty good idea of what your data and analytical needs are over the next couple of years, and you do a good job of prioritizing the various phases of how your data lake will be built.

WARNING

The world is constantly changing, though, which means that the farther out your data lake road map stretches, the more likely it is that any given phase will be preempted by changing priorities and new analytical needs.

As your organization's analytical needs evolve and — hopefully — become more sophisticated over time, you'll continually adjust your data lake plans to reflect the real world.

TIP

Think of a data lake as a living entity that is subject to constant change. Remember that century-long life span of a U.S. Air Force B-52, with changing missions over the years being addressed by constantly incorporating new technology to extend the plane's value.

Speedboats, Canoes, and Lake Cruises: Traversing the Variable-Speed Data Lake

You can *stream* all kinds of data into your data lake as quickly as that data is created in your source applications. Suppose that you dedicate a portion of your data lake to analyzing your overall computer network traffic and server performance to help you detect possible security threats, network bottlenecks, and database performance slowdowns.

You'll be streaming tons of log data from your routers, gateways, firewalls, servers, databases — pretty much any piece of hardware in your enterprise — into your data lake, as quickly as you can as traffic flows across your network and transactions hit your databases. Then, just as quickly, you and your coworkers can analyze the rapidly incoming data and take necessary actions to keep everything running smoothly.

At the same time, not everything needs to zoom into your data lake at lightning-fast speed. Think about a lake that not only has speedboats zipping all over but also has much larger ferry-type vessels that take hundreds of passengers at a time all around the lake. Some of those ferries also offer evening gourmet dinner cruises in addition to their daytime excursions.

You're not going to have much success trying to water-ski behind a lake ferry, nor will you have much success trying to eat a six-course gourmet meal served on the finest china while you're bouncing all over the place on a speedboat. You need to find the proper water vessel for what you're trying to do out on the lake, right?

TIP

You should think of your data lake as a variable-speed transportation engine for your enterprise data. If you need certain data blasted into your data lake as quickly as possible because you need to do immediate analysis, no problem! On the other hand, other data can be batched up and periodically brought into the data lake in bulk, on sort of a time-delayed basis, because you don't need to do real-time analysis. You can mix and match the data feeds in whatever combination makes sense for your organization's data lake.

Managing Overall Analytical Costs

You like the overall idea of a data lake. But you're talking about overhauling almost all your current analytical data environment. Over the past couple of decades, your organization has spent a ton of money on a couple of data warehouses, not to mention hundreds of data marts. And that was just the start!

Every budget planning cycle, your CFO groans at the price tag of keeping those data warehouses and data marts running. The servers, the database software, the staff to keep things up and running . . . sure, everyone in your organization would love to stop writing those huge checks every year to keep those old systems running. But wouldn't a data lake mean starting all over from scratch with a gigantic price tag?

Not necessarily! In fact, your new data lake presents you with the opportunity to get a grip on your overall analytical costs, as well as to get started without having to write a seven- or even eight-figure check.

Too good to be true? Thanks to the financials of cloud computing, you can have your data lake and drink it, too. (Wow, that was a really bad metaphor, but you get the idea.)

Almost all data lakes are built and deployed on a cloud computing platform, such as Amazon Web Services (AWS) or Microsoft Azure. With cloud computing, you can tiptoe into new technology using a pay-by-the-drink model. (Now that metaphor works much better!)

Chances are, your organization's data warehouses and data marts were built in — and are still hosted in — your company data center. Even if your IT organization uses an outside data center for the actual hosting, you still had to write some pretty big checks for every aspect of your current data warehouses and data marts, and you probably have some all-inclusive hosting contracts with your outside data center providers.

TIP

Most likely, your organization has already headed into the world of cloud computing. You may be using Salesforce for customer relationship management (CRM), or enterprise resource planning (ERP) software such as NetSuite or Workday for your finance and accounting, human resources, and other "back office" functions. If you've already dabbled in cloud computing for your operational applications, heading in the same direction for your analytics is natural.

You'll build your data lake in a phased, iterative, and incremental manner (see Chapter 17). With cloud computing, you can pay as you go along each phase, with tighter controls over your financial outlays for your data lake than you had with your earlier data warehouses and data marts.

WARNING

"Managing overall analytical costs" does not equate to "not spending a lot of money. You'll still need to keep a close watch on the *total cost of ownership* (TCO) of your data lake. With cloud computing, the meter is always running as your business users run reports, produce visualizations, and build machine learning models.

But you'll have the opportunity for a fresh start with new technology and new approaches to enterprise analytics, without the need to make a gigantic investment up front as you bravely enter this new world of data lakes.

Chapter **3**

Break Out the Life Vests: Tackling Data Lake Challenges

E ven a great day at the lake can go down the drain. Maybe it's that painful sunburn that sneaks up on you or a nasty thunderstorm that rolls in before you know it while you're still out in the middle of the lake. Or maybe the lake gets really choppy all of a sudden, and your boat starts rocking and rolling and seems like it might capsize. Just because the sky is blue and it looks like a spectacular day when you first get to the lake doesn't mean that everything will stay the same for the rest of the day.

Like it or not, a data lake comes with a giant warning sign that reads the equivalent of "DANGEROUS WATERS! ALL SWIMMING AND BOATING IS AT YOUR OWN RISK!"

In 2016, Gartner Group, a leading technology research and advisory firm, published a report indicating that an estimated 60 percent of data lake projects failed. Bad news, right?

Unfortunately, the data lake waters turned out to be even more treacherous than originally reported. A year later, a Gartner analyst estimated that the actual data lake failure rate was really closer to 85 percent!

Then you come across articles with titles like "The Data Lake Is Dead; Long Live the Data Lake!" (Yep, that's an actual title of an article from a leading data management product vendor.) Reading ominously phrased titles like that one make you feel like you're watching a horror movie set in the dark, cold waters of some remote lake, and the monster from the deep is about to jump onto the screen!

The silver lining of gloomy statistics and foreboding article titles is that your organization isn't necessarily destined to become yet another one of those data lake failures. Your data lake really can survive and thrive!

The first thing you need to do, though, is fully understand exactly what challenges and outright dangers await you in the world of data lakes. Otherwise, your chances of winding up in the data lake failure column are substantial!

That's Not a Data Lake, This Is a Data Lake!

Your work life is definitely a lot easier when everyone agrees on key definitions and terminology. Unfortunately, that's not what you'll find in the world of data lakes. Instead, you have to deal with conflicting boundaries among enterprise analytical components and confusion between a data lake and its cousins.

Dealing with conflicting definitions and boundaries

Guess what? It's pop quiz time!

Don't worry, you'll only get one question, and it'll be a zero-point, multiple-choice practice question to make an important point.

Take a look at the conceptual architecture diagram in Figure 3-1, where data is fed from source applications into an enterprise-scale analytical environment. Ready? Here's your question:

Which component(s) of the diagram is or are considered to be the data lake?

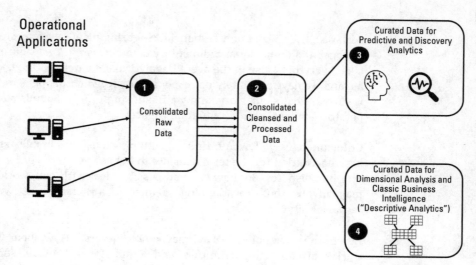

FIGURE 3-1:
Playing "find the
data lake."

Your possible answers:

A. Component 1 (consolidated raw data)

B. Component 2 (consolidated cleansed and processed data)

C. Components 1 and 2 (consolidated raw and cleansed and processed data)

D. Components 1, 2, and 3 (consolidated raw and cleansed and processed data, plus curated data for predictive and discovery analytics)

E. Components 1, 2, 3, and 4 (basically, everything after the data is sent out from the operational applications)

F. Any or all of the above

If you guessed F — any or all of the above — then you know exactly where this discussion is headed. Welcome to the state of data lake confusion!

If you were to spend a couple of hours surfing the web and searching for information about data lakes, you'd come across varying opinions about where the data lake boundaries begin and end. In fact, you can think of this problem as sort of a property line dispute between neighbors. In some cases, one of the "property owners" — the folks responsible for one of those components, such as ingesting and storing the raw data — insists that they need to have responsibility for many or even all of the other components, even if, for example, a separate data warehousing team is responsible for the curated dimensional data for descriptive analytics.

On the other side of the equation, you may encounter a situation where a designated data lake team is responsible for a single component of the overall architecture — usually the raw data in the "bronze" or "raw" zone. That data lake team then declares: "Hey, we're only responsible for bringing in raw data, storing it in object storage, and doing some rudimentary data cleansing. *That's* our company's data lake. Everything else in the overall analytical data architecture is out of scope for us, and we have absolutely no responsibility for what happens to the data or how it's used. That's our story, and we're sticking to it!" (Sounds sort of like a "hot potato, data lake edition" situation, right?)

Unfortunately, you won't find an authoritative, immutable, standards-body-based definition for the term *data lake* to help solve these border wars and property line disputes. So, how can you possibly deal with real-world scenarios that may involve both overlapping claims of ownership, as well as gaps in responsibility?

TIP

Ignore the terminology! Okay, maybe not "ignore." How about "don't get sidetracked by conflicting definitions and points of view"? Maybe some people think that only the ingested raw data is a data lake, while others view the entire enterprise analytical landscape as a modern data lake. In the long run, *somebody* needs to handle the end-to-end architecture for your data pipelines, beginning with data coming in from your source applications all the way to the data-driven insights presented to users.

REMEMBER

This book addresses the end-to-end analytical data architecture in a terminology-neutral manner. For your purposes, every component shown in Figure 3-1 needs to be considered as you plan and build your organization's data lake. If your company takes a divide-and-conquer approach, no problem. Say that curated dimensional data is considered to be a "downstream data warehouse" and outside the data lake realm. You'll be sending data from whatever your business and technology leaders consider to be the data lake into that data warehouse, which means you need to plan, architect, and build the data lake and data warehouse in concert with each other.

Data lake cousins

You'll find that the technology landscape is filled with data lake lookalikes and soundalikes. Welcome to the Wild West of enterprise-scale data management!

Get ready for a state of confusion when it comes to data lakes and the following:

>> Cloud databases

>> Data lake houses

>> Data hubs

>> Data fabric and data mesh

The cloud database

A cloud database is, well, a database somewhere out there in the cloud. That database can be

>> Relational, such as Microsoft SQL Server sitting in the Microsoft Azure cloud environment

>> Columnar, such as Amazon Redshift out there in the Amazon Web Services (AWS) cloud

>> A NoSQL database, such as IBM Cloudant

Can you consider any of the preceding to be the same as a data lake? Well, not necessarily. More accurately, SQL Server, Redshift, or Cloudant may be *part* of a data lake. For example, your data lake built in AWS may include not only Amazon Simple Storage Service (S3) for raw and processed data, but also Redshift for curated columnar data sourced from S3.

TIP

Think of a cloud database the same way you think about big data technology: an enabling component platform that may be useful to include in your data lake environment.

A nice house at the lake

You'll undoubtedly come across references to something called a *data lake house*. What's a data lake house? Well, it's a single environment that combines the best capabilities of a data lake with the best capabilities of a data warehouse — the best of all worlds!

WARNING

The pitch for a data lake house presumes that the boundaries for your data lake do *not* extend end-to-end along your enterprise analytical data architecture. In Figure 3-1, your data lake would stop after Component 2 (consolidated cleansed and processed data) or maybe Component 3 (curated data for predictive and discovery analytics). You would have a logical firewall between your "data lake" and Component 4 (curated data for dimensional analysis/classic business intelligence).

Instead of getting caught up in semantics, take a step back from the physical landscape of your enterprise data landscape. If you decide on a single next-generation data storage platform that fully handles *everything* in Figure 3-1, fantastic! Go ahead and say that you're implementing a data lake house instead of a data lake.

If, however, your architecture will include multiple data storage components such as AWS S3, Redshift, and perhaps even other AWS data services such as DynamoDB and Aurora to achieve your company's full analytics continuum, you still arrive at the same place as with a so-called data lake house, except you're integrating more than one type of data service to build your environment.

TIP

Again, don't get caught up in terminology wars and property line disputes! The concept of a data lake house is certainly a valuable one, and you absolutely should be heading in that direction. How you achieve that objective — with some emerging single platform or by integrating multiple components — is less important than considering your data lake to be a comprehensive, end-to-end solution for your enterprise analytical data. In fact, to add to the confusion you'll come across multiple versions of the term: *lakehouse* (one word) and *lake house* (two words).

Data hubs

A data hub is an enterprise-scale "traffic cop" that routes data among many different components, both transactional and analytical.

TECHNICAL STUFF

Instead of point-to-point interfaces between, say, a source application and a data lake's bronze zone for raw data, a data hub may take data from an enterprise resource planning (ERP) environment such as Workday and then route that data to multiple destinations in a *publish-and-subscribe* manner. For example, HR data about new employee onboarding can be extracted from Workday and then routed by the data hub to

>> Your company's NetSuite ERP system

>> An outside payroll provider

>> Your company's data lake

>> Stand-alone data warehouses and data marts that source their own data rather than take data feeds within your data lake–driven pipelines

TIP

You can use data hubs to help route data around your enterprise, and even outside your enterprise, in a highly governed manner that helps reduce the number of data feeds you need to manage. Data hubs are complementary to data lakes and may fit into your overall enterprise data architecture, but they shouldn't be thought of as a replacement or competing technology for your data lake.

Data fabric and data mesh

A data lake house isn't the only "next-generation data lake" approach you'll likely encounter as you get to work on your organization's data lake. Get ready for the *data fabric* and the *data mesh*. Wow!

TECHNICAL STUFF

You'll probably come across multiple ways in which the data fabric concept is presented. In a general sense, a data fabric is a unified, end-to-end data architecture to support your enterprise analytics. (Sounds kind of like a data lake, right?) But you'll also see Apache Ignite — an open-source, in-memory distributed database engine — referred to as a data fabric.

Both definitions fit when it comes to how you should think about the data fabric concept: something that is complementary to your organization's data lake and can help you overcome some of the architectural challenges you'll face.

You can say the same about a data mesh: It's one more architectural approach for your enterprise data environment that addresses some of the architectural complexity you'll encounter with your data lake.

TIP

In fact, the data lake architectural approaches and best practices you'll see in this book contain a healthy helping of what's new in the world of data fabric and data mesh architectures, so you're getting the best of all worlds.

Exposing Data Lake Myths and Misconceptions

Did you hear that story going around about the group of high schoolers who skipped school on Senior Ditch Day to go to the lake? And then, at dusk, their car wouldn't start? Just after nightfall, the ghost of their high school's principal from a hundred years ago materialized and said that he was going to put every one of them in detention and they'd have to attend summer school before they can graduate?

Data lakes come with urban legends, just like life does. Sometimes these urban legends are outright myths; in other cases, they're simple misunderstandings. But nothing clears up myths and misunderstandings like a little bit of sunlight, right?

Misleading data lake campaign slogans

You undoubtedly will come across this pitch for a data lake: "Your data lake will be the home for all your data."

Really? *All* your data? Not exactly.

Try this more accurate — but admittedly less exciting — pitch instead: "Your well-architected data lake will be the home for much or most of your analytical data."

So, what's the confusion here?

Remember that today's data lakes are used to support analytical processing, not transactional processing. Your data lake will absolutely feed data into your business intelligence, data visualizations, machine learning models, and all sorts of advanced analytics. Your data lake will *not*, however, sit underneath your ERP applications such as SAP S4/HANA or Microsoft Dynamics 365. And you won't be building your enterprise health management system (enterprise health records, or EHR) to manage patient admission and discharge, patient rooms, operating rooms, hospital pharmacies, in-hospital labs, and radiology for an entire large hospital system on top of a data lake.

You will, though, be feeding data from S4/HANA, Microsoft Dynamics 365, or an EHR system such as Epic or Meditech into a data lake for your analytics.

At least for the near term, your operational systems and applications use traditional relational technology or possibly newer database models (for example, the SAP HANA in-memory database) for their own data management. Eventually, down the road, data lakes may be "ready for prime time" to support transactional processing. Software companies are currently working on these capabilities. But the day of a single-platform data lake to support transactional and analytical processing is still off in the future (see Chapter 18). For the present, you still need to feed data from your source applications into your data lake instead of having a single unified platform for "all things data" within your enterprise.

The single-platform misconception

Can a data lake exist on more than one data platform? For example, can a data lake have some of its data sitting in Amazon S3 buckets, with other data residing in Amazon Redshift?

Absolutely! So, what's the confusion here?

Some data lake proponents will argue that a data lake is a "centralized store of data," which means that by definition, a single, monolithic data platform will provide that centralized storage and management. As soon as data flows out of, say, Amazon S3 into another environment such as Redshift or DynamoDB, then, by definition, that data has moved on to a data warehouse or some other non–data lake environment.

TIP

You can define the boundaries of a data lake however you want (see "That's Not a Data Lake, This Is a Data Lake," earlier in this chapter). If you elect the broader, end-to-end perspective on data lakes, then almost certainly you'll wind up building different components of your data lake on various data platforms. You're the one calling the shots here, so don't get sidetracked by dogmatic thinking about data lake platforms!

No upfront data analysis required

Did you hear the one about the data lake versus the data warehouse? So, you know how a data warehouse requires you to do a ton of upfront analysis so you can define the database tables for your incoming data? Well, guess what? In a data lake, you can skip all that! Just blast in all that data and store it! Don't waste your time doing upfront analysis of data structures and business rules for the data! In fact, a data lake is just like a point-and-shoot camera. You "point" your source data toward your data lake, and presto!

Ah, if it were only that simple. In reality, a data lake is much more like the most sophisticated, expensive, photojournalist's camera than its simplistic, inexpensive, point-and-shoot cousin.

Yes, it's true that you can rapidly ingest new data sets into a data lake without extensive upfront analysis to design staging layer database tables and all the rest of the stuff you need for a traditional data warehouse. Amazon S3 buckets or Microsoft Azure Data Lake Storage (ADLS) lets you rapidly ingest and store new data.

TECHNICAL STUFF

You're *deferring* the analysis of that data, however, not skipping the analysis altogether. Data lakes follow a *schema on read* paradigm rather than a *schema on write* paradigm. You still need to process and prepare your data at some point along the data pipeline to get the data ready for your analytics.

True, you can quickly blast in a whole bunch of data, but at some point you'll still need to understand your data, apply master data management, other data governance rules, and catalog your data for your users. In other words, the hard work still needs to be done!

The false tale of the tortoise and the data lake

Here's another urban legend: Data lakes are excruciatingly slow for classic business intelligence and visualization! You would never, ever want to combine data warehousing needs into your data lake. Your business users will clobber you!

Wait a minute. Slow down, there. Actually, make that "speed it up."

TECHNICAL
STUFF

True, early-generation big data technology wasn't exactly a speed demon when you tried to run SQL on top of your non-relational data. For example, the classic Hadoop architecture in the early days of big data had a variation of SQL such as HiveQL (for the Apache Hive environment) translated into a series of MapReduce jobs that would run against the Hadoop Distributed File System (HDFS). After all that translation, the resultant query response time was almost always much slower than SQL running against a plain old relational database such as Microsoft SQL Server.

Consequently, an urban legend grew about big data that continued into the world of data lakes: Forget about doing anything SQL-like against a data lake! So, for business intelligence reporting and visualization, head to the data warehouse, not the data lake. In fact, keep your data lake as far away from your data warehouse as possible.

TECHNICAL
STUFF

Meanwhile, back in the real world, big data vendors were already hard at work addressing this issue as a new generation of big data technology emerged. For example, Cloudera introduced an engine called Impala to bypass MapReduce — and all that translation and mapping — and instead ran SQL natively against HDFS-resident data.

Still, the tale of the tortoise and the hare — that is, the tortoise and the data lake — persisted. Data lakes were exceedingly slow for classic database functionality. End of story!

Fortunately, you don't need to be fooled by this myth. In a modern data lake, you can mix and match technologies all across your data pipelines to meet your analytical needs, even those that supposedly aren't a good fit for data lakes.

TECHNICAL
STUFF

For example, in the AWS environment, you can use Redshift Spectrum to natively access S3 data instead of — or in addition to — actually copying that S3-resident data into Redshift.

The bottom line: Just ignore the naysayers, and build the end-to-end environment that makes the most sense for *your* organization's portfolio of analytical needs.

Navigating Your Way through the Storm on the Data Lake

Every enterprise-scale initiative comes with dozens or even hundreds of challenges. You're out there sailing along on your data lake, and suddenly you turn right into 70-mile-per-hour headwinds, just as the water starts chopping and churning. Will you be able to make it back to shore?

WARNING

When it comes to program-level challenges, data lakes are no different than enterprise data warehouses (EDWs), ERP implementations, or EHR efforts. You absolutely, positively will hit a point when success seems impossible and failure is all but guaranteed.

At this point, you and your team have two options: You can surrender and accept failure, or you can muster your strength and forge ahead.

Your data lake initiative's "valley of despair" may come early along your implementation road map or later on, but at some point, you'll want to throw in the towel. Maybe a key component in your architecture is far more difficult to work with than you had expected, or maybe it doesn't perform as advertised. Maybe technology isn't your problem, and instead, your efforts to facilitate change throughout your enterprise are meeting with significant resistance. Perhaps you're having significant difficulties finding skilled technologists or the right program manager.

You're also acutely aware of Gartner Group's data lake failure statistics. If they're saying that 85 percent of data lake projects fail, what makes your company's initiative so special that you can avoid becoming another data lake casualty?

TIP

Whatever the issues happen to be, don't quit! Take a step back, pause, and regroup. Assess where you're at. Modify your architecture, adjust your phasing and overall timeline, or go find some super-skilled outside consultants to fill your resourcing gaps. The "valley of despair" is real, and it can be a program killer . . . but only if you surrender.

Building the Data Lake of Dreams

Field of Dreams, a late-'80s movie, featured an often-misquoted line — "If you build it, he will come" — that still shows up near the top of most "Famous Movie Quotes" lists. Over time, the actual line from the movie morphed into the misquoted "If you build it, *they* will come." However, for the world of analytical data management, the incorrect version of the quote is absolutely perfect!

When data warehousing came onto the scene in the early '90s, one widely followed approach was highly data-driven rather than usage-driven. Instead of meeting with business users to understand their reporting and business intelligence needs, the data warehouse development team would forge ahead largely on their own and load as much data as possible into the data warehouse under the philosophy that users would eventually start using the new environment anyway.

In other words, if you (the data warehouse team) built it (the data warehouse), they (the users) would come.

Fast-forward to the data lake era. Who says history doesn't repeat itself?

One school of thought for building a data lake calls for just loading as much data as possible from sources all over your enterprise, into the data lake, with little or no effort spent on collecting analytical requirements from finance, HR, supply chain, sales, and the other departments and organizations. After all, the nature of big data technology allows for theoretically infinite data storage, right? If you stock that data lake with enough fish — I mean, data — then analytical users can't help but find something useful there! Build the lake — the data lake — and they will come.

Not so fast!

Maybe you have a junk drawer in your house or apartment. Over the years, you've stuffed those odd screws and bolts, pieces of plastic that probably fell off of something in your home, keys that don't seem to fit any of your locks, half-used tubes of superglue, small tools — pretty much anything — into that junk drawer. Your basic operating model was, and still is, that if you find something around your house or apartment that you don't immediately have a use for, you throw it in the junk drawer because it'll be there later, whenever you figure out what that thing actually is and how you can put it to use.

So, how easy is it to find something in your junk drawer when you actually need it? Ha!

WARNING

Don't let your data lake turn into your junk drawer! If you take a data-first-and-only approach to building out your data lake, then unfortunately you're headed in that direction.

True, a data lake stores data. But for what purpose? Analytics! You need to take a balanced approach to constructing your data lake, addressing *both* data and analytical usage in parallel, and carefully plan your end-to-end data pipelines that you then match to your overall architecture. (Chapter 17 covers your data lake road map.)

Performing Regular Data Lake Tune-ups — Or Else!

Getting that initial release of your data lake out there to your business users is one heck of an accomplishment. Before too much time passes, those business users are clamoring for more and more data, so they can do more and more analytics. Your data lake road map is all set for the next two or three years (see Chapter 17), but you can squeeze in some additional requests for data from your users. After all, you want to keep your customers happy!

WARNING

You need to be careful that, in your haste to build out your data lake, you don't overlook the all-important periodic tune-ups that will keep your data lake running smoothly and efficiently.

You wouldn't take your brand-new speedboat out onto the lake for the first time, and then ignore the maintenance on your prized watercraft. Some of that maintenance is relatively simple, such as changing the oil every 50 to 100 hours. But you also need to have someone check the engine once a year, make sure that the battery is in good working order, check your fuel lines, and lots more. If you're too focused on having a great time out on the lake, sooner or later your speedboat is going to have a major problem, which will cost you much more in the long run to fix than if you'd taken the time for maintenance along the way.

You know where this speedboat maintenance analogy is headed, right? Your data lake is just like your speedboat. Don't be so focused on adding new data, trying out new cloud data services, and all the rest of the "fun" stuff in data lake development that you skip over all-important maintenance and performance tune-ups.

TIP

Your data lake road map needs to periodically take a pause from new development and capabilities for your team to spend some time concentrating on maintenance without being distracted. Maybe the tune-up and maintenance period will be a week or two, or you can spend two or three months on it if you're doing a major overhaul. Your data lake road map (see Chapter 17) needs to include maintenance periods from the very beginning as you lay out your phases, so everyone is fully aware that data lake maintenance is a must.

Technology Marches Forward

One summer, you jump into your SUV with a couple of your best friends and drive a couple hundred miles to your favorite lake where you own a time-share. You've been going to this lake for the past five years since you bought your time-share, and everyone has their favorite activities to do when you get there and settle in for your annual ten-day vacation.

This year, though, you get to the lake, drop your boat that you've towed behind your vehicle, unpack, and get settled into your cabin. Then it's time to get out on the water. You're loading up your boat and getting everything all set. Then the person in the next boat slip says, "Hey, did you hear about this great new lake resort that just opened up 50 miles away? Wow, that place has everything! I hear it's going to be the absolute best place to go boating in the entire state!"

Oh, great. Here you are not only unpacked for the next ten days, but you bought a time-share here because five years ago, *this* was the great new lake resort that was supposed to be the absolute best place to go boating in the entire state.

Sure, you can try to sell your time-share, or see if you can trade it for something closer to that new lake resort. Maybe you can lease out next summer's time-share week at this lake to someone else, while you try out the new resort. You can make the switch to the brand-new resort, but it won't be easy.

Data lake technology is like owning a time-share at a lake resort. (Bet you never thought you'd see that analogy, huh?) Whether you like it or not, technology marches forward. Normally, technological progress is a good thing. But when you've invested millions of dollars and tens of thousands of hours building a data lake on what is now old technology, those advances in technology can be bitter-sweet. In fact, you may have to throw away what you've built and start over.

Back when big data was really starting to catch on (around the early 2010s), most organizations began experimenting in the Hadoop ecosystem. James Dixon, who was then the chief data officer (CDO) at Pentaho, is credited with first using the term *data lake* in a 2010 article entitled "Pentaho, Hadoop, and Data Lakes." For a few years, some organizations tried to bring governance and order to their big data Wild West that was based largely on Hadoop and began using the term *data lake*.

Soon, though, the data lake momentum shifted to the world of AWS and Microsoft Azure and those cloud mega-vendors' respective data lake services and platforms. If you jumped into the data lake waters around, say, 2017 or 2018, you most likely headed down either the AWS or Azure path.

But what if you were an early experimenter with data lakes, and you built out significant capabilities in Hadoop? You can certainly deploy your latest and greatest data lake components in AWS or Azure, but you would have to integrate those pieces in some manner with your earlier Hadoop components. Otherwise, you can settle on one of those "hot new data lake resorts" and — just like foregoing your time-share at the old lake to move to the popular new one — migrate your early data lake efforts into one of the new platforms.

And what about the future? Who's to say that one of the other major technology players such as IBM, Oracle, SAP, or maybe some company that doesn't even exist right now, won't come up with some revolutionary new data lake platform that blows away anything that exists today? What are you going to do then?

WARNING

One thing that you absolutely *can't* do is avoid making investments today because something better will almost certainly be available tomorrow. Sitting on your hands and delaying work on your data lake will almost certainly compromise your organization's ability to support the broad continuum of high-impact, high-value analytics that drive critical business decisions and subsequent actions. Any analytical successes that you do have will likely be fragmented and uneven.

You can mitigate some of your technology investment risk with solid architecture and grounded-in-reality planning for the long term (see Chapter 2.) But you need to resign yourself to the fact that no matter how aggressive your organization is when it comes to jumping on the latest and greatest data lake technology, eventually something better will come along. You *will* be able to take advantage of that new technology, maybe even sooner rather than later, but steel yourself because a lot of your hard work and investment will have to be repeated as part of your next wave of data lake effort.

2

Building the Docks, Avoiding the Rocks

Chapter **4**

Imprinting Your Data Lake on a Reference Architecture

Building your organization's data lake can seem like an overwhelming proposition, with dozens of moving parts. Where and how do you even get started?

Fortunately, you don't need to start from a totally clean slate. You should begin your data lake adventures by following a relevant *reference architecture* that will guide you with options and ideas for:

>> Bringing data into your data lake

>> Deciding what type(s) of data storage platforms make sense for your organization

>> Specifying how your business users will interact with the data lake

>> Deciding how (or if) you should incorporate existing data warehouses and data marts into your data lake ecosystem

>> Incorporating external data along with your data lake contents into your analytics

>> Allocating your enterprise analytics among your data lake and other realms, such as "the edge"

Playing Follow the Leader

Quick! Name an animal that you'd find at a lake. If you happened to answer "fish," then let's try a follow-up question that will get you closer to the purpose of a technology reference architecture (yep, really): Name an animal that lives *on* a lake. This time, you probably answered "duck" or maybe "goose" or even "swan."

So far, so good. Now, here's one more follow-up question: What do baby ducks and baby geese and baby swans all have in common? True, they all swim and float. But they also all *imprint* on their mothers and fathers to get a running start (or would that be a "swimming start") on their young lives. A baby duck, for example, carefully watches what an adult duck does and learns what to do — and what not to do — in a follow-the-leader manner.

You can get your own running start with your data lake by "imprinting" it onto a reference architecture. A *reference architecture* is sort of a starter kit for your data lake, depicting how data is brought in, stored, managed, and eventually consumed. Instead of starting totally from a blank sheet of paper, you can begin by finding an appropriate reference architecture that closely matches the specifics of your environment, and then tailoring that architecture as needed.

A reference architecture is not intended to be a "Do exactly this, or else!" blueprint. Instead, think of a reference architecture as a set of prespecified interrelated components that gives you a head start on your data lake architecture. You'll almost always need to make adjustments and enhancements to that starting point, but at least you're off and running (or swimming).

WARNING

You may be tempted to start architecting your data lake by diving right into vendor solutions, cloud platforms, specific data services, open-source software, and other implementation details. Don't do it! Your best and safest bet is to steer clear of implementation specifics at first and instead work with *conceptual* reference architectures rather than implementation-specific reference architectures.

TECHNICAL STUFF

True, eventually you'll need to specify your data lake in terms of:

>> Specific platforms such as Amazon Web Services (AWS) or Microsoft Azure.

>> Specific vendor products such as Amazon Redshift, AWS Simple Storage Service (S3), Databricks, Dremio, Microsoft Azure Data Lake Solution (ADLS), Starburst, Yellowbrick Data Warehouse . . . the list of candidates goes on and on and on. . . .

>> Specific open-source frameworks and specifications such as Apache Arrow, Apache Iceberg, Apache Ignite, Apache Kafka, and so on.

At the start, though, avoid boxing yourself in to specific solutions. Instead, focus on the conceptual ways in which your data should make its way into your data lake, how and where the data should be stored, and then how that data is consumed by your analytics to drive decisions and actions. Focus on the end-to-end data pipelines that need to be built, all the way from data sources to the consumption of that data. Match the specifics of your organization's data and analytical needs with an appropriate conceptual-level reference architecture, and then go from there.

Guiding Principles of a Data Lake Reference Architecture

The best data lake reference architectures are governed by a set of common principles, regardless of the various scenarios they cover. These principles include the following:

>> **Having a predominantly cloud-based architecture:** Your data lake may have pieces here and there that reside in an on-premises data center rather than in the cloud, but the critical mass of your data lake will usually be cloud-based.

>> **Having a loosely coupled architecture:** You'll construct your data lake by bolting together potentially dozens of different services and products. A loosely coupled architecture, built around *micro-services* and *fine-grained services* that are each individually responsible for small but important pieces of the overall workload, gives you the best mix-and-match portfolio of potential resources for your data lake. Perhaps even more important, a loosely coupled architecture is a step in the right direction to building a "bionic data lake" (see Chapter 2) that can evolve over the years or even decades without having to start all over again from scratch.

>> **Separating computing power from storage:** In the earliest days of data lakes that were predominantly built on the Hadoop Distributed File System (HDFS) and the overall Hadoop ecosystem, computing resources and data storage were tightly coupled and more or less distributed in tandem to underlying servers. Modern data lakes largely separate data storage from the computing power for using the data. You can use low-cost object storage as the workhorse of your data lake's bronze zone, with higher-powered computing resources allocated to your data transformations, analytics, and other downstream components.

>> **Looking at both vendor and open-source solutions:** You may want to use as much open-source software as possible for your data lake, or you might instead decide to go only with vendor-provided and vendor-supported products. Most implementations will be a mixture of both vendor and open-source solutions, and eventually you'll explore options for both paths.

>> **Covering both data at rest and data in motion:** *Data at rest* addresses data storage, while *data in motion* relates to data moving from one place in your overall environment to another. As you build your data pipelines, both data at rest and data in motion need to be considered and addressed.

>> **Solving simultaneous equations:** Just like those high school or college math problems that you may have pushed to the deepest reaches of your mind, data lake architecture requires you to address many different moving parts, all of which must be "solved" in concert with one another. Your reference architecture will give you the starter kit where data ingestion is "solved" alongside data storage, which is likewise addressed in concert with data usage. Your reference architecture will help you balance and make sense of this predicament.

>> **Specifying the optimal number of components:** Your data lake can be highly monolithic, at least conceptually. In other words, every single piece of your data can wind up sitting in low-level object storage such as S3 or ADLS. On the other side of the spectrum, your data lake can include potentially dozens of different data services, especially in your gold zone where your users spend most of their time. You can conceivably include different databases and data services for dimensional analysis, graph-oriented data, time-based data, and other unique uses of your data. But how many components are too many? Copying data from one environment to another, and then to yet another, inside your data lake can be problematic. Yet, at the same time, force-fitting all your data into a single environment just to avoid cross-component copying along your data pipelines can also lead to problems. Your reference architecture will help you find the right balance for your data lake.

>> **Looking ahead:** You're building your data lake for today, but you're also building your data lake for tomorrow, and the next day, and the day after

that. . . . A good reference architecture balances today's technology with what's on the horizon to prevent you from getting locked into a rapidly aging solution that's speeding toward obsolescence. Once again, the key principle of a bionic data lake comes into play.

>> **Being careful with technical jargon:** Take a step back and forget about the term data lake. Instead think "enterprise-scale analytical data solution," and you'll be better able to make use of the reference architectures available to you without getting boxed into preconceived notions and "turf wars" about what is and isn't within the scope of the data lake.

>> **Enabling you to think like a community planner:** If you were building a suburb or planning for the revival of a section of a city, you would need to think about single-family homes, apartments and other multifamily residences, business locations and zoning, transportation routes, hospitals and medical care, schools, and dozens of other critical pieces of a community. You need to engage in the same sort of big-picture thinking when you build a data lake. A reference architecture is your "community plan" for your data lake that gives you the head start with all the critical pieces for you to then fill in the details.

A Reference Architecture for Your Data Lake Reference Architecture

Where do you start with data lake reference architectures? The answer: at the beginning, with an overarching "reference architecture for your reference architectures."

No, you're not going around in circles. Figure 4-1 shows a general framework for almost any data lake that includes three major component areas:

>> Data ingestion, which includes feeding data into your data lake from source applications.

>> Data storage and management, which includes how data is handled across your bronze, silver, and gold zones. (For reference architecture purposes, you can disregard your data lake sandbox for the time being.)

>> Data usage and consumption, which includes your organization's analytics continuum that will range from descriptive analytics — rudimentary reporting, classic business intelligence (BI), and online analytical processing (OLAP) — to the overarching category of data science and your more complex and advanced analytics.

Why does Figure 4-1 show reporting and BI in a separate compartment than data science when both are part of the same analytics continuum? I explain why it's useful to separate BI from data science and advanced analytics later in this chapter (see "The Old Meets the New at the Data Lake").

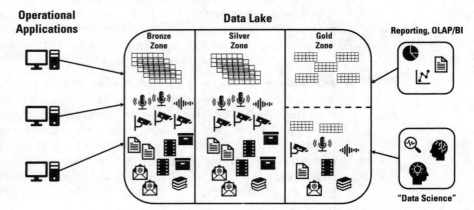

FIGURE 4-1:
A reference architecture for data lake reference architectures.

As the saying goes, though, "The devil is in the details." You can't really tell *how* the pieces of your data lake will fit together or what variations might make sense for your particular situation from the high-level depiction in Figure 4-1. So, start digging into the details!

Incoming! Filling Your Data Lake

For your data lake, your goal is data ingestion, not data indigestion! You want to figure out the best mixture of inbound data flows to make your data lake sing . . . or swim . . . or something. . . .

Figure 4-2 illustrates the two overall classes of data flows into which all your inbound data will be categorized:

>> Batch data
>> Streaming data

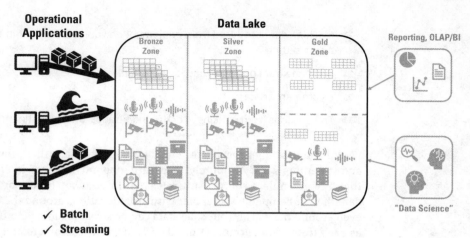

Operational Applications

Data Lake

Bronze Zone

Silver Zone

Gold Zone

Reporting, OLAP/BI

"Data Science"

FIGURE 4-2:
Two classes of inbound data flows for your data lake.

✓ **Batch**
✓ **Streaming**

Notice how the top data feed in Figure 4-2 consists only of incoming batch data. Sound familiar? If you've worked with data warehouses and data marts, it's old home week! Even in the world of data lakes, some inbound data is best handled "in bulk" through period batches. For example:

>> End-of-day inventory counts

>> The results of your company's latest round of employee reviews, including promotions and salary adjustments

>> Daily or weekly breakdowns of the details about patients seen at each hospital that are part of your larger health system network, with those details including counts for various diseases and conditions, totals for patients admitted and discharged, billing and payment updates from the hospital's accounting system, and other types of "bulk data"

Because a key aspect of your data lake is "the need for speed," often batch data simply isn't fast enough for the types of analytics you need to support and the portfolio of data-driven decisions that your business users need to make. When periodic batch data feeds don't do the trick, you can stream data into your data lake, as indicated by the second inbound data feed in Figure 4-2.

Streaming data operates in a real-time or near-real-time manner. As soon as an *event* of some type occurs in a source system, data about that event is "pushed" out onto a streaming service and quickly sent on its way to your data lake, with little or no delay. Examples of streaming data for your data lake include the following:

>> Log data from your IT servers, routers, and other networking devices, and your security infrastructure

- » Machine data produced from equipment on your factory floor in a manufacturing setting

- » Real-time transportation and logistics data

- » E-commerce data

- » Transactions from banking, stock market trades, and other financial data

Would you possibly have a data source for your data lake that provides both batch and streaming data? Absolutely! The third inbound data feed in Figure 4-2 shows that any given data source isn't relegated to only batch data or only streaming data. If your company is a retailer with store locations around the United States or even around the world, your sales data can be streamed into your data lake as soon as each transaction occurs. Other data about your customers and products or the employees who rang up the transactions and their end-of-day sales totals, might be less time-intensive for purposes of reporting and analytics and can wait for an end-of-day batch feed.

After you identify your general mixture of batch and streaming data feeds for your data lake, you need to take the next step and decide on an inbound data feed architecture. You have two primary options:

- » **The lambda architecture:** Supports both batch and streaming data feeds through separate but parallel batch and streaming layers

- » **The kappa architecture:** Merges your batch data feeds into your streaming layer rather than building and maintaining two separate layers

I cover both the lambda and kappa architectures in Chapter 5.

REMEMBER

For top-level reference architecture purposes, you only need to be aware of whether your data lake will be supporting primarily batch or streaming data feeds, or perhaps equal amounts of each feed type.

Supporting the Fleet Sailing on Your Data Lake

Your data lake will contain tons of data, right? Where and how exactly will all that data be stored?

TECHNICAL STUFF

If the first thought that comes to your mind is "in a database," then you're sort of correct, but, well, mostly incorrect. You're "sort of correct" if you're thinking of a "database" in a conceptual sense, as in a "large collection of data." In fact, during the stone age of computing when the mainframes ruled the land, the term *data base* — two words, not one — meant exactly that: some large collection of data, regardless of how all that data was stored and managed.

For a long while, though, *database* has meant more than just a collection of data. You're probably familiar with relational databases such as Microsoft SQL Server or MySQL, which may well play a role in your data lake when you start selecting products for your reference architecture. You may also be aware of — or even have some experience with — columnar databases such as Amazon Redshift.

So, if you're probably not going to store your data lake's data (or at least most of your data lake's data) in a database, where exactly will all that data be stored? It has to exist somewhere!

Objects floating in your data lake

Figure 4-3 illustrates how low-cost, cloud-based *object storage* technology serves as the storage platform for most data lakes.

Object storage such as S3 or ADLS allows you to easily store structured, semi-structured, and unstructured data as peers to one another without any special "database tricks" or workarounds. Some of the earliest attempts at data lakes were based around the HDFS, another way to easily store your three types of data as peers to one another.

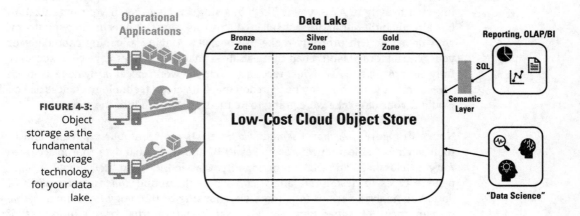

FIGURE 4-3: Object storage as the fundamental storage technology for your data lake.

While you're working on the earliest phases of your data lake reference architecture, you don't need to place a stake in the ground and declare that you'll be using a particular technology such as S3 or ADLS. You can simply use the generic term *object storage* to indicate that — as shown in Figure 4-3 — your bronze, silver, and gold zones will all use object storage for your raw, refined, and curated data, respectively.

REMEMBER

Unless your organization is only beginning its journey with cloud computing technology, however, you won't have total freedom when it comes to selecting a specific platform for your data lake's object storage. If your company has already invested heavily in AWS, you'll likely be using S3. Likewise, if your organization has already built out or at least selected Azure as your cloud technology platform, your data lake will probably make use of ADLS. Having a leading candidate for your object storage isn't a bad thing at all — many data lakes have been successfully built on S3 and ADLS. Just recognize that you won't necessarily have as much "freedom" if your company has already made its cloud technology choices as you would if your data lake were going to be the first venture into the cloud.

Notice in Figure 4-3 that a *semantic layer* exists between your reporting and BI tools such as Tableau or Microsoft Power BI and the actual data that is accessed for your classic BI and OLAP functionality. Classic BI — the "tell me what happened" types of descriptive analytics — is built around *dimensional analysis* of data. You analyze various *facts* (data warehousing terminology for a quantitative measurement of some type, such as sales and returns, or the numbers of employees hired and terminated) and then "slice and dice" those facts according to *dimensions* (such as customers, products, time, departments, and so on).

TECHNICAL
STUFF

In object storage, however, unlike a database, you don't natively support concepts such as fact and dimension tables. But your business users still need to do BI, right? You put your dimensional models in your semantic layer, which then maps those conceptual facts and dimensions into the underlying objects in S3 or ADLS as if you had a "real" database underneath instead of object storage. Now, you can support the full continuum of analytics — descriptive, diagnostic, predictive, and discovery — from one common pool of object storage, even though descriptive analytics traditionally runs against a database.

Mixing it up

But is object storage an all-or-nothing proposition? If you head down the path that so many others have traveled before you, and you lay out a draft platform of object storage for your data lake, does that mean that every piece of data in your data lake will be in S3 or ADLS?

Not necessarily! Figure 4-4 shows how a segment of your data lake's gold zone, where your ready-to-analyze curated data resides, may have database technology sitting side-by-side with the object storage that makes up the majority of your data lake.

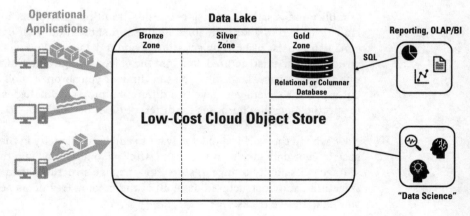

FIGURE 4-4:
Incorporating
database
technology along
with object
storage.

Instead of using a semantic layer to provide translation and mapping into underlying object storage, your BI actually runs against a real database. Your data lake is now *component-based* rather than monolithic. In other words, you've introduced a second data storage platform into your overall architecture. You still have a *logically* centralized data lake, but under the covers, you're doing a little bit of mix-and-match.

So, why would you want to complicate the storage layer of your data lake by adding a second platform? Figure 4-5 shows how you might incorporate and embed an existing data warehouse into your overall data lake environment. The next section in this chapter ("The Old Meets the New at the Data Lake") carries this discussion of data warehouses and data lakes further, looking at various options you should explore.

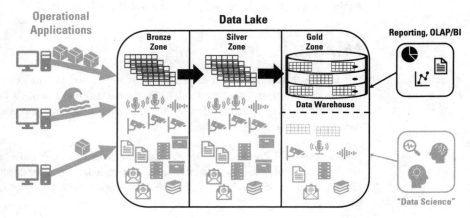

FIGURE 4-5:
Embedding a data warehouse into your data lake environment.

Complication alert! Having side-by-side, multiple platforms in your data lake isn't restricted to your gold zone. Figure 4-6 shows how your data lake's bronze zone can consist of both object storage and a database. You would ingest semistructured and unstructured data into the object storage and bring structured data into your database. Logically, you can think of your bronze zone as a single unit, but under the covers you have two different storage technologies, each dedicated to specific ingestion purposes for different types of data.

Now, why in the world would you want to add heterogeneity in the form of a database to your data lake's bronze zone? After all, one of the "win themes" of object storage is its ability to ingest, store, and manage structured data alongside semistructured and unstructured data, all of them being treated as peers without any special database tricks.

TECHNICAL STUFF

Again, the answer lies in the realm of legacy data warehouses and what you decide to do with them. I explain more in "The Old Meets the New at the Data Lake" later in this chapter, but for purposes of understanding storage technology within your data lake's bronze zone, think in terms of reusing the extract, transform, and load (ETL) jobs, as well as the *staging layer* of an existing data warehouse, and embedding those existing capabilities within your data lake environment.

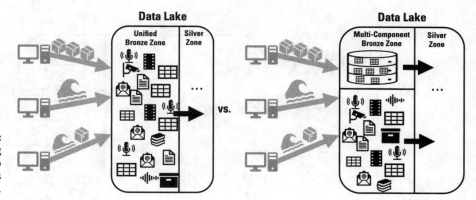

FIGURE 4-6:
Adding
heterogeneity to
your data lake's
bronze zone.

Can you have more than two types of data storage in your data lake? Absolutely!

Figure 4-7 illustrates your data lake's gold zone with not one, not two, but *five* different data storage and management technologies at work:

>> The same object storage that you use for your bronze and silver zones and that will feed data into your machine learning, advanced analytics, and other data science capabilities

>> A relational or columnar database to support your reporting and BI

>> A time-series database for specialized temporal analysis

>> A graph database, which is well suited for analyzing the networking connections of social media relationships

>> A "wide-column" database, which is often used for specialized industrial analysis

Are you carrying things too far if you incorporate four or five or perhaps even more different data management technologies all into your data lake gold zone? Perhaps. The simplest approach, of course, is to stuff all your data into a single environment, which would take you down the object storage path (for example, S3 or ADLS). On the other hand, highly specialized analytics, especially when consuming very large data volumes, may run into performance issues if you try a one-size-fits-all approach for data management.

Decisions, decisions, decisions. . . . How about some help here?

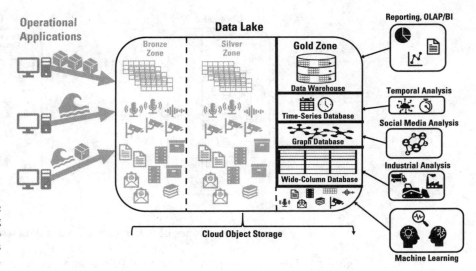

FIGURE 4-7:
Adding
heterogeneity to
your data lake's
bronze zone.

Suppose you work for an energy exploration firm. You're building a data lake that will contain mountains of sensor and seismic data from test drilling sites. All that data will be fed into incredibly complex algorithms that will help your company's management decide whether to spend millions of dollars drilling for oil or natural gas at each test site. You'll also have some rudimentary reporting and BI needs scattered among your business users, but for the most part, analytics equals data science at your company.

TIP

You might as well go simple in this case. Your needs may change down the road, but at least at the start, set up your data lake with object storage such as S3 or ADLS across the board, including your entire gold zone.

Suppose you work for a financial firm, and you're building a data lake to support an entirely new generation of super-advanced financial analytics. Your company doesn't deal with a lot of semi-structured or unstructured data; almost all your data is structured (numbers, dates, fixed-length character strings).

You can certainly store all that structured data in object storage, but you might be better off using a database. Part of your database can be organized using fact and dimension tables for dimensional business analysis; other parts can store your business data in tables that are optimized to feed your machine learning and other advanced analytics.

If you're anticipating super-large volumes of data in your financial firm such as market trading data, then new generations of databases can certainly handle massive amounts of data far more robustly than older database technology. You'll still want to allow for semi-structured and unstructured data, so object storage might come into play later on. But your data lake's gold zone will look more like a data warehouse than an energy exploration company's would.

What about another use case that doesn't fit quite so neatly into the object-versus-database decision — in fact, all the way back to where data is first ingested into your data lake's bronze zone? Suppose you're building a data lake for a hospital system. You have tons of structured data:

>> Patient admission and discharge data

>> Billing and payment data

>> Measurements and readings from all those unpleasant blood tests that the hospital labs do

Your electronic hospital records (EHR) system most likely stores all this data in an underlying relational database, meaning that each piece of data is structured from the moment of its creation.

On the other hand, in a hospital you also have

>> X-rays

>> Computerized axial tomography (CAT) scans

>> Magnetic resonance imaging (MRI) scans

>> Videos from the operating room to record surgical procedures

This unstructured data is also accompanied by plenty of semi-structured data, such as notes taken by doctors and nurses during their rounds of patient rooms. The unstructured and semi-structured data calls out for object storage rather than a database.

TIP

The right side of Figure 4-6 may well be your answer. If you have inbound data that is highly structured, why not receive that data into some sort of a bronze zone database that will then propagate that information along a pipeline of databases into your data lake gold zone, where the data is then curated and ready for consumption? There's no sense in "un-structuring" data into an object store, only to have to re-create the structure that was originally present, right?

At the same time, the other part of your bronze zone can consist of S3, ADLS, or some other form of object storage, and ingest the incoming unstructured and semi-structured data.

Then, over in your gold zone, you can build mix-and-match data storage as needed to accommodate a relatively equal proportion between structured data and, on the other side, unstructured and semi-structured data.

As your data lake matures and your analytical needs expand, you can always add new specialized data management technologies or change out older ones for newer ones. You don't want to start out thinking about excessive data storage specialization, but your data lake can eventually wind up looking something like the reference architecture in Figure 4-7. As long as you're actively and aggressively managing your data pipelines and all the underlying components, you'll be in good shape.

WARNING

Specialization comes with a price, though. Every different data management technology that you add means that you'll be transmitting data from one component to another. *Transmitting* means copying data, which means additional storage, as well as potential delays, or even points of failure, along your data pipelines as each piece of data makes its way from its point of origin to its final storage home. You have to balance your need for specialized analytics against the price you pay as you stream or batch-copy data from one environment to another.

TIP

While you're still at the architecture stage, you should explore the good, the bad, and the ugly of at least several different alternatives. Walk through a real-world scenario for your organization with a unified architecture consisting of only object storage versus one or more compartmentalized and specialized alternatives. Run live demos with actual data using specific data services and products. You have an advantage with cloud-based services, being able to experiment with real-world scenarios at a relatively low cost. Have vendors of licensed products do show-and-tell live test demos with your data and their software and hardware to compare various alternatives.

The Old Meets the New at the Data Lake

As you set out to build your data lake, you might be among the fortunate data architects and strategists who don't have to contend with legacy analytical data, most likely under the management of data warehouses and data marts. Maybe you work for a startup company that just came into existence. Or perhaps you're part of a brand-new division within a larger company that was set up to help your company break into new markets.

However, even if you're off to a running start without having to worry about legacy analytical data, your organization may decide to follow the philosophy of a clear separation between data lakes and data warehousing instead of treating them as part of a unified environment.

Dealing with both data warehouses and data marts along with your data lake are a fact of life for data architects and strategists. Fortunately, your data lake reference architecture "library" presents you with a few common patterns that can help guide how you handle data lakes and data warehousing in a cohesive manner that makes sense for your organization. These patterns include

>> Subsuming part, but not all, of an existing data warehouse into your data lake

>> Subsuming most or even all of an existing data warehouse into your data lake

>> Using your data lake as a front end to a new data warehouse outside the boundaries of your data lake

>> Running a data lake and a data warehouse in parallel with each other

Keeping the shiny parts of the data warehouse

Lei, Anika, and Tim are the lead dimensional data modelers on the data warehousing team for a semiconductor manufacturer. Five years ago, they built a world-class dimensional model to help their company's executives and directors make key decisions from supply chain data. However, their dimensional data model was really the only good thing about the company's data warehouse. The data feeds, the staging layer, the ETL jobs . . . all the rest was sort of thrown together by a different group on the overall data warehousing team and has been a headache to maintain.

When Lei and the others heard that their company was thinking about building a data lake, they pulled all sorts of strings to get onto that project. They looked forward to the opportunity to work with modern data management technology. All three were selected to be part of the data lake team, and for the past three months, they've sat in meeting after meeting after meeting.

The data lake program manager has already decided that the data lake will totally replace the creaky old data warehouse. "Not so fast!" Lei pointed out in a meeting last week (though somewhat more diplomatically). Lei asked Tim to describe the dimensional model that the three of them had built. The program manager (as well as every other data lake team member present) was super-impressed, and they started brainstorming ways to have their cake and eat it, too, as the saying goes. Or, to translate that old saying into techno-speak: Was there a way to salvage all the good stuff from the data warehouse while they retired and moved beyond the not-so-good parts?

Figure 4-8 shows what Anika drew on the board and that everyone agreed was the best of all worlds.

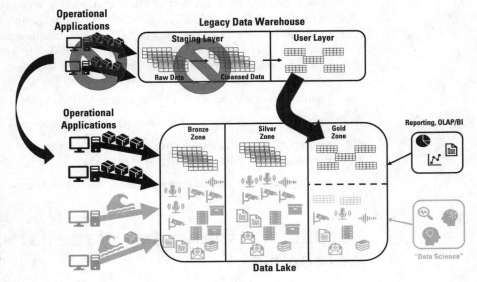

FIGURE 4-8: Incorporating the user layer of a legacy data warehouse into your data lake's gold zone.

Like most data warehouses, when you peeled the lid back and looked inside, the semiconductor manufacturer's data warehouse consisted of two distinct layers:

» **A staging layer,** where inbound data first lands and then undergoes all the necessary data transformation and cleansing

» **A user layer,** which is where the dimensional model that Lei, Anika, and Tim built resides and where users go for all their ready-to-analyze data

Lei pointed out that their data lake gold zone can be whatever makes sense for the types of analytics that the company's users will be doing. Many of them will still need to do the same types of BI and reporting — in other words, descriptive analytics — that they've always done. Just because the data warehouse will be retired doesn't mean that those descriptive analytics will be going away!

"We'll dedicate a portion of the gold zone to some sort of database, and we'll port our data model directly into the gold zone," Lei explained. "Then the supply chain data and other inbound data can come into the data lake's bronze zone, be cleansed and transformed into the silver zone, and then feed the same data structures that we've always used. But now, we'll be doing all that within the data lake, and we can do it right!"

After a round of applause, everyone in the room agreed: They'll keep and repurpose the data warehouse's user layer and embed a new sort-of-data warehouse right inside the data lake. Problem solved!

Flooding the data warehouse

Over at the primary competitor to the semiconductor manufacturer where Lei, Anika, and Tim work, their data lake team is facing a similar problem, but with a twist.

Raj and Sharon are in a conference room, scribbling a drawing of their own. In their case, not only do they have a world-class user data model in their legacy data warehouse, but they also have an equivalently strong end-to-end data infrastructure, including their staging layer and the entire portfolio of ETL jobs.

Still, just like their competitors, their data warehouse will be going away when the new data lake is deployed. In their case, as Raj explains, the data warehouse is hosted in a third-party data center with monthly operations costs far exceeding what the company would spend if it moved to a public cloud provider.

"That's okay," Raj confidently explains, as he starts scribbling on the board, drawing the picture shown in Figure 4-9. "Our legacy data warehouse is highly compartmentalized and very well architected and engineered, so we can subsume each of the major components right into the corresponding area of the data lake. Batch data ingestion will now come into the bronze zone rather than the data warehouse staging layer. In fact, that staging layer will be allocated between the bronze and silver zones for the raw and refined data, respectively. Then we'll move the data model into the gold zone, and that's where the curated data will be. The existing ETL might need to be tweaked a bit, but we can reuse most of it, at least logically, even if we decide to replace the tools that we use."

"Problem solved," everyone agrees as they move on to looking at new capabilities of the data lake.

Using your data lake as a supersized staging layer

The previous two scenarios (refer to Figures 4-8 and 4-9) both follow the premise that a data lake can include the data models and infrastructure that would otherwise be called a data warehouse or a data mart. In other words, the data lake isn't purely for data science, and it isn't solely built using cloud-based object storage.

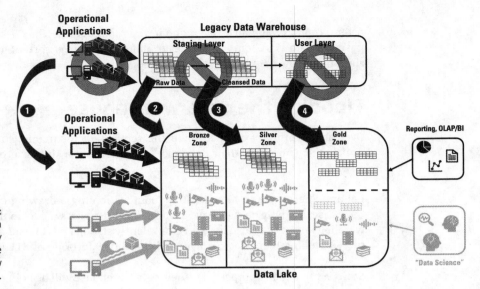

FIGURE 4-9:
Subsuming an end-to-end legacy data warehouse into your new data lake.

REMEMBER

But what if the powers that be at your company are, shall we say, somewhat dogmatic about a clear demarcation between data lakes and data warehouses? Chapter 3 describes how one of the most significant challenges to building a data lake has nothing to do with technology but rather a general lack of agreement about what a data lake even is and where the boundaries might be.

If you work in a company where the worlds of data lakes and data warehouses are clearly and immutably separate, how do you handle either of these scenarios?

Figure 4-10 shows how your data lake and data warehouse might exist as separate entities from one another but might still have touch points that require coordination and interoperability.

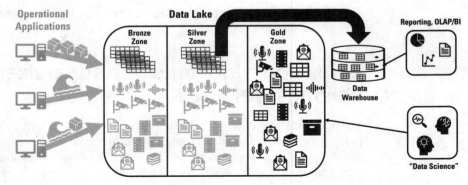

FIGURE 4-10:
Your data lake feeding your data warehouse.

Lucerne, Maya, and Rio all work for an energy exploration company that's building a data lake. In fact, within the IT organization at this company, the data lake team is the place to be — this is where all the excitement is happening!

For better or for worse, Lucerne and her colleagues all work on a totally separate data warehouse team. They have already been working on retiring their company's legacy data warehouse and had proposed something similar to either Figure 4-8 or Figure 4-9 to support BI going forward.

"Nothing doing!" the data lake project manager snarled when he saw that proposal. "Our data lake is for machine learning and all sorts of advanced analytics, not that old-fashioned BI stuff!"

After that rather contentious meeting, the data warehousing team huddles to figure out a plan B.

"All the data that we need for BI will be coming right into the data lake," Maya points out. "It would be a waste of resources to reinvent the wheel for a brand-new data warehouse."

"We might not have to," Rio heads to the whiteboard, sketching out the picture in Figure 4-10. "We'll fight the battle if we have to, but we can tap into the data lake and use it as a supersized staging area. They're going to be doing all the cleansing and refinement, so we get an outbound feed from the data lake silver zone — sort of use it like our staging layer — and then do the final round of transformations into the star schema's dimensional model in our separate data warehouse."

Satisfied that they have a plan in place, Lucerne schedules a follow-up meeting to present this idea. They'll build a brand-new data warehouse to replace the legacy environment that's being retired, but they can leverage a lot of what the data lake is doing on the front end for economies of scale.

Split-streaming your inbound data along two paths

Suppose, though, that the data lake leader at the energy exploration company refuses to even allow the proposed data feed from the silver zone into the new data warehouse. What then?

Figure 4-11 shows how a data warehouse and a data lake can exist, side by side, as peer analytical environments, using *split-streaming* data feeds for common data needed by both.

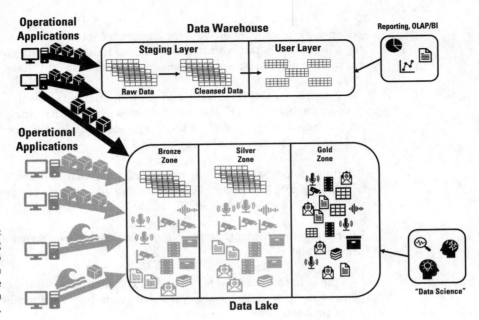

FIGURE 4-11:
Split-streaming data feeds to support both your data lake and your data warehouse.

For building a new data warehouse, the architecture shown in Figure 4-11 is probably the worst option of all. If, however, the powers that be insist that there's no way the data lake will serve as a front end to anything other than its own gold zone, then at least you have a reference architecture that will support all the analytics classes that your business users need.

You do have a silver lining of sorts with the architecture shown in Figure 4-11. Suppose that at the energy exploration company where Lucerne, Maya, and Rio work, they just built and deployed their data warehouse last year, using the latest and greatest technology. Basically, that data warehouse isn't going anywhere!

In this case, the data lake, not the data warehouse, is the new kid on the block. Any source data used by the data warehouse that will also be needed by the data lake can be split-streamed into the data lake as the bronze zone is built out. Then, as the data lake continues to be built, its data pipelines and analytics will progressively come to join those of the data warehouse.

Over time, as both the data warehouse and the data lake do their own things, the architects at the energy company will likely come across data lake content that would be useful for the data warehouse, and vice versa. Figure 4-12 shows how both raw data and refined data can be fed from either environment — the data lake or the data warehouse — to the other as time goes on. Basically, even if your company's philosophy calls for a clear separation between your data lake and your data warehouse, you can still share content as needed without violating the principle of separate environments to support BI and data science.

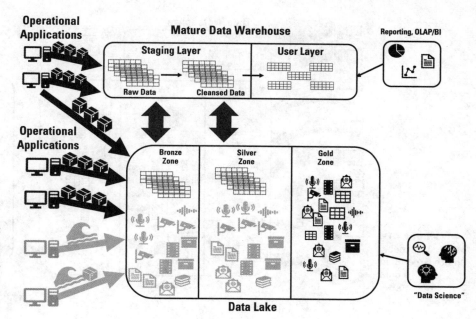

FIGURE 4-12: Ongoing data interchange between your data lake and your data warehouse.

Which is the bigger breadbox?

If your mind insists on equating *data lake* with *big data,* you're probably thinking that a data lake is larger — probably significantly larger — than a data warehouse, as shown in Figure 4-13.

Sure, that's possible, especially if you're using cloud-based, highly scalable object storage for your data lake, and you plan to bring in monstrous amounts of data over time.

But can a data lake actually be *smaller* than a data warehouse? Absolutely! Figure 4-14 shows that exact situation: a very large data warehouse compared to a more modest, lower-capacity data lake.

REMEMBER

When it comes to the distinction between a data lake and a data warehouse — presuming that your organization insists on making that distinction, rather than thinking in more general terms of enterprise-scale analytical data — don't think in terms of size and "newness" (for example, "Data lakes are newer so, therefore, a data lake will store more data than a data warehouse"). Instead, think in terms of usage and types of data, with size not even factoring into the distinction. If you really want to be dogmatic about it, a data warehouse stores primarily structured data to support BI, while a data lake stores all types of data to support data science.

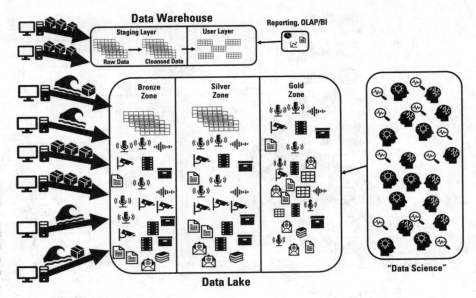

FIGURE 4-13:
A data lake that is much larger than a data warehouse.

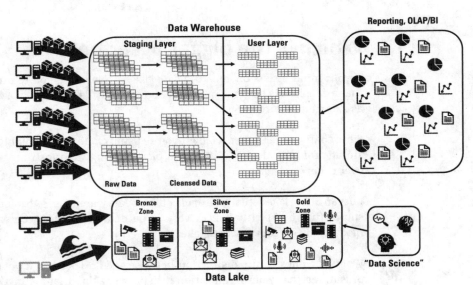

FIGURE 4-14:
A data warehouse that is much larger than a data lake.

TECHNICAL
STUFF

However, a newly built data warehouse that is constructed on top of a modern high-capacity database such as SAP's HANA or Oracle's Exadata, can conceivably contain much larger data volumes than a modest data lake. Perhaps your organization plans to do some mind-blowing analytics but doesn't need massive amounts of data for those algorithms and models. Your environment might look more like the one depicted in Figure 4-14 than the one in Figure 4-13.

Bringing Outside Water into Your Data Lake

If you're from Chicago, you probably love Chicago-style deep-dish pizza. If so, you're not alone. In fact, some of Chicago's most famous pizzerias opened restaurants in cities such as Phoenix and Denver, where thousands of former Chicagoans live. And it gets even better! These "branches" of Chicago's pizzerias out in the desert or at the foot of the Rockies ship in real Chicago water to make their dough. As the story goes, the secret to authentic Chicago pizza is genuine Chicago water.

Then you have bagels. New York bagel bakeries are just as famous in their own way as Chicago's pizzerias. And wouldn't you know it: You can find New York–style bagel bakeries in cities such as Phoenix (yes, again) and Las Vegas that ship in genuine New York water because it's supposedly the secret ingredient to authentic New York bagels.

Whether you're talking about remote Chicago pizzerias or remote New York bagel places, they both ship in their "hometown" water via truck or train or maybe even by plane. In other words, they're bringing in *outside* water using *batch feeds*, following the same paradigm that a data lake (or data warehouse) does for its own batch data feeds.

Streaming versus batch external data feeds

So, now the discussion comes back around to data lakes. The analogy to Chicago or New York water being shipped to Denver or Phoenix or Las Vegas is external data coming into a data lake from an outside provider, as compared to data coming from internal applications and systems. Figure 4-15 illustrates how external data (on the bottom of the diagram) comes into the bronze zone, silver zone, or gold zone of the data lake.

Two questions arise from the architecture shown in Figure 4-15:

>> **How do you decide whether to bring data into the bronze zone, or the silver zone, or the gold zone?** (The figure shows all of them occurring.) The answer is simple. If an external data provider is providing raw data with little or no error correction or other refinement, then the appropriate destination would be where your internal raw data goes: the data lake bronze zone. If, however, the external data is refined — error-corrected and possibly enhanced with descriptive metadata as you would do with your own raw data along your data pipelines — then the data is best brought into the silver zone. If, however, the data is "ready to consume" and can stand on its own, then you can safely bring the data into your gold zone.

» **What sort of data feeds are those from the external data: batch or streaming?** That's a great question, and the answer is — drumroll, please — either! Go back to the Chicago pizza and New York bagel example for a moment where shipping hometown water by truck, rail, or air is analogous to a batch data feed. In other words, "batches" of water periodically arrive at the pizzeria in Denver or the bagel place in Las Vegas and are used as needed. Suppose, though, that the Chicago pizzeria in Phoenix had a very, very long hose running about 1,500 miles all the way back to Chicago. Then, when the time comes to make another batch of that fantastic Chicago deep-dish dough, all the kitchen staff would need to do is turn on the faucet, and — presto! — right from the tap comes good old Chicago River water! (Okay, so this analogy isn't specifically related to lakes, but at least it's water-related.)

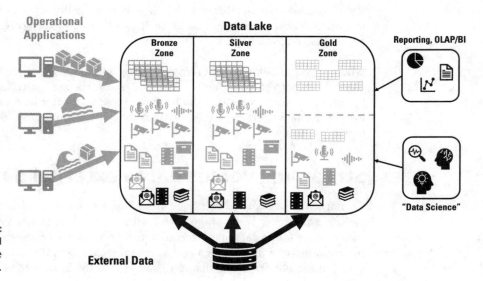

FIGURE 4-15: Feeding external data into the data lake.

You probably get the idea by now. External data can come into your data lake in batches or it can come in via a streaming interface. Basically, if the external data provider supports streaming data feeds, and if your analytics would benefit from real-time or near-real-time external data, then by all means plan on a streaming feed. Basically, you have the same alternatives for external data that you do for internal data: batch or streaming, based on:

» Whether the source can support streaming

» Whether your analytics require — or at least would benefit from — streaming data

Ingestion versus as-needed external data access

Water, unlike data, is physical. The Chicago water that goes into a deep-dish pizza or the New York water used to make bagels is an actual physical entity that somehow needs to make its way from its home city to a distant location.

Data isn't physical, though. True, we build data lakes and data warehouses to avoid heavy analytical workloads on our source applications, meaning that we copy and then restructure our data to be optimized for analytics. Does the same paradigm apply to external data as well as internal data?

Not necessarily. Some data providers may have ready-to-go, optimized-for-analytics data sets available on demand. Figure 4-16 illustrates an alternative approach to accessing external data. Instead of ingesting that data, as shown in Figure 4-15, you access the external data on demand.

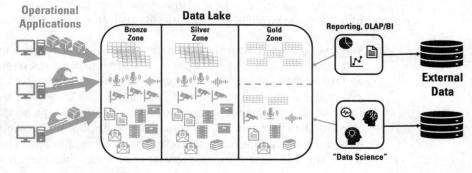

FIGURE 4-16:
On-demand access to external data for your analytics.

FISHING IN THE AWS DATA EXCHANGE

Looking for interesting and potentially valuable external data for your data lake? Check out the AWS Data Exchange (https://aws.amazon.com/data-exchange). You can "find, subscribe to, and use third-party data in the cloud" using an AWS Data Exchange application programming interface (API) that allows you to load data directly into S3 and then use a wide variety of Amazon analytical services. Healthcare data, business transactions, weather data, and much more . . . it's all there as needed.

TIP

You'll typically use on-demand access to external data for curated, ready-to-go external data — the same quality of data that if you were ingesting it, you'd be putting right into your gold zone. Remote data that requires data cleansing and significant transformation can still be accessed on demand, but be aware that you'll still need to do the necessary data "sprucing up," which will likely impact the response time to queries and reports or take longer for more complex analytics.

Playing at the Edge of the Lake

Here's sort of a trick question: If your organization decides to invest significant time, capital, and resources to build a world-class data lake, will that data lake support all your organization's analytical needs?

The answer: Not necessarily. Think about one of the primary value propositions of a data lake: curating integrated and synthesized data from dozens or potentially hundreds or even thousands of data sources into a single logical environment.

Suppose, though, that you have analytical needs that only require finite sets of data that don't need to be integrated with other data for the requisite algorithms and models? Suppose also that those highly compartmentalized analytical needs exist "at the edge" of your enterprise? Figure 4-17 shows a real-world example from the energy exploration company where Lucerne, Maya, and Rio all work. The company has invested millions of dollars in drilling-site sensors that continuously monitor various temperature and pressure readings deep inside oil and gas wells. The wells also are under constant video surveillance with cameras trained on critical moving parts of the drilling equipment.

The readings and output from the sensors and video monitors are all fed into models that predict equipment problems and failure. The company has shifted its preventive maintenance program for its hundreds of remote wells to be driven by analytical failure prediction rather than scheduled physical inspections. If the analytics detect imminent equipment failure, the machinery at that well will be automatically shut down until a maintenance crew arrives to swap out parts or do whatever they need to do to get the machinery back online and functioning correctly. If the model works as it's supposed to, the machinery will be shut down before it "blows up" and causes extensive — and expensive — damage to that drilling site. Pretty smart, right?

One incredibly important question needs to be asked, however: Should the failure prediction analytics take place in the company's data lake environment?

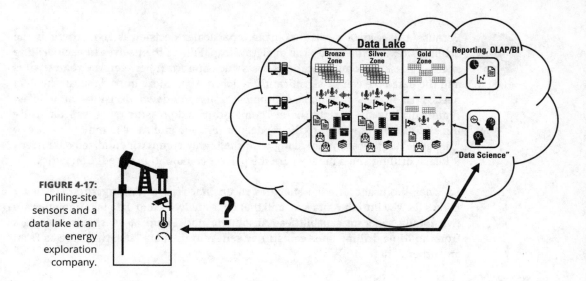

FIGURE 4-17:
Drilling-site
sensors and a
data lake at an
energy
exploration
company.

For all the power of data lakes, this particular scenario is better handled through "edge analytics," as shown in Figure 4-18.

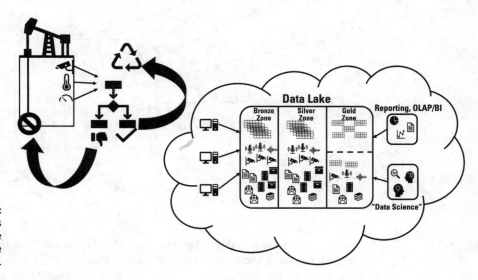

FIGURE 4-18:
Edge analytics
existing outside
the control of the
data lake.

Instead of constantly transmitting data from the remote drilling site all the way to the cloud service where the company's data lake is located, and then sending back a "Shut down now!" order to the equipment if the problem detection model indicates possible or imminent equipment failure, the analytics are performed "at the edge" of the enterprise — in other words, not in or adjacent to the data lake, but at the actual point of operation. Why?

TECHNICAL STUFF

Because all the data needed to make a particular decision is right there at the drilling site. By embedding the analytical capabilities themselves in each drilling site — excessive communications costs back and forth between the remote sites and the data lake can be significantly reduced. Even more important, all the data needed to make continuous continue-versus-shutdown decisions at a given remote drilling site is right there! Temperature and pressure readings from drilling site #2 don't factor into the models for drilling site #1. The remote nature of "the edge" in this scenario, along with the highly compartmentalized data needs for each drilling site's models, are the perfect combination for edge analytics.

So, does the usage of edge analytics mean that remote drilling site data never makes its way into the data lake and that edge analytics and data lake analytics are two totally separate capabilities? Absolutely not! Figure 4-19 shows how data from multiple drilling sites can still be sent into the data lake, the same as from any other data feed.

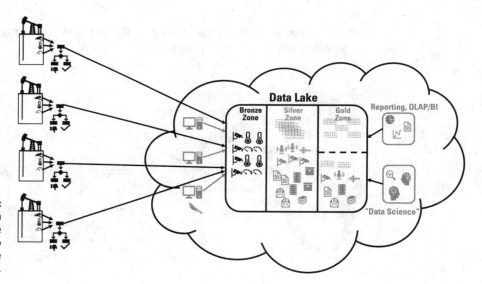

FIGURE 4-19:
Remote data from edge analytics can also be sent to the data lake.

The actual continue-versus-shutdown decision is still made at the drilling sites themselves, using local data. However, temperature and pressure readings, along with video of the drilling equipment, can still be valuable for other analytical needs that do require integrated data. In this case, the energy exploration company doubles down on its usage of remote data by using the data at the various edge sites themselves, as well as transmitting the data into the data lake for additional analysis.

» Supporting multiple ingestion models

» Bringing data into your bronze zone

» Deciding among your bronze zone storage options

» Cataloging data in your bronze zone

» Analyzing your bronze zone data

Chapter 5

Anybody Hungry? Ingesting and Storing Raw Data in Your Bronze Zone

Your bronze zone might go by some other name in your data lake environment, such as:

» The raw zone

» The landing zone

» The sushi zone, where you consume raw data

Just kidding about the last one. . . .

Regardless of what name you decide to use, the bronze zone is where you first ingest data from your operational applications into your data lake, as shown in Figure 5-1.

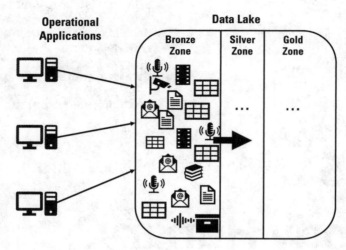

FIGURE 5-1:
Data flowing into your data lake bronze zone.

You probably won't be surprised to learn that the diagram in Figure 5-1 is a very high-level, overly simplified depiction of how your bronze zone works. In fact, you need to really dig deep into three distinct but related aspects of your bronze zone:

>> Data ingestion

>> Data storage and management

>> Data cataloging

You need to match up the particulars of your data and analytical needs with the best reference architecture options (see Chapter 4) in order for your organization to help you make key decisions about what paths to follow for each of these three key bronze zone aspects.

In this chapter, I explain the importance of setting up your bronze zone as the gateway into your data lake. You see different approaches for data ingestion, along with various options for storing data in your bronze zone. You also see how cataloging your bronze zone content is a critical first step to finding your way around your data lake. Finally, even though your bronze zone contains raw data, you still will want to bring in your analytical power against your bronze zone contents.

Ingesting Data with the Best of Both Worlds

You bring data into your data lake using one or both of two different architectural approaches:

>> Streaming data feeds

>> Batch data feeds

Row, row, row your data, gently down the stream

Data streaming and data lakes go together like, well, a cool, mountain stream flowing right into a crystal clear lake. In fact, part of the reason that you're even reading a book about a so-called "data lake" goes directly back to the origins of the term. Back in 2010, James Dixon, the founder and former chief technology officer of Pentaho, put it this way: "The contents of the data lake stream in from a source to fill the lake. . . ." So, the stream-flowing-into-the-lake analogy is very much at the core of why "big data" has become almost a passé term, and your organization has set out to build a data lake built largely on big data technology.

Analogies are one thing, though. You know that the devil is in the details, so how does data streaming work in the context of your data lake and, in particular, for your data lake's bronze zone?

REMEMBER

The key principle behind streaming data is a *continuous flow* of data from a point of origin to one or more destinations, as contrasted with periodically transmitting *batches* of data. (Batch data feeds still play a role in your data lake, as I explain shortly.) The middle data flow in Figure 5-2 conceptually illustrates a streaming data feed into your bronze zone, as contrasted with the top data feed and its periodic batches of data.

You should take note of two important points about Figure 5-2:

>> Regardless of whether your data comes into your data lake's bronze zone in batch mode (the top flow) or via streaming (the middle flow), all of that inbound data still winds up logically "mashed together" and managed as a supersized collection of raw data.

>> Any given data source can conceivably use *both* streaming and batch data flows for different sets of data, as shown in the bottom feed.

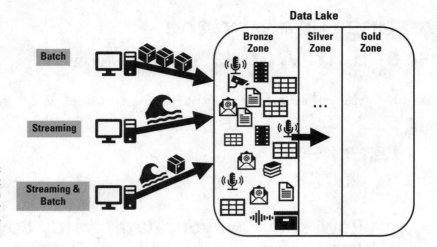

FIGURE 5-2:
Three different
operational data
feeds into your
data lake bronze
zone.

Streaming data works great when your data lake has a "need for speed" for certain sets of data. If you're trying to minimize the *latency* (the lag time, or delay) between when some piece of data is first created in an operational application's database and when that data is brought into the data lake, cleansed and refined, and made available for analysis, then streaming is the way to go.

TECHNICAL STUFF

You have various options for how you can stream data into your data lake:

>> Open-source data streaming services and frameworks, such as Apache Flink, Apache Kafka, or Apache Storm

>> Vendor- or framework-specific data streaming services, such as Amazon Kinesis

>> Vendor-enhanced open-source streaming, such as Amazon Managed Streaming for Apache Kafka (MSK)

Regardless of which streaming service or framework you choose, you should look for several key capabilities when you stream data into your data lake:

>> **High availability:** The under-the-covers architecture of your selected streaming service uses multiple pathways to guarantee that a source-to-destination route is (almost) always available.

>> **Durability and fault tolerance:** Data placed on the streaming service isn't lost forever if some type of "hiccup" occurs.

>> **Low latency:** Source-to-destination streaming is best suited for data feeds where time delays between data origination and data analysis need to be minimized.

>> **Maintaining and replaying historical data:** Being able to "replay" data from a stream, if necessary, prevents you from having to re-extract and retransmit the desired data from its origination.

You can set up most streaming services to allow more than one destination to subscribe to a particular data feed. Suppose your data lake–supported analytics will coexist with "edge analytics" in your overall enterprise analytics portfolio (see Chapter 4). Figure 5-3 illustrates a typical data and analytics environment that you might use if you worked for an energy exploration company with numerous drilling wells scattered around remote or even difficult-to-reach locations.

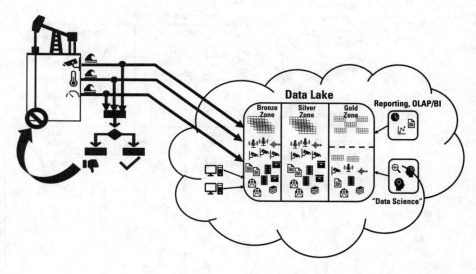

FIGURE 5-3: Multiple subscribers to sensor and video data streams.

You would implement "edge analytics" capabilities at each well, which would receive steady streams of temperature, pressure, and video monitoring data from sensors and cameras buried deep within each drilling well. In the event of abnormal readings that indicate potential or imminent equipment failure, the controlling mechanism at that well would shut down the equipment until maintenance crews can be dispatched to inspect and, if necessary, fix or replace faulty equipment.

However, you'd also want to analyze all that temperature, pressure, and video data from each well alongside similar data from all your other wells, which is where your data lake comes in. As shown in Figure 5-3, each of the three data streams from a drilling well has not one but two subscribers for the same data:

>> The localized "edge analytics" that continually ingest data to constantly make continue/shut down decisions at each well

>> Your data lake, where all that sensor data is ingested and used for other types of analytics

You can also set up multiple subscribers to a data stream if you're going to be running your data lake in parallel with a totally separate data warehouse. Chapter 4 covers how logical "split-streaming" can be used for a source application that needs to send data to both a data warehouse and your data lake. You can use a streaming service to turn that figurative split-streaming into literal split-streaming, as shown in Figure 5-4.

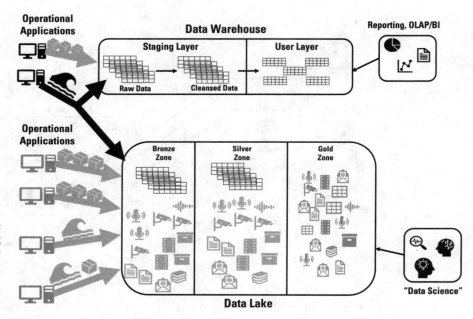

FIGURE 5-4: Using a streaming service to split-stream data into both a data lake and a data warehouse.

What sorts of data are particularly suitable to stream into your data lake? You'll typically use streaming for:

>> Internet of Things (IoT) sensor data from smart homes or smart buildings

>> Other IoT sensor data from industrial equipment and components such as jet engines, remote drilling well monitoring, and factory floor machinery

>> High-volume business transaction data such as online e-commerce sales

>> Time-sensitive medical data from hospital patient monitoring systems

Each "piece" of streaming data sent to your data lake is typically smaller, such as a single reading from a hospital patient's heart monitor or a calibration reading from an IoT-enabled robotic drill press. However, your data lake will be on the receiving end of tens or hundreds of thousands — or perhaps even millions! — of streaming *events* each second along each data stream. Each data stream will likely see ebbs and flows of event volume over a given period of time, but for the most part, you'll have a continuous and steady flow of data from some point of origin into your data lake.

TECHNICAL STUFF

You'll want to get assistance from your organization's cloud computing team when it's time to select the streaming services that you use for your data lake. You have many different options, both open source and vendor-provided, and you'll find that each has its own strengths and weaknesses. Additionally, new versions of streaming services regularly become available, and the various services tend to leapfrog each other.

Still, you have a few guidelines to help you at least narrow down your options on your own. Open-source streaming such as Flink or Kafka is popular, especially in heterogeneous environments involving multiple clouds, or if you need to send data from applications hosted in your company's on-premises data center to Amazon Web Services (AWS) or Microsoft Azure.

TIP

On the other hand, if your operational applications are all hosted in AWS and you're building your data lake in AWS, then it makes sense to at least consider an AWS streaming service such as Kinesis.

Supplementing your streaming data with batch data

Some of the data that you need to bring into your data lake is better suited to batch data feeds than streaming. Examples include the following:

>> Product returns and refunds from each retail location totaled up at the end of each business day

>> Data from your company's human resources organization, with all the details of the latest employee review cycle: promotions, raises, evaluation rankings, and all the rest

>> Inventory reconciliation data from each of your company's warehouses and distribution centers

TECHNICAL STUFF

If you've ever worked with a data warehouse, all that extraction, transformation, and loading (ETL) from your source systems into your data warehouse (or data mart) is the classic example of a batch data feed. Even if your organization will be decommissioning your tired old data warehouse and subsuming all that business intelligence (BI) support into your shiny new data lake, you'll still find that a lot of the data warehouse's tried-and-true architectural concepts — such as batch-oriented ETL — will be making the journey to the data lake.

Figure 5-2 shows how batch data feeds coexist alongside streaming data feeds — both even sometimes coming from the same data source — for your data lake, with both batch and streaming feeds sending data into your bronze zone.

The gray area between streaming and batch

In a purely conceptual sense, a streaming data feed works as follows:

1. A "piece of data" is produced in a source application or from some sort of sensor.

2. That single "piece of data" is plopped into the streaming interface between the point of origin and your data lake.

3. That single "piece of data" quickly travels along the stream until it arrives at your data lake.

4. That single "piece of data" is transferred from the stream into your data lake's bronze zone.

Sounds pretty simple, right? Well, the mechanics under the cover (or would that be "below the surface of the water"?) are probably a little more complicated. But don't worry — in this case, the complication is to your benefit!

Figure 5-5 takes you back to that remote drilling well somewhere way up in the Rocky Mountains that's operated by your energy exploration company. Sensors and cameras buried within the well produce a continuous flow of temperature and pressure readings, as well as both still images and video.

Presume that you have a streaming interface between the drilling site and your data lake. (To avoid complicating the scenario even further, forget about the "edge analytics" at the drilling site itself for a moment.)

Theoretically, each "piece of data" — a single temperature reading, or a single pressure reading, or maybe a short snippet of video — is placed into the data stream and travels to your data lake, where the data is "unloaded" into your bronze zone.

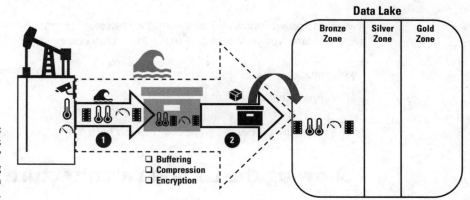

FIGURE 5-5:
Under-the-covers
"micro-batching"
within streaming
input to your data
lake.

❑ Buffering
❑ Compression
❑ Encryption

However, in this case, "theoretically" actually means "it's really more compli-cated than that." Figure 5-5 shows how a small collection of data produced by the sensors and cameras is actually buffered together *at the drilling site* into a sort of "micro-batch." After the designated buffer size is filled, the "micro-batch" of data is transmitted along the data stream to your data lake.

Basically, your *logical* data stream actually has characteristics of batch data feeds under the covers. For all intents and purposes, you still have a streaming inter-face. But in the interest of technological efficiency, small groups of data are

>> Buffered together

>> Possibly compressed into a smaller number of bytes

>> Possibly encrypted

REMEMBER

When it comes to your data lake's bronze zone, any under-the-covers "micro-batching" of data along a streaming interface doesn't matter all that much. You still have a streaming interface that minimizes latency and is well suited for your data lake.

Joining the Data Ingestion Fraternity

You can safely presume that if you're building an enterprise-scale data lake and will be ingesting data from many different sources, you'll have a combination of both batch and streaming interfaces. But how should you handle each?

Two data transmission and processing architectures from the world of big data are candidates for your data lake ingestion architecture:

>> Lambda architecture

>> Kappa architecture

In the following sections, I walk you through both.

Following the Lambda architecture

Figure 5-6 illustrates the Lambda architecture in which batch and streaming data feeds have their own separate pathways between the places where data is generated and where data is consumed.

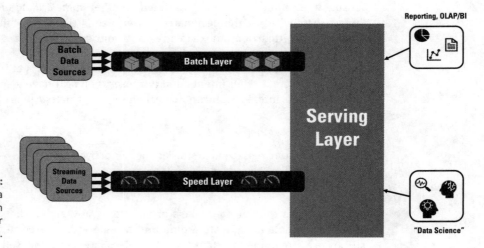

FIGURE 5-6:
The Lambda
data ingestion
architecture for
your data lake.

In the Lambda architecture, the pathway for batch data is known as, well, the *batch layer.* (Surprise!) The streaming data pathway, however, is known as the *speed layer.* After all, streaming data is all about minimizing latency and, thus, increasing speed between the place where data is created and the place where it's consumed, right?

The headline for the Lambda architecture reads as follows: Batch data has different characteristics than streaming data, so it makes sense to have two separate pathways at work.

TECHNICAL STUFF

For your data lake, you might use a traditional, tried-and-true batch-oriented ETL tool to move large volumes of data at regular intervals from the source applications into your data lake's bronze zone. You would then, in parallel, set up a streaming service such as Flink or Kinesis to handle the speed layer and the streaming data along that pathway. Pretty straightforward, right?

Using the Kappa architecture

You'll regularly come across a criticism of the Lambda architecture that asks the following question: "Why do we need to maintain two totally separate pathways for our inbound data, with two different tools or services?"

Okay, that question is reasonable to ask, along with a follow-up question: "Is there a way to converge these two different pathways into a single source-to-destination route?"

Technically, you can batch up your streaming data and periodically send packages along your regular batch layer. Many streaming systems sort of do that anyway, as shown in Figure 5-5, where you gather small amounts of streaming data and then buffer, compress, and encrypt that "micro-batch" before sending the data to your data lake. Can you follow that paradigm, but on a much larger scale?

WARNING

You probably can, but you'd be defeating the purpose of streaming data into your data lake in the first place. Streaming data is all about speed and reducing latency, so the more data you package up, the greater the latency along that pathway.

What about trying it the other way? Figure 5-7 illustrates the Kappa architecture, in which your batch data is actually treated as streaming data and sent to your data lake (or some other destination) via a streaming service such as Kafka, Kinesis, or Storm.

TIP

When it comes to your organization's data lake, you need to have a good idea of the types of data that are being produced and that will be consumed in your analytics, along with a solid understanding of the timeliness of the data-to-analytics pathway. Specifically:

>> If your data will be more or less evenly divided between batch and streaming, you're probably better off with separate tool sets for each, which means that your data lake will be built around the Lambda architecture.

>> If your data lake will be ingesting mostly batch data with only minimal streaming data, then you're also headed down the path of the Lambda architecture. However, you also need to carefully examine the platforms and storage engines that you'll be using in your data lake (see the next section).

FIGURE 5-7:
The Kappa data
ingestion
architecture for
your data lake.

> » If your data lake will be ingesting mostly streaming data with only minimal
> batch data, you should probably look strongly at implementing the Kappa
> architecture, where even your batch data will be sent to the data lake via a
> streaming service such as Kafka.

Storing Data in Your Bronze Zone

Data is flying toward your data lake from all corners of your enterprise. You know
that the first stop for all that data will be your data lake's bronze zone. But how
exactly are you going to store the data? Will you use the same storage models as
data moves downstream into your silver and gold zones? You need to get your data
lake house in order because you've got company coming!

Implementing a monolithic bronze zone

The simplest, most straightforward bronze zone architecture is to use a single
object storage layer straight out of your data lake conceptual reference architecture playbook (see Chapter 4), as depicted in Figure 5-8.

In the AWS environment, you would use Amazon Simple Storage Service (S3). If
you're building your data lake in Microsoft's Azure environment, you would use
the Azure Data Lake Storage (ADLS) platform.

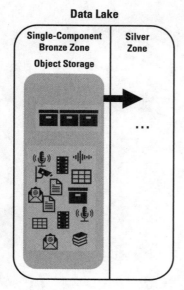

Data Lake

Single-Component
Bronze Zone

Silver
Zone

Object Storage

...

FIGURE 5-8:
Going for storage
simplicity with
only object
storage in your
bronze zone.

**TECHNICAL
STUFF**

Theoretically, you can also use the Hadoop Distributed File System (HDFS) as your data lake's bronze zone object store. However, HDFS is mostly out of favor with modern data lakes because of the close coupling of computing power and data storage. Still, if you have an older first-generation data lake still operational, then HDFS may well be the storage platform for your data lake as a whole, including your bronze zone.

No matter what data sources will be feeding your data lake, or what types of data each will be providing (structured, semi-structured, unstructured), or how the data arrives in your bronze zone (batch, streaming, or both), all data lands in your bronze zone as "peers."

Building a multi-component bronze zone

You aren't restricted to low-cost, cloud object storage for your bronze zone. As described in Chapter 4, one of your reference architecture options is to implement a multi-component bronze zone. The most common portfolio you'll find for this option is to augment your object storage (usually S3 or ADLS) with a relational database. Figure 5-9 illustrates a simple multi-component bronze zone.

Why would you want to sacrifice the simplicity of a monolithic, single-platform bronze zone? Figure 5-10 shows you the tradeoffs between ingesting relational database data into a single-component bronze zone versus a bronze zone composed of both a database and object storage.

Data Lake

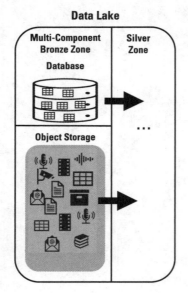

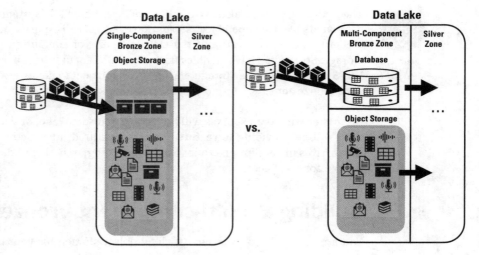

FIGURE 5-9:
Implementing a multi-component bronze zone.

FIGURE 5-10:
Ingesting data from a database: object storage versus database in your bronze zone.

TECHNICAL
STUFF

With a single-component bronze zone, you need to "unload" your incoming relational data into (for the AWS environment) a non-database format such as Apache Parquet inside of an S3 bucket. All your incoming database data is now inside your data lake and, specifically, inside your bronze zone, but the data is no longer in "genuine" database format, as shown on the left side of Figure 5-10.

If, however, your bronze zone contains a database as well as object storage, your inbound data can go directly into the target database (see the right side of Figure 5-10). With a database-to-database feed, you can easily retain all the semantics of the source data that may be useful downstream in your data lake gold zone, including:

- >> The full database table structures
- >> Primary key and foreign key relationships
- >> Any range-of-value and list-of-value constraints

Coordinating your bronze zone with your silver and gold zones

Deciding between a single-component and multi-component bronze zone has repercussions for your silver and gold zones. Figure 5-11 shows one likely data pipeline through your data lake if you set up a multi-component bronze zone with a database alongside your object storage.

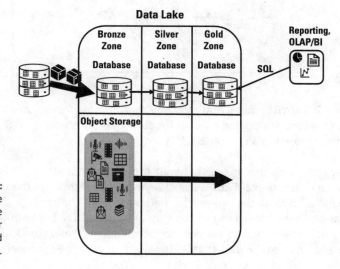

FIGURE 5-11:
Carrying a bronze zone database through to your data lake gold zone.

You'll likely carry that database-managed data all the way from your bronze zone into your gold zone with a database also used for data cleansing and refinement in your silver zone (see Chapter 6). In other words, when you make the decision that the additional bronze zone complexity of a database is worth it, you most likely wouldn't subsequently "unload" that inbound database data into object storage in either the silver zone or the gold zone.

Your BI and reporting users would access the database-managed data in the gold zone, the same as if they were accessing a data warehouse for their data.

So, if at least some of your users will be doing BI and reporting functionality, does that lock you into using database technology in your data lake alongside object storage? Definitely not!

Figure 5-12 shows how you can go down the single-component bronze zone route and carry that model all the way through your entire data lake and still support BI, reporting, and other SQL-based analytics.

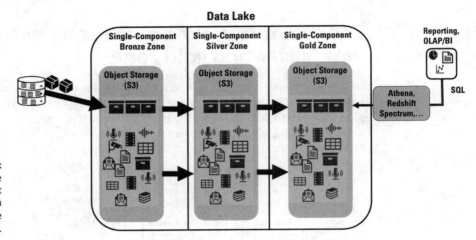

FIGURE 5-12: Carrying bronze zone object storage through to your data lake gold zone.

In the AWS environment, you can use Amazon Athena or Amazon Redshift Spectrum to access underlying S3 data for classic BI purposes, even if the underlying data isn't stored in a database.

Hmmm . . . does that mean that your bronze zone platform decision — single-platform or multi-platform — must be maintained through the rest of your data lake zones? Again, the answer is: Definitely not! Figure 5-13 shows how your bronze and silver zones can exclusively use S3 or ADLS, but within your data lake gold zone, you decide to use database technology (Yellowbrick, for example) to store and manage the data that will be used for classic BI purposes.

You have total control over which platforms to use for your data lake from the moment inbound data hits your bronze zone. You'll definitely come across strong opinions that a data lake is only composed of object storage or that after data is loaded from data lake object storage into a downstream database, that data has now left the data lake. You should certainly take those opinions into consideration. But your only concern is to build an enterprise-scale analytical data environment that not only works for your organization today, but also will be "bionic" and allow you to adjust over time to new analytical needs and new technologies (see Chapter 2). The concept of a "bionic" data lake begins in your bronze zone, so design and build what makes sense!

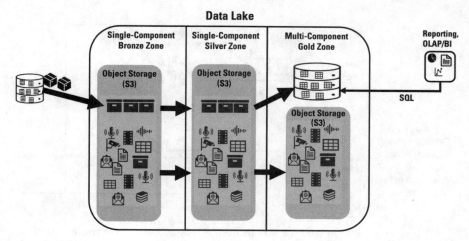

Data Lake

FIGURE 5-13:
Going back to a database in a multi-component gold zone.

Just Passing Through: The Cross-Zone Express Lane

Streaming data will usually play an important role in bringing data into your data lake. Streaming data can actually complicate your bronze zone architecture, though. But don't worry: The "complication" can be beneficial if you take a holistic view of your bronze zone, in particular, and your data lake as a whole.

The most basic paradigm for your bronze zone is that inbound data, whether batch or streaming, arrives at the entry point to your data lake and is "unloaded" — sort of like FedEx bringing a package to your house or apartment and dropping it on your doorstep.

TECHNICAL STUFF

Streaming data services, however, usually have some degree of *persistence.* In other words, a stream actually retains data for a period of time. The persistence allows a stream to be "replayed" by your analytics if necessary.

Figure 5-14 depicts two different approaches to inbound streaming data. The top of the figure shows the straightforward "stream and unload" model. The bottom of the figure, however, shows how the data stream itself acts as sort of an extension to your bronze layer. In addition to "unloaded" data now sitting in object storage (or perhaps a database), the streamed data isn't actually stored into your data lake until the silver zone. The silver zone is where you'll cleanse, refine, and enrich inbound data (see Chapter 6). Your bronze zone is for raw data — and wouldn't you know it? The persistent data inside of the stream is raw data. So, why "unload" and copy all that data if the data is actually accessible within the stream itself for some period of time?

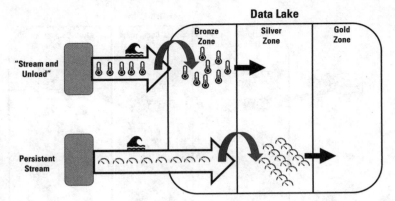

FIGURE 5-14:
Data streaming doing double duty as bronze zone storage for raw data.

The persistent streaming data is actually a bit more complicated than what you see in Figure 5-14. You need to have an end-to-end view of your data lake and how content will be consumed into analytics. Figure 5-15 shows three different models within a hospital setting for persistence streaming data into different zones of their data lake.

The top data flow in Figure 5-15 is the same as the bottom one from Figure 5-14. The data stream functions as an extension of the data lake bronze layer and stores readings generated by a patient's bedside monitoring system. Those readings are refined and cleansed as necessary before unloading the data into the silver zone.

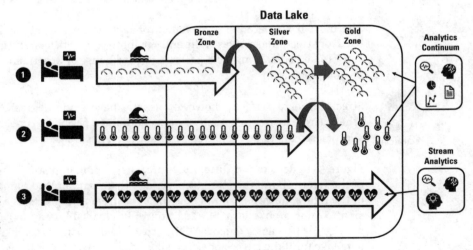

FIGURE 5-15:
Three different models for linking your analytics with streaming data.

The middle data stream, however, carries the data persistence farther into the data lake. Presume that temperature readings don't really need any data cleansing or enrichment. In this case, why not treat that data stream as an extension all the way into the silver zone, the same as you did for the bronze zone? You can then unload those readings and store them in the gold zone as part of curated data packages that will be consumed by users' analytics.

The bottom stream functions differently. If you're the data and analytics architect for this hospital, you're aware that some of your colleagues recently implemented *stream analytics* (or *streaming analytics* — you'll see both terms used) for patient heart monitors. With stream analytics, the models actually read data directly from a data stream rather than from object storage or a database.

In this third scenario, the data stream isn't only extending the bronze and silver zones; it's also extending the gold zone itself. Basically, the heart monitoring data stream itself serves as the directly accessible data repository for the real-time analytics.

REMEMBER

Any of the models depicted in Figure 5-15 may be applicable to your organization's data lake. You and your colleagues need to be the ones who take a holistic, enterprise-wide view of data all the way from the points of origin to the points of consumption into analytics and decide what combination of models makes sense for your data lake.

Taking Inventory at the Data Lake

Imagine walking into a big-box warehouse-style retailer that sells tens or even hundreds of thousands of different items all under one roof. Now that's what they mean by one-stop shopping!

Suppose you visit a Home Depot or a Lowe's and you need to buy a drill, some duct tape, and a pair of pliers. (You can turn this little analogy into a lake-related one by presuming that you need these tools and supplies to do a little work around your vacation home at the lake. How's that?)

You've never been inside this giant retailer before, however. So how do you know where to find the products you need? Well, that's easy: You look at the overall store directory to tell you which aisles to go to. Then, within each aisle, you'll see signs that give you a hint where along the shelves you'll find what you're looking for.

Suppose, though, that the retailer doesn't have a store directory or at least not a directory that you can easily find. Then suppose that the aisles don't have any signs at all, even at the ends, that list what products you'll find in each one. Now, to find that drill, the duct tape, and the pliers, you might well have to wander up and down each aisle, starting at one end of the store and maybe even continuing all the way to the other end, carefully looking at every shelf. Talk about inefficient!

The analogy here should be pretty apparent, right? Your enterprise-scale data lake will contain all sorts of data, ingested from numerous business applications, sensors, and even from outside your organization. Without some sort of directory, you might as well be wandering around in a giant hardware store that doesn't believe in signs. True, what you need is in there somewhere, but finding the right products — or the right data, in the case of your data lake — is going to be painfully time-consuming!

You need to begin your data lake's overall catalog and directory in the bronze zone, even though your users mostly will not be accessing data in the bronze zone. If you wait until data makes its way into the silver and gold zones, your data cataloging will be much more difficult to achieve fully, especially when it comes to *data lineage* (tracking user-accessible data all the way back through its entry into the data lake in the bronze zone, and even all the way back to its point of origin outside the data lake).

Presume that you're using S3 for a monolithic object store in your bronze zone. Suppose that you're ingesting temperature and sensor readings from a factory floor machine through a streaming interface and that you'll be unloading the sensor data into CSV files in an S3 bucket.

You can use the AWS Glue Data Catalog to "crawl" your S3 buckets and collect metadata information that will populate the index within the Glue Data Catalog. This way, you have a head start within your bronze zone for the catalog information that can then be carried into your silver and gold zones.

Regardless of the software or cloud services you use, you want to create a catalog that tells you:

>> What major sets of data your bronze contains, such as Machine X Temperature Data or Intensive Care Unit Patient Bed Heart Monitoring Data

>> Where the data originated outside of the data lake

>> How the data arrived into the data lake (for example, through a particular streaming interface)

>> The last time the set of data was updated if coming in via a batch feed

Bringing Analytics to Your Bronze Zone

Inside your organization's data lake, the gold zone is the sector most heavily used for analytics as the home of curated packages of data. Other analytics will also reach into the silver zone for "un-curated" discrete data. And don't forget that users will also play in the sandbox, so to speak, where they build and test analytical models and perform other experimental analytical functions.

Can it be, though, that the raw data in your bronze zone also has value when it comes to your organization's analytics? Absolutely! After all, *raw data* does not mean "useless data."

Your bronze zone should support

>> Expert-level analytics

>> Data inventory analytics

>> Data quality and observation analytics

Turning your experts loose

Your organization's data scientists and power users often need access to data that hasn't been previously used in analytics, but which, fortunately, is in the data lake — specifically, in the bronze zone.

REMEMBER

The operating model of a data lake is to gather together a sizable collection of data, even if you don't have formally defined analytics needs for some or even most of that data. You build data and analytics pipelines that begin with the operational systems or sensors where data is first created and that terminate inside your analytics.

However, only some of your overall ingested data is destined from the start to head all the way down a pipeline, through your bronze and silver zones, and into your gold zone. The rest of that data is just sitting around in your bronze zone, waiting and waiting and waiting. . . .

Some of that not-yet-used data in your bronze zone will eventually be targeted to be brought into your gold zone as part of a new data package or perhaps expanding an existing one. But what happens when your organization has a sudden need for data that isn't already in the silver zone or the gold zone but turns out to be sitting in raw form in the bronze zone? Just because nobody has yet used that data for analytics doesn't mean that right now isn't the best moment to start!

As long as your analytics whizzes understand that bronze zone data is in raw form, why not let them access it directly? The transformations that preemptively take place on the way into the silver zone (see Chapter 6) can also be done on the fly when accessing raw data in the bronze zone.

Maybe the analytics on bronze zone raw data will turn out to be a one-time thing, and you won't have to worry about that data down the road. Or it can turn out that the raw data is tremendously valuable, and your organization's management is wondering just why in the world that data hadn't already been moved along a data pipeline and made available for analytics. In the latter case, you can get right to work and bring this newly valuable data into the gold zone via the silver zone and have it ready to go for new visualizations or machine learning models.

Taking inventory in the bronze zone

Sometimes you just don't know what you have when it comes to your organization's data. Time to take inventory!

The metadata associated with your gold zone and even your cleansed and enriched silver zone data is the equivalent of walking into a department store, heading to the shoe department, and browsing the shoes that are on display. Sure, a salesperson usually needs to go into the storeroom to see if they have your size or to grab the matching shoe for one that's on display. But for the most part, what you see is what the department store's shoe department has for sale.

However, have you ever gone into a department store's discount outlet? Maybe you're familiar with Nordstrom Rack, which is Nordstrom's outlet, or Saks OFF 5th, which is the equivalent for Saks Fifth Avenue. These outlet stores also have shoes. But you have to browse through stacks of boxes sometimes covering several aisles. The shoeboxes are usually — but not always — grouped by size, though it's common to find sizes all mixed up from customers putting boxes back wherever they feel like it. You can't always tell what color a pair of shoes is until you pull out a box and open it.

Your bronze zone data is sort of like those stacks of shoes in Nordstrom Rack or Saks OFF 5th. They definitely have a lot of shoes, but wow, you really have to work for those discounts!

Wouldn't it be nice, though, if each of those outlet stores had some sort of magical directory that can tell you exactly where those size 9 Kenneth Cole cordovan loafers were, or better yet, if the store even has any of those shoes in stock?

Your data scientists and other "power users" can run *data inventory analytics* against your data lake catalog (see "Taking Inventory at the Data Lake," earlier in this chapter) to see what's in the bronze zone that may be of interest for analytics, either directly from the bronze zone or after enriching and curating the data.

REMEMBER

Data inventory analytics don't produce critical insights about your organization's business operations through visualizations or by feeding data into machine learning models. But knowing what data is, even in your data lake's bronze zone, is highly valuable for when your analysts may need it.

Getting a leg up on data governance

The operating philosophy of your data lake is a straightforward one: Blast lots and lots of data into the bronze zone as effortlessly as possible and without worrying right then about errors, data anomalies, missing data elements, and other quality issues. Then, after you've sort of taken possession of all this data, you can do all the error correction and other refinement that needs to be done as the data makes its way into the silver zone.

But how "dirty" is your data? Are errors and anomalies introduced way back in the operational systems? Or is it possible that your data ingestion might actually be introducing quality issues? Maybe you're bringing high-quality data into your bronze zone, but you're introducing errors as part of your transformations into your silver zone and packaging in your gold zone.

The growing field of *data observability* comes into play in your data lake. Essentially, you turn a whole lot of computing power loose on your data — including bronze zone data — to fully understand data lineage and all the variations of data along a pipeline. With data observability, you're still taking inventory of your data, but you're going beyond simple cataloging and trying to understand the life cycle of your data, including where errors and anomalies might be introduced so you can address them.

REMEMBER

Data observability will require your bronze zone data along with both downstream data (your silver and gold zones), as well as upstream data (your source systems).

» Adding master data into your data lake

» Coordinating your bronze and silver zones

» Exploring hierarchical storage for your silver zone data

» Making silver zone data available for analytics

Chapter 6

Your Data Lake's Water Treatment Plant: The Silver Zone

The silver zone is the unglamorous part of your data lake. The silver zone isn't the landing place where you ingest mountains of data from all over, teasing the possibility of unprecedented insights drawn from all that data. Nor is the silver zone where you build and deploy packages of ready-to-consume data tied to specific analytics, which in turn are linked to explicit business objectives; that's done in your gold zone.

Your silver zone is a gateway between promises and delivery. In fact, you can think of the silver zone as the water treatment plant for your data lake. Think of the silver zone as doing the equivalent of:

» Cleaning the water

» Adding fluoride and minerals

» Maybe even doing desalination to turn saltwater into freshwater

Water comes into a water treatment plant, and water comes out. But the outbound water is now cleansed, refined, and possibly even enriched.

Now substitute *data* for *water,* and you get the idea of your data lake's silver zone.

Funneling Data further into the Data Lake

Your silver zone has three primary missions for the raw data that has landed in your data lake's bronze zone:

>> Data cleansing and transformation

>> Data refinement

>> Data enrichment

WARNING

The silver zone is your gateway between the raw data in your bronze zone and the curated data in your gold zone. You need to be aware, though, that some decisions you make and actions you take as you set up your silver zone technology and processes will ripple back into your bronze zone and forward into your gold zone. Specifically, you will impact

>> The *persistence policies* in your bronze zone, as you decide whether to retain raw data after you've processed that data in your silver zone

>> How many *data packages* you need to create in your gold zone on behalf of your analytics versus pointing your analytics at refined and enriched data in your silver zone

Sprucing up your raw data

The easiest way to understand how your data lake's silver zone functions is to look at incoming structured data that is ingested in a batch (versus streaming) manner. In fact, if you've ever worked with a data warehouse or data mart, all the extract, transform, and load (ETL) functionality that you've done in the past will exactly match what you need to do for inbound structured data.

Presume that your data lake is on the receiving end of several large sets of end-of-year human resources (HR) data from all-around your company. Presume also that your company is a global consumer packaged goods (CPG) company — in fact, one of the *leading* CPG companies in the *world.* The company was built largely through mergers and acquisitions over the past two decades. Additionally, the country managers around the world are fully empowered to implement whatever systems they want for enterprise resource planning (ERP), customer relationship management (CRM), supply chain management (SCM), and other key business functions.

Consequently, your company's HR data is scattered across more than a dozen implementations of Microsoft Dynamics, Oracle PeopleSoft, SAP, and Workday, not to mention two custom-developed HR systems originally implemented in acquired companies that are still up and running.

So, what does all this heterogeneity mean for your data lake? Well, your bronze zone will be ingesting raw data from those dozen-plus HR systems. The operating model of big data in general, and data lakes in particular, encourages and supports the relatively effortless ingestion of data without needing to do significant upfront analysis and norming. So, you don't even break a sweat in the face of your company's dozen different HR data sources. That's the good news.

The not-so-good news, however, is that you'll have multiple data structures and related business rules all coexisting in your bronze zone in sort of an apples-to-oranges-to-celery manner. Basically, you need to merge all that HR data together for enterprise-scale reporting and analytics. But in your bronze zone:

>> **Data field names, types, and sizes differ.** For example, for an employee's last name, one system has EMP_LAST_NAME CHAR (30) NOT NULL, and a second system has EMPLOYEE_LNAME VARCHAR (45).

>> **Field value codes differ.** One system has four possible "employment status" values (F, P, R, and T, which stand for full-time, part-time, retired, and terminated, respectively); a second system has five possible values for employment status (FT, PT, RT, RS, and IT, which stand for full-time, part-time, retired, resigned, and involuntarily terminated, respectively).

>> **Postal codes vary.** Some systems enforce global postal code abbreviations such as AZ for Arizona in the United States or BC for British Columbia in Canada; others allow states to be spelled out or abbreviated, however data is entered.

Just as you would do for a data warehouse or data mart, you need to make command decisions for unified field names, data types and sizes, and permissible values you want to use because all of that similar-but-differently-structured data gets synthesized in the data lake silver zone and then moves forward into the gold zone.

Some of the transformations you make will be pretty straightforward and can be fully automated within software. For example, if you have three possible values for "employment status" in each and every source of employment data — let's say, active, retired, or terminated — and all three are semantically equivalent across each data source, then all you have to do is settle on which encoding set you want to use in your data lake. Let's say you decide on a two-letter code. Then, if a source coming in has *A* or *Active* for an employee status value, you would convert the value to, say, *AC* as you write a new target record in your silver zone. Simple, huh?

In other cases, you may need either more advanced automation or perhaps even manual input to do your transformations. Suppose some source HR systems have three possible employment status values, while others have four or even five possible values. If *active* can mean either *full-time active* or *part-time active*, then you need to determine somehow what a given employee's status actually is. Maybe you have other fields in an employee record to make the full-time versus part-time determination in an automated manner. If not, then your transformation logic will need to set that record aside and route the data for manual inspection and input to determine whether an employee is full-time or part-time.

All this logic for batch-structured data is pretty straightforward and comes directly to the world of data lakes from tried-and-true practices in data warehousing. When you get to your semi-structured and unstructured data for your data lake, however, the waters get murkier.

Refining your raw data

Presume that your data lake will ingest plenty of unstructured data: images, videos, and audio files, in particular. Some of that unstructured data may arrive in your data lake via batch ingestion, while other unstructured data is streamed into your bronze zone. Regardless of the batch-versus-streaming route that the unstructured data takes, what happens after those images, videos, and audio files reach your bronze zone?

Figure 6-1 shows an example of an image sent into the data lake bronze zone from some sort of surveillance application. Suppose that the original image isn't particularly sharp and isn't particularly useful for image analytics in its raw form. No worries! Your organization wants to be at the leading edge of facial recognition applications and wants your data lake to play an important role in image and video analytics. You can use image-enhancing software to sharpen an image's features, colors, and other characteristics. Essentially, you're refining the image, as shown in Figure 6-1.

The refined image can then be stored within your data lake's silver zone along with other refined and enhanced data. Problem solved!

FIGURE 6-1:
Refining an image
between the
bronze zone and
the silver zone.

You can do similar refinement and enhancement with audio: increasing sound volume, reducing background noise, dampening static, and adjusting the recording speed. Likewise, you can refine and enhance videos. Pretty much any raw unstructured data can be refined and enhanced, resulting in "better" versions for your data lake that are plopped into your silver zone.

Enriching your raw data

Just as they say in the informercials: But wait, there's more! After you've refined your raw data, you can also enrich that same data. Figure 6-2 shows how a refined image of a customer can be processed through facial recognition to identify exactly who that person is, and then the customer's name and ID number can be attached to the image itself essentially "enriching" the data with attributes (name and ID) that weren't part of the original raw data.

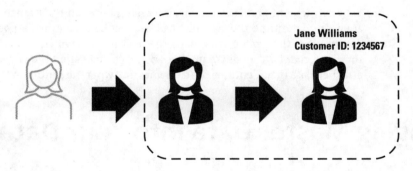

Jane Williams
Customer ID: 1234567

FIGURE 6-2:
Enriching an
image for storage
in the data lake
silver zone.

But what about semi-structured data? Does the concept of enrichment apply as well? Absolutely!

Suppose your company, GiantPetsRUsMart, is a regional pet food and supply superstore. You set up monitoring software to watch for your company's name, either directly or in a hashtag, showing up in tweets, Facebook or Instagram posts, or other social media. One of the key things you want to do is continuously monitor social media to gauge overall customer sentiment about your stores and products and, in particular, to identify any unhappy customers so you can address their concerns right away.

Figure 6-3 shows a raw tweet ingested into your data lake's bronze zone. If you read the tweet as a human being, you can tell that the customer who wrote it was pretty happy. The raw text can be used later in text mining algorithms, but you also can attach structured *sentiment analysis encoding* to the raw tweet.

FIGURE 6-3:
Enriching a tweet by determining and attaching sentiment analysis.

Your refinement and enrichment processing between the bronze zone and silver zone can determine the sentiment of a tweet or social media post. You can also determine if the person who made the post is a known customer and, if so, who that customer is. Then, in your silver zone, you can store the tweet along with the attached data that identifies the customer and what the sentiment of the tweet was.

Bringing Master Data into Your Data Lake

Mindy and Matt are the lead data lake architects for one of the largest fast-food chains in the world. Mindy is new to the company, but Matt is a long-time employee and a veteran of the company's SAP program over the past five years.

"So, here's a big problem," Matt tells Mindy before a key meeting to discuss the upcoming data lake implementation. "If you ask ten people 'How many stores do we have?,' you'll get ten different answers. I can tell you how we handle stores within SAP, but if you show up in a meeting, people have reports from all these systems that don't make any sense compared to each other."

"Why?" Mindy wants to know.

"Well," Matt explains, "some systems only count stand-alone stores that are in their own buildings or in a mall food court, while other systems also include counters inside highway rest stops, gas stations, and other places you find along the road. Then you have other systems that only count our company-owned stores but not franchised locations. Then you have. . ."

Matt continues with his explanation, but Mindy's mind is furiously churning. "We have a master data problem," she thinks to herself. The good news is that Mindy has dealt with master data management (MDM) at several previous companies, even though those efforts were for building a data warehouse, not a data lake.

No worries! Mindy's MDM experience from the world of data warehousing transfers almost directly to the data lake realm.

Mindy heads up to the whiteboard and starts sketching out a taxonomy for the company's locations, using the generic term *outlet* rather than *store* as the root of the categorization hierarchy. Figure 6-4 shows what Mindy sketches on the whiteboard.

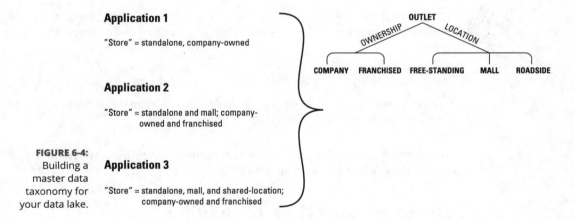

FIGURE 6-4:
Building a master data taxonomy for your data lake.

Application 1

"Store" = standalone, company-owned

Application 2

"Store" = standalone and mall; company-owned and franchised

Application 3

"Store" = standalone, mall, and shared-location; company-owned and franchised

"When we can get everyone to agree on the taxonomy," Mindy explains, "we can categorize every outlet according to its ownership and its location type. This way, all the source systems can do things their own way and blast raw data into the bronze zone without worrying about trying to come up with apples-to-apples definitions. But after we have the data, we can apply the master data processing and store the MDM-aware versions of data in the silver zone and then carry that data through into the gold zone as necessary."

"Makes sense to me," Matt nods.

REMEMBER

MDM is every bit as important for your data lake as it is for enterprise data warehousing. Your silver zone is the starting point for your MDM efforts. As you bring data over from your bronze zone and proceed to refine and enrich the data, you can apply master data transformations and encoding to get your key enterprise data in good shape for your analytics.

Impacting the Bronze Zone

The philosophy of everything up to this point in this chapter can be summed up as follows: Just blast data into your data lake's bronze zone, and don't worry about the "niceties." You don't really have to start worrying about data quality and any sort of data governance until you start moving data into the silver zone.

Probably in the back of your mind, however, you're thinking, "It can't be that straightforward." Well, guess what? You're right! For better or for worse, what you do in your silver zone impacts what you do in your bronze zone in several important ways.

WARNING

Cloud-based storage for your data lake is relatively inexpensive, but it's not free. Additionally, every time you copy data from a source to a destination along a data pipeline:

>> Latency, even a tiny bit, is introduced into the end-to-end data flow.

>> You open up the possibility of introducing errors or anomalies in the data, even as you try to refine and enrich the data.

You need to make some key decisions along your data pipeline between the bronze zone and the silver zone of your data lake.

Deciding whether to leave a forwarding address

Some of your data arrives in your bronze zone with definite plans to move on to your silver zone. You ingest HR data from the latest employee review cycle and know for certain that the HR data will wind up being used in HR analytics. You know for certain, then, that you'll need to run that data through the usual data warehouse–like ETL process and then store the transformed data in your silver zone.

Or you may be ingesting tweets or images or audio files that are definitely targeted for analytics of some type. You'll refine and then possibly enhance the unstructured and semi-structured data, and then send it on for analysis.

WARNING

Not every piece of data that hits your data lake's bronze zone is automatically destined for refinement, enhancement, and analytics, however. One of the most important value propositions of a data lake versus its data warehouse and data mart predecessors is that you can be a "data hoarder" and bring in data that may not be immediately destined for analytics. You ingest lots and lots of data "just in case." Maybe you'll eventually turn your discovery analytics loose on this mountain of data to look for interesting and important patterns. Or maybe you'll just stockpile the data and perhaps never even use it at all.

The first thing to understand is that you may well have data that never makes its way past the bronze zone. So, what do you do with that data?

Stand by because your silver zone decisions will come into play, even for bronze zone data that never makes it that far.

Deciding whether to retain your raw data

What does your data life cycle look like between your bronze zone and your silver zone for data that you're definitely moving through the pipeline (as opposed to leaving it in the bronze zone because you don't immediately need it for analytics)?

At first, the answer to this question seems simple: You refine and enhance the raw data, regardless of whether the data is structured, unstructured, or semi-structured, and then you store the refined and enhanced data in the silver zone. Mission accomplished!

Not so fast.

What should you do with your raw data after you've refined and enhanced it? Or here's a trickier question: What about raw data that needs little or no refinement or enhancement?

Figure 6-5 shows sensor readings for temperatures and equipment pressure from a remote drilling well arriving at your data lake. Assume that you don't really need to do anything to these readings. Each one is a discrete measurement with relevant "context" attached — a specific location, the timestamp for when the reading was made, the sensor ID, and the type of equipment being measured. For simplicity's sake, assume that no transformations or master data need to be applied — the raw data itself is everything you need, in its natural state.

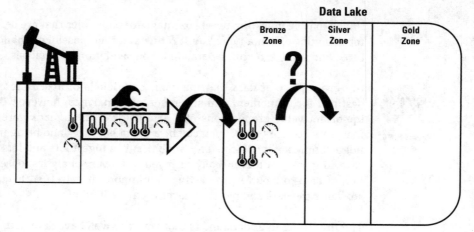

FIGURE 6-5:
Decisions, decisions: What should you do with bronze zone data destined for your silver zone?

You have a decision to make. Should you copy that data exactly as is from your bronze zone to your silver zone? After all, the data isn't undergoing any changes at all. So, do you really need to make another copy, especially if you're talking about phenomenally large volumes of data?

REMEMBER

Figure 6-6 shows one option. Your data lake's "property lines" between your zones can actually be very fluid and flexible. In the case of sensor data that's undergoing absolutely no refinement or enrichment, you can simply "promote" that data from the bronze zone into the silver zone. In other words, you sort of "redefine and pivot" the boundary line between the bronze and silver zones to now include all that sensor data in the silver zone. You essentially check off that data as now being usable for analytics, either directly or via curated packages in the gold zone (see Chapter 7).

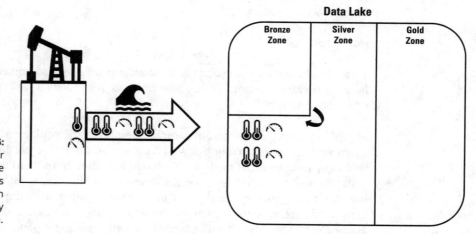

FIGURE 6-6:
Redefining your data lake zone boundaries rather than unnecessarily copying data.

You can apply the same "redefine and pivot" paradigm to other data that does undergo refinement and enhancement. Figure 6-7 shows the first step of ingesting a raw tweet into your data lake's bronze zone.

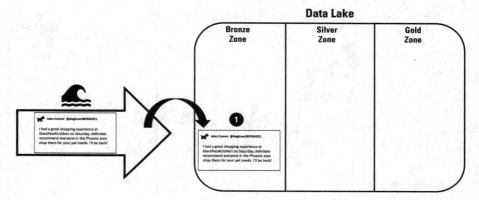

As you saw earlier in this chapter, you can apply sentiment analysis to the tweet to determine, in this case, that the person who tweeted about your company had very positive things to say. You can also determine the name and ID number of the customer and attach all this enriched data to the tweet itself.

TIP

But you don't need to make another copy of the tweet! You can "promote" the tweet and its attached data into the silver zone, again by "pivoting" the boundary line to now consider the tweet to have been "promoted" out of the bronze zone (see Figure 6-8).

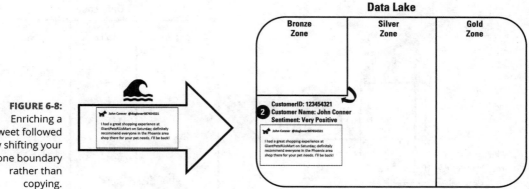

FIGURE 6-8:
Enriching a
tweet followed
by shifting your
zone boundary
rather than
copying.

If, however, the boundary lines of your data lake are more rigid than fluid due to policy and process reasons more than technical ones, you can still avoid unnecessary copying and storage costs. Figure 6-9 shows the first step for, once again, ingesting sensor data from a remote drilling well.

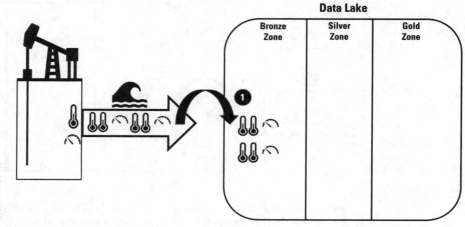

FIGURE 6-9:
Step 1: Ingesting raw data into your bronze zone.

TECHNICAL STUFF

Now, instead of "pivoting" the boundary line between the bronze and silver zone, you sort of put the data on a logical conveyor belt and move it into the silver zone. If you're using object storage such as Amazon Simple Storage Service (S3), you can simply move the S3 bucket from the control of your bronze zone into the control of your silver zone. The data is now in your silver zone and no longer in your bronze zone, as shown in Figure 6-10.

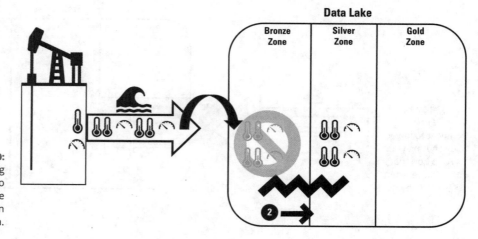

FIGURE 6-10:
Step 2: Moving data into the silver zone rather than copying data.

With the sensor data in Figure 6-10, you know that the data hasn't been refined or enriched; the raw data is usable for analytics as is. But what if you're refining and enriching your raw data? Do you have any other options besides pivoting the boundary line (refer to Figure 6-8)?

Figure 6-11 shows an example of an image that goes through refinement processing, as well as being enhanced with the name and ID of a customer via photo recognition. The refined and enriched image is written into the silver zone. Then the raw image is retained in the bronze zone in its original state.

Or is it?

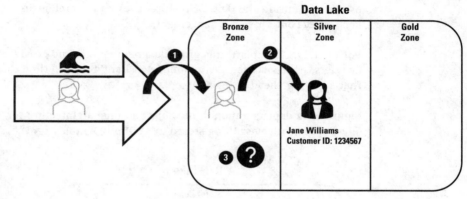

FIGURE 6-11:
Deciding whether to keep a raw image after refinement and enhancement.

Now you have another decision to make. You've refined and enriched the image, so do you really need the raw image?

The answer: Maybe.

If you can absolutely, positively state that you will never, ever need the raw version of data after it has been processed and made its way into the silver zone, then you can safely delete that data. Chances are, though, that some of your raw data will, indeed, be of value down the road, even after refinement and enhancement. Sometimes you're better off keeping raw data around, just in case.

The good news, though, is that you have some clever data storage strategies to help you out with raw data — in fact, even with your silver zone refined data.

Getting Clever with Your Storage Options

Hey, did you hear that cloud-based storage is inexpensive, but it's not free? Yeah, you've heard that more than a few times by now.

Your data lake puts you in the middle of two opposing forces. On the one hand, the mission of your data lake is to be the home for mountains of data. In fact, adopting a sort of "data hoarding" mentality goes hand in hand with big data and, by extension, data lakes.

On the other hand, even fraction-of-a-penny cloud storage costs can add up. So, although you don't need to be nearly as selective about analytical data storage as you did during the days of on-premises data warehousing, you still need to keep an eye out for cost management.

Fortunately, cloud platforms give you a helping hand by providing multiple storage tiers, with each tier having unique cost and retrieval time characteristics. But that's getting ahead of the story.

Figure 6-12 depicts a monolithic object storage architecture for your data lake's silver zone, with everything stored in S3. Pretty simple, right?

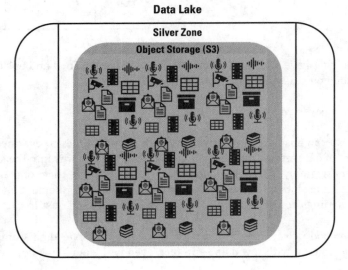

FIGURE 6-12: Your data lake silver zone using Amazon S3.

Here's where the picture gets complicated, but in a good way. Take a look at Figure 6-13. Basically, S3 comes in various "flavors" that you can use for any data that you store in Amazon Web Services (AWS), including your data lake. The three "flavors" of S3 shown in Figure 6-13 are

>> **S3 Standard:** The default S3 object storage class for data that you commonly use for your analytics

>> **S3–Infrequent Access (S3-IA):** Used for, well, data that you access infrequently

>> **S3 Glacier:** Used for archive-level storage and access — the data management equivalent of going up to your cobweb-filled attic to find something that you haven't looked at in a long time

TECHNICAL STUFF

You actually have even more options available for "flavors" of S3 storage, but Figure 6-13 keeps the picture on the simpler side by showing just three of them.

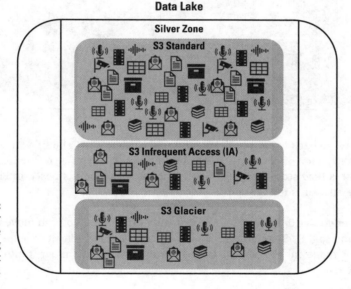

FIGURE 6-13:
Dividing your silver zone content among three different flavors of S3.

Your storage costs for S3-IA are significantly lower than with S3 Standard, but Amazon charges more for accessing the data in S3-IA than in S3 Standard. For data stored in S3 Glacier, your storage costs go way down, but your access costs are even higher than they are for S3-IA; plus, you'll wait significantly longer for your data to show up when it's retrieved.

Amazon also offers a version of Glacier called S3 Glacier Deep Archive, with a default retrieval time of 12 hours. You can save a lot of money on storage by keeping *very* infrequently used data, data that really can wait for delivery into your analytics, in S3 Glacier Deep Archive.

Here's some even better news: Tiered storage in S3 (or the equivalent in Microsoft Azure) doesn't only apply to your silver zone! As shown in Figure 6-14, you can implement tiered storage in your bronze zone as well.

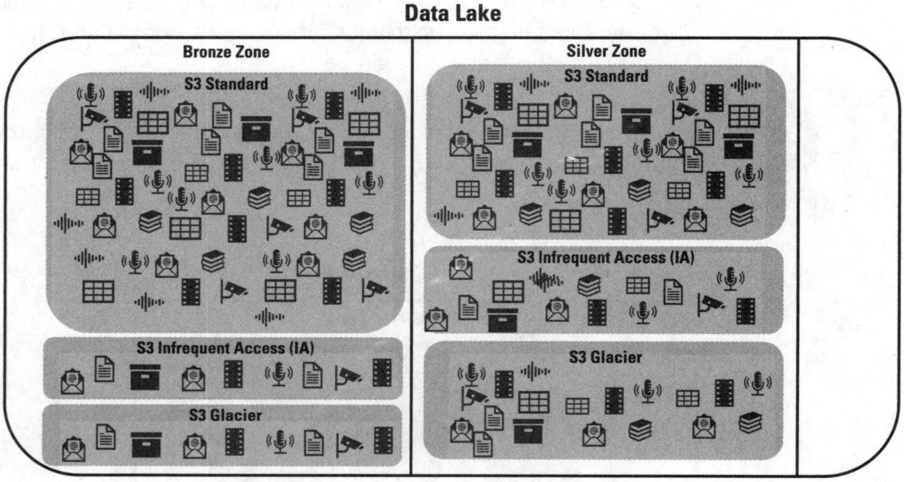

Data Lake

FIGURE 6-14:
Carrying hierarchical storage back into your data lake bronze zone.

Now, go back to the predicament posed earlier: What should you do about the raw data version of an image in your bronze zone that you've refined and enriched and that is now stored in your silver zone? The question is posed in Figure 6-15, and the answer is in Figure 6-16.

After you've done your refinement and enrichment, you can move your raw image from, say, S3 Standard into S3 Glacier. (Or, if you *really* don't expect to access the raw image but you want to keep it around just in case, move it into S3 Glacier Deep Archive.)

TIP

Now, you can be a "data hoarder" in your data lake on behalf of the broadest possible analytics portfolio but also be somewhat cost-conscious, with an eye toward the long-term expenses for your data lake. You can store raw data "just in case it's needed" in your bronze zone or refined versions of that data in your silver zone, even if you don't have an immediately identified analytical need.

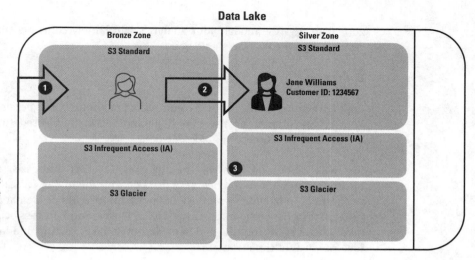

FIGURE 6-15:
Step 1: Refine
and enrich
an image in
your data lake
silver zone.

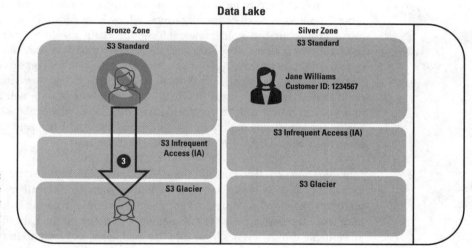

FIGURE 6-16:
Step 2: Move
bronze zone
image to S3
Glacier to save on
storage costs.

Working Hand-in-Hand with Your Gold Zone

Your organization's analytics portfolio is powered by data. Now that's stating the obvious, right?

The data-into-analytics picture actually gets more complicated than slogan-level statements. If you follow along with the bronze zone–to–silver zone–to–gold zone data pipeline model, your analytics will largely consume curated data that resides in your data lake's gold zone.

But not totally.

You'll see more details about the gold zone in Chapter 7, but here's the punchline: Your organization's most well-defined and "officially blessed" analytics will be the primary consumers of gold zone data.

But what about ad hoc, on-the-fly analytics that addresses sudden critical business needs? Even if a business need doesn't qualify as critical, the mantra of analytics is to be able to produce data-driven insights on demand, with as little just-in-time data preparation as possible. The curation process between your data lake's silver zone and the gold zone definitely adds friction and lag time into the idea-to-insight time frame.

REMEMBER

Your analytics need to be able to reach back into the silver zone, not just the gold zone. In addition to the carefully prepared, heavily curated packages of data just sitting there in the gold zone waiting for their inevitable consumption into analytics, your silver zone data contains a wealth of data that can be accessed on demand. Unlike the raw data in your bronze zone, your silver zone data has been "approved for analytical usage" through refinement and enrichment. You'll still need to determine the ways in which discrete pieces of data will be synthesized, and your overall analytical performance will almost always be slower than with the prepackaged sets of data in the gold zone. But you'll still find value from going after the wealth of data in your data lake's silver zone.

If any of those on-the-fly analytics needs against silver zone data turn out to be so valuable that your organization's leadership wants to turn them into production analytics, no worries. Your gold zone is a constantly evolving component of your data lake, and you can always subsequently package up the data that you've found so valuable into a new addition into the gold zone, as I explain in Chapter 7.

» Examining gold zone data storage

» Balancing gold zone prepackaged data with silver zone data

» Adjusting your gold zone storage as necessary

Chapter **7**

Bottling Your Data Lake Water in the Gold Zone

You've probably heard the age-old proverb (updated slightly for modern times): "If you give a person a fish, you feed that person for a day. But if you teach that person to fish, you feed that person for a lifetime."

Fish? Lake? Data lake? Aha! You *knew* that saying would show up in this book sooner or later! What an absolutely perfect proverb to describe your organization's data lake, right?

Well, sort of. When it comes to your organization's data lake, you need to act upon *both* parts of that proverb: teaching some of your users to fish, and giving other users a fish. In fact, you really need to go beyond just giving some of those users a fish. You need to give them the data lake equivalent of a ready-to-eat fried-fish dinner, complete with french fries, coleslaw, and biscuits.

And that's where your gold zone comes in.

Laser-Focusing on the Purpose of the Gold Zone

You can best understand your gold zone by using one of the alternative terms for this portion of your data lake that I introduce in Chapter 1.

The gold zone is sometimes referred to as the data model zone, or the performance zone, or the curated zone. The third term, *curated zone*, is the one to focus on. *Curated* refers to something that has been selected, organized, and made ready to use by an expert. Why? To provide "the masses" with a more rewarding experience than by hunting out "the best stuff" on their own. The contents of your gold zone perfectly fit that definition! Of all the data housed in your data lake, certain "collections" are selected, pulled together, and made easier for others to access.

Jumping back to lake-related analogies for a moment, presume that you're packing your car for a two-week lakeside camping trip that will include plenty of hiking and other outdoor activities. In addition to your clothes, camping gear, and food, you definitely need to bring along a lot of water.

Or do you? Maybe you should just bring along a bunch of filters and water purification tablets. Every time you need water for cooking or drinking, you can fill a couple of containers straight from the lake and do your own filtering and purification, right on the spot. But that would be sort of like grabbing data straight from your data lake's bronze zone, right when you need the data for analytics — doable but inefficient and time-consuming.

Or you can grab a couple dozen plastic or glass bottles of various sizes while you're still at home and fill each bottle with water from your kitchen sink. The water coming out of your faucet is "refined" — it has been purified and is ready to drink or cook with. Choosing this option would be like accessing data from your data lake's silver zone. Your water — or data — is ready to use, but you still have to go through some amount of preparation.

Here's another option: You can stop by the supermarket and buy a bunch of 16-ounce bottles of water, as well as some gallon jugs of water. The smaller bottles are the perfect size to stuff into a side pocket on your backpack when you're hiking, and you can use the gallon jugs for cooking your campfire meals each night instead of having to use a bunch of those smaller bottles.

Do you prefer flavored waters? You can buy some flavored waters, with or without sweeteners, when you're grabbing "plain" water at the supermarket. Do you prefer fizzy water? No problem: Bottles of carbonated water — flavored or unflavored — are also on the supermarket shelves.

The clever marketing people at all those bottled water companies figured out a long time ago the packaging options that consumers are willing to pay for. They've figured out the bottle sizes, flavor combinations, and carbonation options that are the most popular and sell the best.

Welcome to the data lake gold zone: the home of ready-to-consume, *curated* data packaging. The experts in your company decide not only which packages of data will be useful and valuable but also which are better served on the proverbial silver platter to many of your users instead of teaching those users how to reach into the silver zone and gather their own data.

Looking Inside the Gold Zone

The common theme throughout your gold zone is near-instant analysis of pre-packaged data rather than data gathering and preparation. Figure 7-1 shows how your gold zone is divided into two major categories: actual data and outputs such as a PDF report or visualization.

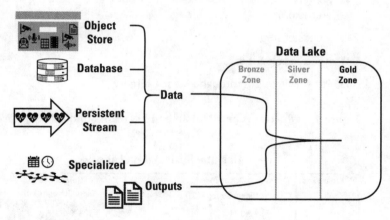

FIGURE 7-1: Peeking inside the gold zone.

Your gold zone data is further divided into four main subcategories:

>> Object stores

>> Databases

>> Persistent streaming data

>> Specialized data stores

Object stores

Mohan and Janelle both work in the IT organization at a major hospital system. Mohan is a lead architect for their data lake, while Janelle specializes in medical analytics and informatics. The hospital system is composed of a dozen full-service hospitals throughout New York City.

One morning, both Mohan and Janelle receive a joint assignment. The company's chief medical officer wants to set up a study of comparative operating room efficiency across all the hospital system's locations. Janelle will lead the effort to define and build all the various analytics, while Mohan's team will gather the data that Janelle's team will need.

The good news is that the hospital system's data lake already has all the data that Janelle's team will need, all sitting in Amazon Simple Storage Service (S3) object storage. However, Mohan wants to make data access as easy as possible for Janelle's team. He defines a gold zone data package called *operating room study* and directs his team members to populate this data package with everything that Janelle and her team will need for their analytics, including the following:

>> Surgery statistics (start and end times, number of operating room personnel, and so on)

>> Videos of surgeries

>> Anesthesiologist data

>> Patient vital signs throughout each surgery

Figure 7-2 illustrates how Mohan and his team build this data package.

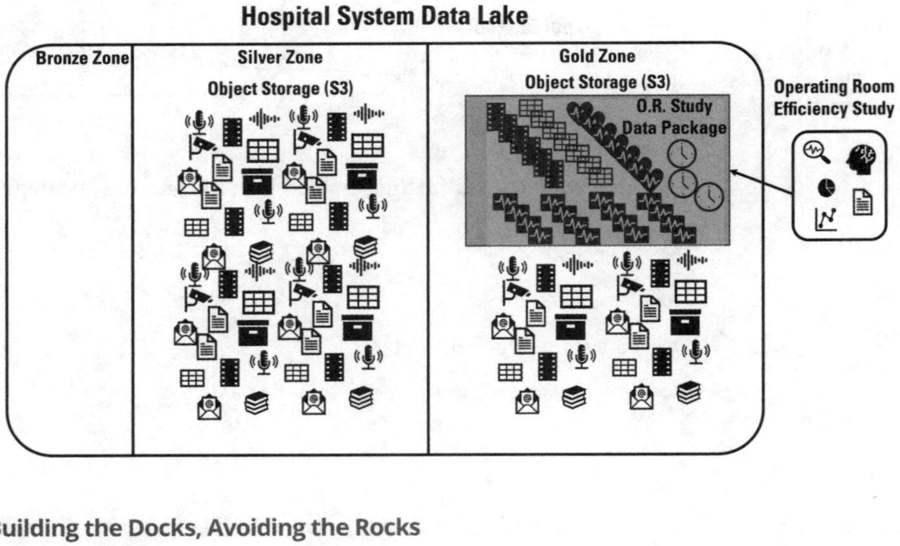

Hospital System Data Lake

FIGURE 7-2:
Building a curated gold zone data package.

REMEMBER

Janelle's analysts aren't limited to the curated gold zone package that Mohan and his team have created for them. If their analytics require additional data down the road, they're fully empowered to reach into the silver zone and grab whatever they need. They can even reach way back into the bronze zone for raw data that has yet to be processed, though they'll have to do the cleansing and enriching themselves. But for the data they need, at least at first, Mohan has provided one-stop shopping in the hospital system's gigantic data lake.

Databases

Janelle and her team aren't limited to machine learning and other data science–type advanced analytics in their operating room efficiency study. Chances are, a significant portion of their analysis will be good old-fashioned business intelligence, involving dimensional analysis and answering questions such as the following:

>> What is the average surgery time by major surgical classes, by hospital within our system, and also broken down by the number of years of experience for the lead surgeon?

>> What is the average post-surgery recovery time, broken down by the patient's age and the severity of the surgery?

TECHNICAL STUFF

Questions such as these, and hundreds or even thousands of others along these lines, can be answered against gold zone object store data. Users can issue direct queries in SQL or use a business intelligence tool such as Tableau or Microsoft Power BI that issues SQL statements. The SQL is "translated" by an abstraction layer such as Amazon Redshift Spectrum or Amazon Athena to access the underlying object data stored in S3, just as if that data were stored in a database.

Or your gold zone can actually make use of a database rather than emulate one in object storage. If your classic business intelligence and online analytical processing (OLAP) analysis may involve many terabytes of data, a "real" database is likely more efficient and will offer faster response time than translating SQL statements into access queries against object store data. Figure 7-3 shows how Mohan has expanded his operating room study data package into two related components:

>> S3 object storage for any semi-structured and unstructured data within Amazon Web Services (AWS), such as the operating room video recordings that are analyzed as part of the efficiency study analytics

>> A database (Amazon Redshift, in this case) for all structured data such as patient monitor readings, patient demographic data, and information about the operating room personnel

Figure 7-3 shows Mohan's implementation of database-resident data alongside object store data, all nicely packaged up for Janelle's analytics.

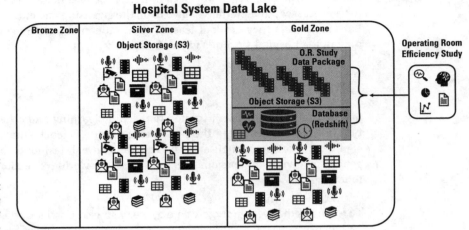

FIGURE 7-3:
Adding database
data to object
store data inside
a gold zone
curated package.

WARNING

Several of the data lake reference architecture alternatives presented in Chapter 4 include databases as part of your overall data lake and your gold zone in particular. Remember, though, that some architects and strategists view a data lake as being solely housed in object storage and view any database as being outside the boundary lines of a data lake. Conversely, if you take a broader, more inclusive "enterprise analytical data" view of data lakes, you absolutely can include databases in your overall environment, including in your gold zone.

Persistent streaming data

After Janelle and Mohan finish their analytics and data curation for the operating room efficiency study, the chief medical officer has another assignment for them. The hospital system's executive leadership team wants to implement a real-time dashboard in each hospital that will produce alerts for any patient whose vital signs suddenly indicate a possible problem. The idea is that in addition to the nurses' stations on each patient floor, each hospital will now have a control center responsible for every patient in that facility. The control center will be staffed around the clock, every single day, and the "duty officer" will be responsible for notifying the applicable nurses' station upon receiving an alert about a patient.

It turns out that, two years ago, all the patient bedside monitoring systems in each of the system's hospitals were upgraded as part of a massive modernization effort. Now, each patient room is equipped with an integrated set of vital sign monitors that continuously display a patient's oxygen saturation level, heart rate, blood pressure, and other key indicators on an in-room screen. Additionally, those vital signs are continuously streamed to the closest nurses' station on that floor.

Now, to support the hospital-wide vital sign control center, Janelle and Mohan immediately come up with the most appropriate solution: Tap right into those data streams from all across the hospital and feed them directly into the new integrated dashboard.

REMEMBER

Your data lake will ingest data via two primary mechanisms: batch feeds and streaming data. Some of your streaming data may be "unloaded" into either the bronze zone or the silver zone, while other streaming data passes through to its eventual usage. Essentially, *persistent data streams* become an extension of portions of your data lake.

Persistent data streams also apply to your gold zone. Figure 7-4 shows how multiple data streams pass through your bronze and silver zones and become extensions of your gold zone. Now, the streaming analytics that Janelle's team builds into the integrated patient dashboard can tap directly into the data streams in conceptually the same manner as they would access object store data, database resident data, or both.

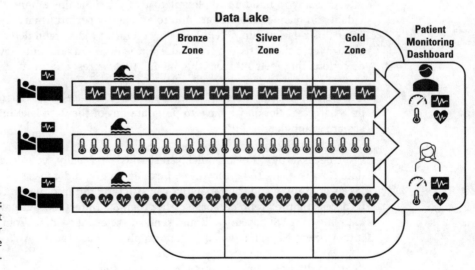

FIGURE 7-4:
Using persistent data streams for your gold zone curated data.

Specialized data stores

Brad and Keisha work together in a bank in very much the same manner that Mohan and Janelle work together in the hospital system company. Brad is in charge of banking analytics, while Keisha is the chief architect for the bank's data lake.

One afternoon, the bank's chief risk officer calls both Brad and Keisha into her office for an important meeting. The bank has received warnings from multiple government regulatory agencies that financial institutions are about to face a new generation of fraud schemes. That's the bad news. The good news is that the regulatory agencies also offered solutions for early detection of potential fraud. Armed with these insights for how the fraud schemes will unfold, the bank can take preventive steps such as temporarily disabling at-risk bank accounts.

Brad and Keisha head to a conference room as soon as they leave the meeting with the chief risk officer. Keisha heads to the whiteboard and starts sketching fraud detection concepts that popped into her head during the meeting. Within a half-hour, she and Brad have a pretty good idea of how to use the data that's already in the data lake as part of the bank's fraud interdiction effort.

In this particular case, a specialized *graph database* will be the most efficient and effective way to build a complex picture of relationships among the bank's individual and business customers and to efficiently perform market-based analysis. After this relationship network has been built, Brad's fraud detection algorithms can traverse the paths if a fraud attempt is detected and shut down access in all directions that feed out from the "node" that represents the at-risk customer.

"There's only one problem," Brad realizes. "The data lake is currently built only on S3 storage. So, do we have to pull data out of the data lake into some downstream graph database?"

"Not necessarily," Keisha quickly responds. "Basically, you described what the data flow is going to be. However, I can add a graph database right into the data lake's gold zone, and your analytics can still tap right into the data lake. You'll just be accessing the graph database rather than S3. In fact, because everything in the data lake is AWS-based, we'll just send the relevant S3 data from the silver zone into Amazon Neptune, which is their graph database for the AWS environment."

"Let's do it!" Brad proclaims, as he watches Keisha sketch out the rest of the diagram on the whiteboard. Figure 7-5 shows what Keisha drew for their solution.

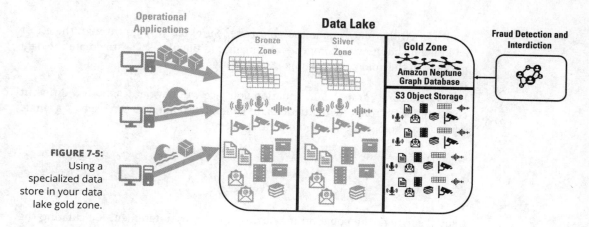

FIGURE 7-5:
Using a specialized data store in your data lake gold zone.

Deciding What Data to Curate in Your Gold Zone

As you add contents to your data lake gold zone, you need to continuously ask yourself the following important question:

> Is it worth making copies of data that already exists in my data lake, or should I have users access individual pieces of data that they need directly in the silver zone?

Take a look back at all the examples earlier in this chapter. With the exception of persistent data streams, all the gold zone curated data packages are created by

» Making copies of existing data

» Applying any necessary transformations to that data

» Reorganizing the data to optimize the known and likely access paths

WARNING

The painful truth of data lake gold zones is the same painful truth that you've faced if you've ever worked with data warehousing. You can save a lot of time and effort by directly accessing and using packages of data that are optimized to support business intelligence, machine learning, or other analytical needs. However, building those packages involves duplicating and transforming data that you already have somewhere else.

Consider the operating room efficiency study (refer to Figure 7-2). Can Janelle's analytics have directly accessed videos, patient and surgical staff data, and other relevant information directly from the silver zone, instead of having Mohan make copies of all that data inside the gold zone? Sure! So, why go through the effort and take up additional storage — and incur additional costs — to create the data package in the gold zone to support that study?

Every gold zone curated data situation you face will have at least a few different characteristics from other situations. In general, though, you can "solve" a single equation to help guide your gold zone strategy:

```
If (Benefit of Curating Data) > (Cost of Curating Data)
Then Curate Data
Else Access Directly from Silver Zone
```

Okay, "solving" the equation may be a bit of an overstatement. Calculating the benefit of curating data will almost always transcend purely quantitative and financial measurements and involve qualitative factors such as the following:

>> Ease of accessing the desired data in a curated package versus engaging in a "scavenger hunt" through your data lake's silver zone (and possibly even your bronze zone) for data that has yet to be refined

>> Preventing the "I give up!" factor among users who don't have the knowledge (or the patience) to locate and then synthesize the data they need, especially if transformations need to occur to some or all of the data

REMEMBER

You can use the following general rule for the gold zone data curation decision equation. If you have well-known, time-sensitive, and high-impact analytical needs, the value of curating data — even with all the copying and additional storage — is usually worth it (as opposed to requiring users to go access their own data). In other words, in these situations, you're better off serving up that fish dinner with all the side dishes rather than handing someone a fishing pole and pointing them to the lake . . . or the data lake.

Seeing What Happens When Your Curated Data Becomes Less Useful

Suppose that at some point down the road, a curated package of data is no longer used on an everyday basis (or maybe even at all). What should you do then?

Going back to Janelle and Mohan, suppose that their operating room efficiency study has concluded, and the hospital system company has now issued a series of surgical procedural changes for each of their hospitals. Should Mohan just remove that curated data package from their data lake gold zone?

Perhaps, but Mohan has another option. Tiered storage isn't only for a data lake's bronze and silver zones. Mohan can make use of less-expensive, infrequently accessed storage layers in his gold zone as well. Figure 7-6 shows how the operating room study data package can be relocated to S3 Glacier and "mothballed" in case it's needed down the road. While the data is sitting in S3 Glacier, Mohan will probably want to turn off the ongoing data updates, at least temporarily. If the chief medical officer or another executive at the company subsequently asks a question about operating room efficiency, Mohan can simply access the package on Glacier in its "frozen" state, if current data isn't needed. Or he can feed additional data into the package and access it after any updates are processed.

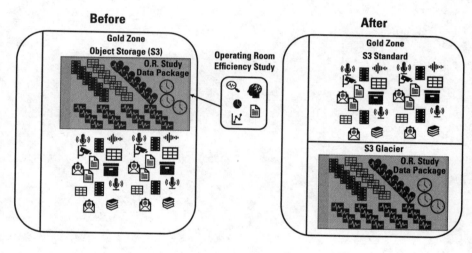

FIGURE 7-6:
Relocating an infrequently used or retired data package to less-expensive storage within the data lake gold zone.

REMEMBER

The important point to note is that even in your gold zone, curated data that becomes less frequently used over time, or is even "retired," can be sort of locked away in the equivalent of your data lake's attic or basement instead of being thrown away.

Chapter **8**

Playing in the Sandbox

At first glance, the sandbox area of your data lake really messes up the basic understanding of how data flows into, through, and then out of your data lake. Think about it: Part of the reason for using *bronze, silver,* and *gold* for the names of the three primary data lake zones is to clearly indicate a progression of your data. If you know anything about the Olympics, you know that gold medals are the best, silver medals, the second best, and bronze medals, third. But who ever heard of a sandbox medal?

Never fear. Your sandbox sits alongside your three primary data lake zones and serves three primary purposes:

» To be a development environment for new analytical models

» To compare different data lake architectural options

» To be a place to experiment and "play around" with data

All three of these purposes have one important factor in common: isolating not-yet-ready-for-prime-time experimentation and development away from the production side of your organization's analytics and data usage. In all three cases, you can work in your data lake without fear of interfering with or interrupting the mission of your data lake.

Developing New Analytical Models in Your Sandbox

Carrie and François usually work together at a large national boutique clothing retailer. Carrie handles the analytics, and François builds out the data lake capabilities to support any new analytics.

A month ago, Carrie and François were asked to develop a new customer loyalty model to replace the one that has been in use for more than a decade. Given the great work that François has been doing on the company's data lake, executive management figures that with the wealth of data — structured, semi-structured, and unstructured — now managed under a single data lake umbrella, it's time to take a fresh look at their entire customer relationship management (CRM) portfolio, including customer loyalty.

In this situation, the data side of the picture is actually fairly straightforward. François is confident that whatever data Carrie needs is already refined and available in the silver zone. Carrie, however, has a much more difficult job. Exactly what new analytical models should be implemented for customer loyalty? And what data will be needed for the new models?

Fortunately, François has set aside an area of the data lake — the sandbox — for analytical development. François can load up the data that Carrie thinks she needs, and Carrie can try all sorts of machine learning and other analytical models. If Carrie wants to try additional data for a model, she can add it to the data that's already in the sandbox or François can help out. Figure 8-1 shows how Carrie makes use of the sandbox while developing her models.

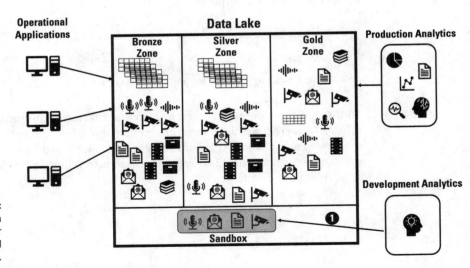

FIGURE 8-1: Using the data lake sandbox for analytical development.

Soon, Carrie is satisfied that she has the perfect models to use for an entirely new generation of customer loyalty capabilities. Now what? The sandbox serves as sort of a development environment for analytics, much as a DEV environment is used for software. Eventually, work from DEV needs to be promoted to PROD and put into production.

In this case, François has created a curated package of data that he has tweaked along the way as Carrie's analytical models were developed. Figure 8-2 shows how not only the analytics, but also the curated data undergoes the analytical equivalent of putting software into production.

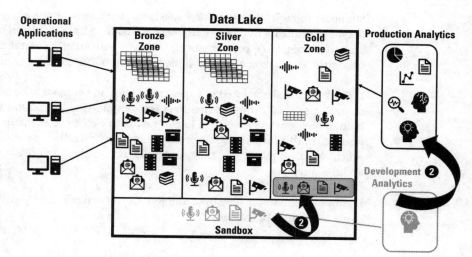

Mission accomplished! Most likely, other analytical development is making use of the sandbox. The sandbox can now be cleared of the "development" data package if it's no longer needed, or the data can be retained to train other models in the sandbox, if desired. Because the sandbox is isolated from the production side of the data lake, whatever happens there will have no impact on the bronze/silver/gold zone progression of data.

Does all your analytical development need to take place in your data lake sandbox? Not necessarily. The sandbox is particularly well suited for situations where you're not quite sure what data will eventually be needed for specific analytics, and you want to try different combinations along with the various models.

Conversely, if you're all but certain what data you'll need for new analytics, you may want to skip the sandbox and curate the data directly in the gold zone (see Chapter 7).

Comparing Different Data Lake Architectural Options

In Chapter 7, I tell the story of how Brad and Keisha were assigned the responsibility to develop a new fraud detection model for the bank where they work. One of their concerns was that the bank's data was built entirely on Amazon Simple Storage Service (S3) object storage, and they were fairly certain that a graph database might be a better option for the types of network-based analytics needed for the new fraud detection models.

Suppose, though, that Brad and Keisha weren't sure about a network database. Maybe data sitting in CSV or Parquet files inside S3 buckets would be perfectly fine and offer acceptable performance. Or maybe instead of a specialized graph database such as Amazon Neptune, a plain old relational database would do the trick.

If Brad and Keisha wanted to experiment with and compare the performance and other aspects of different architectural options for their new fraud detection model, they can use their data lake sandbox to check out as many options as they need to. In this situation, unlike Carrie and François, the "development" isn't so much in the realm of the analytics, but rather in the underlying data architecture.

Figure 8-3 illustrates how Brad and Keisha can explore their architectural options using the data lake sandbox.

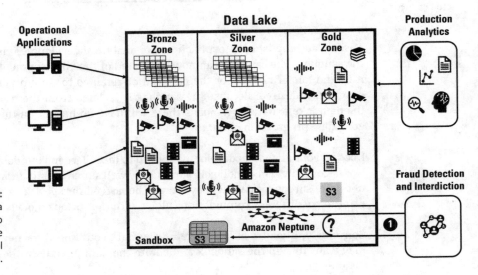

FIGURE 8-3: Using a data lake sandbox to explore architectural options.

After Brad and Keisha decide that a graph database is the way to go, they migrate that curated package of data into the gold zone and — presto! — they're all set with their new fraud detection production capabilities (see Figure 8-4).

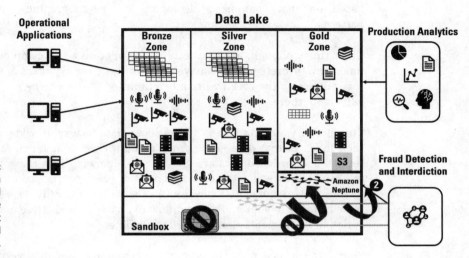

FIGURE 8-4:
Moving a graph
database curated
data package
from the sandbox
into the gold
zone.

TIP

An advantage to using a cloud platform such as Amazon Web Services (AWS) or Microsoft Azure for your data lake is that both Amazon and Microsoft provide a variety of different data services that you can easily spin up, test, and then decide to either use or just "throw away" if they don't fit your purposes. In this example, Keisha can quickly create a Neptune graph database within AWS and populate it with data drawn from the data lake silver zone. Then they can stick with Neptune (as in this case) or, if they decide that object data in S3 would work just as well for their fraud detection, simply stop using Neptune.

Experimenting and Playing Around with Data

"I have an idea. . . "

"I wonder if. . . "

"Is there something that we missed that could've alerted us earlier to that problem?"

Sometimes analytics — even complex analytics — can be almost laser-focused. Do the sensors buried in a remote drilling well indicate a possible equipment failure? Are we seeing any combination of symptoms that might be an early indicator of a public health problem? How loyal to our brand is a given customer likely to be, based on that customer's demographics, psychographics, and purchasing patterns?

Other times, though, analytics can be like piloting a spaceship out into the vast unknown. Or pretend that you were one of the great explorers of years past, setting out across the ocean with only a faint idea — or maybe no idea at all — of what's out there.

The core of your data lake is sort of like a data factory. Raw data comes in, and then much of that data gets refined and enriched. Finally, curated packages of refined and enriched data are "published," knowing that those packages absolutely will be consumed into various parts of your analytics continuum. As with a factory that manufactures physical goods, you don't really have much of a surprise element to your end-to-end flow of data. And you strive to achieve as little variability as possible along your data pipelines.

TECHNICAL STUFF

Your data lake also needs to support the exploratory and discovery aspect of analytics. In addition to those well-known, officially sanctioned production analytics, you want to dive deep into your data. The term *data mining* goes back to the early '90s, and the concept goes back even further. You want your data lake to support data mining in the truest sense of the term: mining through your data in an exploratory sense to discover previously unknown patterns, causal relationships, and other hidden gems.

Before big data and data lakes came onto the scene, data mining was hindered by the need to constantly acquire and prepare data, over and over. Now, though, the one-stop-shopping nature of data lakes is a perfect match for data mining, which brings us to the sandbox.

Modern computing is hallmarked by tremendous computing power. Data lakes are hallmarked by almost boundless storage capacity. Talk about a match made in heaven!

The operating model of exploratory analytics running against your data lake sandbox is straightforward, as shown in Figure 8-5.

Perhaps you're looking at Figure 8-5 and wondering, "Why would I do exploratory analytics against the sandbox? Isn't there a wealth of data sitting in the silver zone?" Congratulations! You've hit on another one of the key decision points of your data lake.

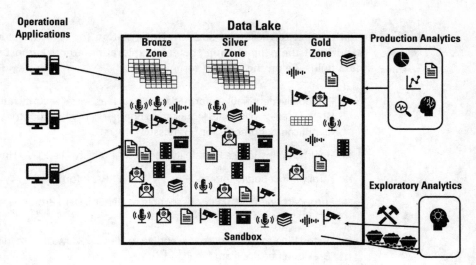

FIGURE 8-5:
Exploratory
analytics and
your data lake
sandbox.

If your exploratory analytics are totally open-ended, your starting point is the refined data in your silver zone or maybe even the raw data in your bronze zone. After all, if you're truly in exploratory mode, you don't really know what data is going to eventually prove useful to drive previously hidden insights. The last thing you want to do is copy a whole lot of data from your bronze or silver zone into your sandbox, over and over, only to find that you wound up wasting money on storage and data transmission costs.

TIP

So, start with your refined or even raw data in your silver or bronze zone, and see what's out there. Eventually, you'll form a hypothesis or two that you want to really dig into. At that point, you can copy the data of interest into your sandbox where it will be isolated.

And here's the great news! In the "production" core of your data lake, from your bronze zone through your gold zone, your data is almost always read-only. Remember that a data lake is a home for your analytical data, not your operational data. Sometimes, though, you want to "what-if" your data — sort of time-travel back to a previous point and ask questions along the lines of "What is likely to have happened if we did X instead of Y?"

In your sandbox, you can modify whatever data you want without worrying about corrupting actual data that's used in your production analytics. So, change away!

WARNING

Don't forget to mask any sensitive information for data that you copy into the sandbox if the people doing the data exploration aren't authorized to see those data fields. Be on the lookout for:

» Personally identifiable information (PII) such as Social Security numbers (in the United States), national identification numbers (in other countries), or tax identification numbers for businesses

» Healthcare Insurance Portability and Accountability Act (HIPAA) information

» Family Education Rights and Privacy Act (FERPA) information

» European Union (EU) data susceptible to General Data Protection Regulation (GDPR) laws

» United Kingdom (UK) data susceptible to UK-GDPR laws as a result of the UK's "Brexit" departure from the EU

Chapter **9**

Fishing in the Data Lake

S ome people go back to the same spot at their favorite lake, year after year. Their trips never vary. They stay at the same cabin or camping spot, even though other people tell them about a new place to stay that just opened last year.

Other people, though, treat every trip to the lake as a new adventure. They pull up information on the Internet throughout the months leading up to their next trip and plot out new hiking trails or new boating routes or maybe a day trip to another nearby lake that they've heard is a lot of fun.

Then you have people that don't even want to go to the lake, at least in person. They're content to just look at online pictures of the lake on their computers and phones.

People come to a data lake in different ways as well. Your data lake needs to support a variety of different users, including passive users, light analytics users, technically skilled users, and data scientists.

Starting with the Latest Guidebook

Every data lake user needs an up-to-date guide to what's available for them in the data lake, whether any given user chooses to make use of the wealth of reports, visualizations, data packages, refined data, or even raw data.

Actually, that data lake guidebook comes with a small caveat, but one that you're almost certainly familiar with from your own adventures in computer usage and information access. Each user is granted access to various portions of the data lake but denied access to other portions. You'll grant permissions using two factors:

>> What any user is authorized to see, based on that user's job and role

>> What any user should see, based on that user's data lake usage style

Setting up role-based data lake access

Marvin, Tammy, and Yan all work in the same hospital. Marvin is a manager in the patient admissions and discharge office. Tammy is a director who manages the hospital imaging department. Yan is a senior director responsible for emergency room operations.

The hospital where they work implemented a new data lake that went live a year ago. The data lake has continued to be steadily built out over the past year and now contains tons of data from all corners of the hospital. Employees from all across the hospital are encouraged to use the data lake for reports, visualizations, and all sorts of analytics.

Table 9-1 shows the data lake permissions that are initially set up for Marvin, Tammy, and Yan. Over time, if any of their jobs change or they need additional data, those permissions can be expanded as necessary. For now, though, the permissions are closely aligned with their respective jobs and the types of analytics they need to do.

TIP

In a general sense, you provide access to the data needed for analytics related to any data lake user's job, and prevent access (at least for the time being) to "extraneous" data that either is beyond a user's permissions level or would otherwise clutter or complicate a user's ability to navigate what data is available.

TABLE 9-1 **Hospital Data Lake Permissions**

User	Gold Zone Data Packages	Silver Zone Refined Data	Bronze Zone Raw Data
Marvin	Admission and discharge history dimensional model Patient health history model Accounting and finance data package	None	None
Tammy	Imaging results statistical model Patient health history model	Refined patient health history Refined and enhanced images	Raw images
Yan	ER tracking data package Patient health history model Admission and discharge history dimensional model	Refined patient health history Refined and enhanced images	Raw images

Setting up usage-style data lake access

You also want to set up access permissions based on the ways in which each user will use the data lake. Again, you can change and expand these permissions as time passes and as a given user wants to make broader and deeper use of the data lake.

Marvin, who works in the patient admissions and discharge office, is mostly a casual user of data and analytics. He definitely has some skills with Tableau and loves creating slick visualizations for his own analysis, as well as results that he presents to his own management team. But for the most part, Marvin doesn't want to go digging for data all over the place. He prefers having neatly created packages that he can manipulate within the guardrails set up for him.

Notice how, in Table 9-1, Marvin has access to several different packages of data in the data lake's gold zone: one for admissions and discharge history, another for patient health, and another for accounting and finance.

TECHNICAL STUFF

Marvin doesn't particularly care whether the underlying data is stored in a database such as Microsoft SQL Server or Amazon Relational Database Service (RDS), or maybe even Amazon Redshift. For all he cares, the data can be stored in Amazon S3 buckets in Parquet files that are accessed via Redshift Spectrum or Amazon Athena. As long as Marvin can get to the data through Tableau, he's a happy data lake camper!

Notice, though, that at least for now, Marvin doesn't have access to any of the refined data in the silver zone, nor does he have access to any of the raw data in the bronze zone. Basically, you're trying to make Marvin's experience with the data lake as pleasant as possible and avoid overwhelming him with assemble-to-order data outside the gold zone.

Tammy and Yan, on the other hand, both have been granted access to data in the silver zone, as well as raw data in the bronze zone. Why? Their respective jobs often require them to do some data digging beyond what someone else has preset for them in the gold zone. Neither Tammy nor Yan has access permission to stray too far around the silver or bronze zones, into areas they don't have a business need to see. So, neither Tammy nor Yan will be able to peruse through accounting and finance data, for example, nor will they be able to check out employee salary and promotion data that made its way into the data lake from the hospital's Workday human resources module.

Taking It Easy at the Data Lake

Sometimes, a person just wants The Answer with as little effort as possible. Modern business intelligence (BI) and visualization tools such as Tableau, QlikView, and Microsoft Power BI aren't only powerful, they're also very intuitive. Yet for some people, even using a relatively simple and straightforward BI tool feels like "too much."

Is such a person out of luck when it comes to using your organization's new, content-packed data lake? Not necessarily. Think of the couch potato who would rather look at pictures of majestic mountain lakes on the Internet than actually take a drive to one. Yeah, it's not quite the same thing, but someone can sort of get their "lake fix" via Google Images.

The concept of a *passive analytics user* has been around ever since the early days of business intelligence in the early '90s. Back then, many BI tools were somewhat on the tricky side to use and required a bit of skill and a fair amount of training. But as data warehouses were being built, lots of tool-shy people still wanted to tap into data-driven insights that can be drawn from all that integrated data.

Figure 9-1 shows how the passive user concept is still around in the data lake era.

Suppose your hospital system data lake has pulled together a wealth of data into a gold zone data package that will support an important operating room efficiency study. The hospital's medical process analysts, data scientists, and others can build an entire continuum of analytics against this carefully curated data, all the way up to advanced machine learning models.

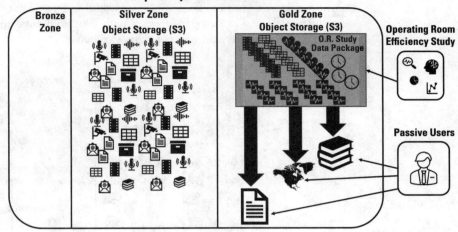

Hospital System Data Lake

FIGURE 9-1:
Data lakes and passive analytics users.

Suppose, though, that a user is more interested in time-traveling back to the days when static reports — maybe even printed out, rather than online — made up the bulk of the "analytics" he received. Digging through data? Drilling up and down and all around to varying levels of detail? Nah, it's not for everyone.

No problem. You can set up a data lake to regularly produce however many static reports, typically in PDF format, you'd like. The distribution of user types across an organization hasn't changed all that much over the years, even as technology and tools have become more powerful. You'll find plenty of passive users who definitely want to check out the latest sales statistics, or the number of employees hired versus the number of employees who have left a company, or pretty much any rudimentary statistics and lists.

TIP

The downside to being a passive data lake user is that the person only slightly benefits from the wealth of insights available from the data lake. However, what often happens is that a passive user eventually wants a little bit more information, and then a little bit more, and then, well, you know how it goes. Rather than have your data lake support team continually produce more and more static reports, you've probably arrived at the point where you can help a passive user "graduate" to becoming a light analytics user (see the next section).

Staying in Your Lane

If you've ever used Tableau or Power BI or an equivalent business intelligence tool, then you're already a light analytics user (at least!), even if you've never pointed one of those software tools against a data lake.

Figure 9-2 shows how a "classic" BI user would use Tableau or a similar BI and visualization tool to access data from a data lake gold zone in much the same manner that the user would access a data warehouse.

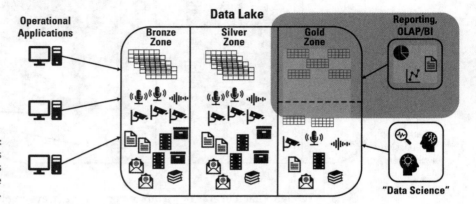

FIGURE 9-2:
Light analytics user access to a data lake gold zone.

Unlike a data lake passive user, the light analytics user has access to actual data — not just static PDFs — and can manipulate the data as much as necessary. Tabular reports? Sure. Simple graphs like pie charts and stacked bar charts? Of course! Drilling up and down to higher or lower levels of detail? Absolutely!

In fact, the light analytics user's software tool provides abstraction against the actual physical layout of the data. Figure 9-2 shows a light analytics user doing online analytical processing (OLAP) against a data lake gold zone composed of object data stored in, say, CSV or Parquet files within an S3 bucket that are treated just like the data that comes from a database.

On the other hand, suppose your data lake actually does have a database as part of the storage layout in your gold zone, as shown in Figure 9-3.

TECHNICAL STUFF

You want to set up your overall environment so light analytics users are abstracted away from the underlying storage mechanisms used. If some or all of the data that will be accessed is in object storage, then Tableau or another tool will interface to that data through an abstraction layer such as Redshift Spectrum or Athena in the S3 environment. On the other hand, if a "real" database is stored within the data lake gold zone, then the BI tool can connect directly using Java Database Connectivity (JDBC), Open Database Connectivity (ODBC), or a more modern capability such as Apache Arrow.

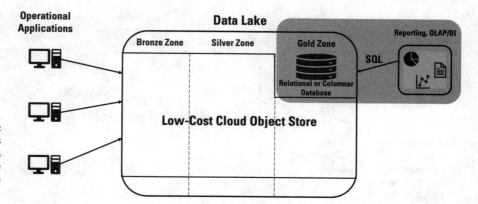

What happens, though, if your data lake gold zone contains more than one database? Suppose the hospital system where Marvin, Tammy, and Yan all work built their data lake in a highly component-oriented manner, incorporating several existing data marts under the data lake umbrella. Now presume that the admission and discharge data that Marvin needs is stored in one of those databases, while the patient health history data is stored in another database.

If Marvin wants to cross-analyze admissions and discharge data with information about patient health history, does he need to endure a multistep process such as the following?

1. Issue multiple SQL statements, one to each data store.

2. Drop his initial results sets, one from each gold zone data store, into an intermediate data store such as Microsoft Excel.

3. Merge the data within Excel, and then bring that data into Tableau to do his data visualizations.

Figure 9-4 shows this somewhat tedious multistep process that Marvin, or some other light analytics user at the hospital, can follow if necessary.

TECHNICAL STUFF

Fortunately, Marvin has a better alternative. He can have Tableau interface with the data lake through a multi–data store engine such as Dremio or Starburst that will provide both *location transparency* and *platform transparency* to Marvin and his data lake–using colleagues.

Figure 9-5 shows how Marvin can get out of the "roll your own data" business.

From Marvin's perspective, the distributed data shown in Figure 9-5 might as well be the single database gold zone data shown in Figure 9-3. He can disregard the underlying topology across the data lake gold zone and concentrate on what he does best: analyzing data to drive decisions and actions.

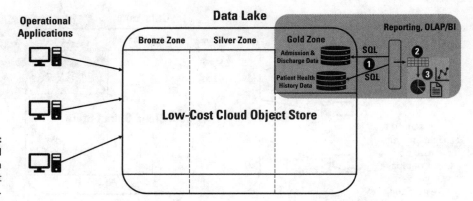

FIGURE 9-4:
A multistep gold zone integration process for a light analytics user.

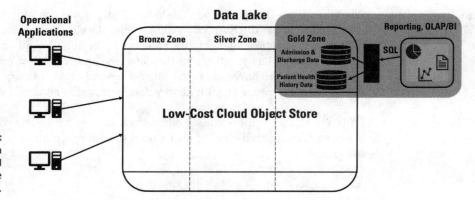

FIGURE 9-5:
Using a data abstraction tool for data lake access simplicity.

In fact, the data abstraction concept transcends databases, as shown in Figure 9-6. Marvin also frequently analyzes accounting and finance data. As it turns out, the hospital system's old accounting and finance data mart didn't survive into the new data lake era, though the accounting and finance data itself lives on in brand-new data packages stored in low-cost object storage in the data lake gold zone.

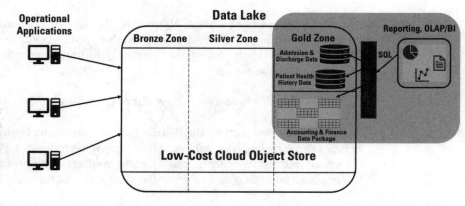

FIGURE 9-6:
Using a data abstraction tool to integrate database and object data in the gold zone.

Suppose Marvin needs to do some analysis that involves all three of his major subject areas. Once again, no problem! Dremio, Starburst, or some other abstraction engine can provide both the location and platform transparency to treat two databases and a package of object-stored data as a single unified data set for what Marvin needs to do in Tableau.

Doing a Little Bit of Exploring

Data lake users like Marvin exist in a sort of happy place. They certainly have more power than a passive data user does when it comes to putting the data lake through its paces. And for the most part, their access patterns against the data lake are fairly predictable and, thus, easy for the data lake team to support by building curated data packages in the gold zone.

At the same time, light analytics users are leaving a lot on the table when it comes to really driving insights from the data lake. In fact, becoming a "power user" (another data warehouse–era concept that has survived into the data lake era) is the next logical step for a light analytics user who continually wants more and more out of the data lake.

For the most part, light analytics users are constrained to the data lake gold zone. Power users, however, can roam at will through the refined and enriched data in the silver zone. They can even head into the bronze zone, as long as they're fully aware that bronze zone data is raw and possibly contains errors that have yet to be corrected.

Armed with SQL and various data access and analysis tools, data lake power users spend significant time exploring discrete pieces of data. Marvin's colleagues Tammy and Yan are considered to be power users. They both spend significant time studying image data in the silver zone and doing dimensional analysis against patient health history data.

Whereas both Tammy and Yan do have their own respective favorite analytics that they run on a regular basis, more often than not, they're off chasing down an ad hoc request from someone or following hunches that often require previously unused combinations of data.

Tammy, Yan, and their fellow power users need unhindered access to the data lake. The only real restrictions for them, or for any other power users, are role-based permissions. For example, neither Tammy nor Yan has access to personnel data that was brought into the data lake from Workday, which is fine with them, because neither has any need for HR data.

Putting on Your Gear and Diving Underwater

Roger also works for the hospital system and is a true data scientist in every sense of the word. In fact, Roger's job title is lead data scientist. How about that?

Just like Tammy and Yan, Roger needs unhindered access to all corners of the data lake. Any attempt to pigeonhole Roger into the access afforded a light analytics user would be met with howls of protest. And if anyone even suggests that Roger can get by with the static reports of a passive user, well, let's just say that you wouldn't want to be in the room to witness Roger's reaction to that suggestion!

The primary difference between Roger and power users such as Tammy and Yan is that Roger spends most of his time actually building advanced analytic models. Tammy and Yan certainly have unpredictable data needs. But when they find data of interest, most of the "analytics" they do are in the old-fashioned BI and OLAP realm — in other words, mostly descriptive analytics with some light predictive analytics thrown into the mix.

Roger, however, is all about discovery analytics and actually building new models for predictive analytics. He spends a great deal of time experimenting in the data lake sandbox (see Chapter 8). Roger is definitely skilled in SQL, but he also writes a good deal of Python and R, along with streaming analytics.

In fact, Roger can be an end-to-end, one-person-show, data lake expert if he truly needs to be. He can grab raw data from the bronze zone and do his own cleansing, refinement, and enrichment. He can build his own training and testing data sets for his new models. His PhD in machine learning for medical informatics certainly qualifies him to build and deploy those new models.

For Roger, the data lake is sort of his "mad scientist kit." The data security team may restrict Roger from accessing certain data lake contents — HR data again comes to mind — but if Roger finds himself in need of HR data for some exploratory analytical model, he can always request access.

So, is Roger a "better" data lake user than Marvin or Tammy or Yan? Or any of the hundreds of passive users who work in the hospital system? Not necessarily. Roger is just a different type of data lake user — one for whom the data lake represents a world of possibilities — but all the others have their own ways of using the data lake in the course of their jobs.

REMEMBER

Just as with a holiday weekend crowd gathering at a popular lake resort, you'll find a broad spectrum of data lake users with varying expectations and plans for making the most of the data lake. To each their own!

Chapter **10**

Rowing End-to-End across the Data Lake

The bronze zone. The gold zone. And in between the two, the silver zone. Oh, and don't forget about the sandbox.

When you examine the layers and zones of a data lake one by one, you get a pretty good idea of the roles and responsibilities of each one. But until you take an end-to-end look at a data lake, you don't necessarily gain a full understanding of the flows of data from their sources into the data lake and then all the way through the pipelines that you'll be constructing.

So, settle in for an end-to-end example of a hospital data lake.

REMEMBER

Before you dive deep into the hundreds or even thousands of data lake–related services and products at your disposal, you want to construct your data lake at the conceptual level. In other words, focus first on the forest that's next to your favorite lake, and don't worry about the details of specific trees — oak, maple, pine, and so on — for now!

Keeping versus Discarding Data Components

Unless you work for a brand-new startup company that's just beginning operations, your organization will have an existing portfolio of data warehouses and data marts that take care of today's analytical data management. Following the principles I outline in Chapter 4, you need to decide if you're going to retain and reuse any existing components from today's data warehouses and data marts.

Figure 10-1 illustrates today's environment as you set out on your hospital's data lake journey.

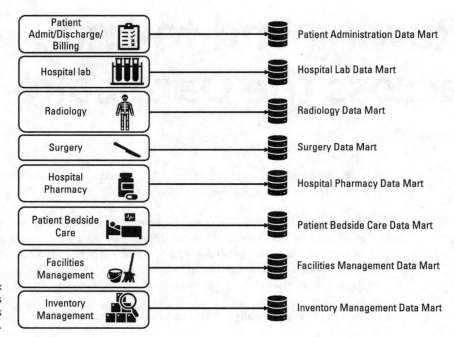

FIGURE 10-1:
Your hospital's legacy systems environment.

Your hospital has followed a *best-of-breed* strategy for its many operational functions and business processes — at least until now. Figure 10-1 shows how you currently have separate, independent applications and systems that handle all the key functions you would expect to find in a hospital, including the following:

>> All the patient administration functions, including admitting, discharge, and billing

>> Hospital lab testing and results

- » Radiology, including X-rays, CAT scans, MRIs, and all other imaging
- » Surgery and operating room management
- » The hospital pharmacy
- » In-room patient bedside care and monitoring
- » Facilities management for the hospital buildings
- » Comprehensive inventory management for all medical and nonmedical supplies

Staying with the best-of-breed strategy, over the years your hospital's IT team also built a series of independent data marts. Keeping things straightforward — if not necessarily optimal — each functional application is paired with a companion data mart that handles reporting, business intelligence (BI), visualization, and some rudimentary predictive analytics.

WARNING

What isn't shown in Figure 10-1 is how complicated and convoluted those data marts have become over the years. Talk about a mess! Any BI and analytics that require data from one or more other functional areas need to acquire that data via a "one-off" data feed. Some of the reports produced by the patient bedside care data mart need data from:

- » The radiology data mart
- » The hospital lab data mart
- » The surgery data mart
- » The hospital pharmacy data mart

For example, suppose you want to run a single report that shows the complete history of a patient's hospital stay. Did that patient undergo surgery? If so, then you'll need to access the surgery data mart. Most likely, the patient received at least a few medications, so go check out the hospital pharmacy data mart, and then merge that data with your results from querying the surgery data mart. X-rays? Add in results from the radiology data mart. And unless the patient was lucky enough to avoid lab tests, you'll have to merge in the results from the hospital lab data mart with your earlier results.

To repeat: Talk about a mess! The best thing to do is throw everything away and start fresh with a brand-new data lake, right? Well, sort of.

Before you automatically dump your entire current portfolio of data marts, take a close look and see if you can salvage and reuse anything. And what do you know? As shown in Figure 10-2, four of the current data marts — patient administration, radiology, hospital pharmacy, and patient bedside care — have solidly constructed dimensional models that are well worth migrating into the gold zone of your new data lake.

FIGURE 10-2:
Selecting data mart dimensional models to retain for your new data lake.

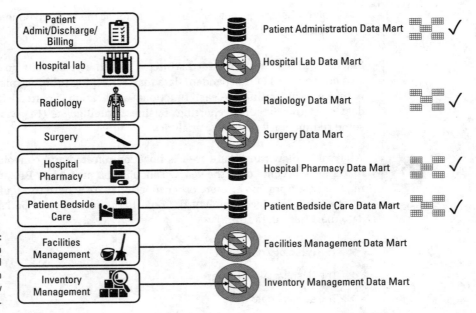

You can — and, no doubt, will — enhance and adjust those data models within the data lake environment. But there's no sense in reinventing the wheel, right?

It turns out that your hospital is going to be doing a lot more than implementing a new data lake. Your new chief information officer (CIO) has decided that the long-standing best-of-breed strategy needs to be changed. The trend for a long while now in medical information systems is to implement an integrated electronic health records environment rather than individual applications to handle the many different hospital functions.

You may also see the term *electronic medical records* (EMR) in lieu of *electronic health records* (EHR); the respective terms and acronyms are used interchangeably. Regardless of the terminology, you'll find vendors such as Epic, Cerner, Meditech, NextGen, Praxis, and many others as the top players in the EHR space.

Figure 10-3 shows how all of today's functions that are handled by individual applications will soon be part of an integrated EHR system.

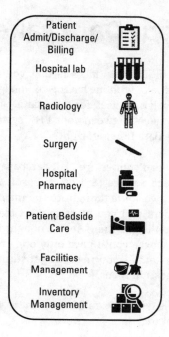

New Integrated
Electronic Health
Records (EHR) System

FIGURE 10-3:
Replacing
best-of-breed
applications with
an integrated EHR
package.

All the top EHR products are increasingly paired with comprehensive data lakes to support hospital and medical analytics. Basically, the EHR system handles hospital operations, and the data lake handles hospital analytics. Figure 10-4 shows the pairing and raises some important questions: Exactly what should your hospital's data lake look like, and how should the data lake be constructed?

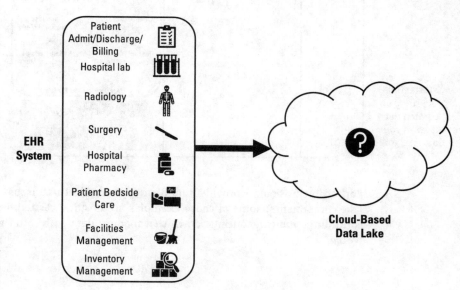

FIGURE 10-4:
Pairing your new
EHR system with
a data lake.

Getting Started with Your Data Lake

A key part of the "marketing pitch" for data lakes is that you can blast mega-volumes of your data into the data lake without having to do significant upfront analysis or even define specific analytical uses for your data. So, following that premise, you can just turn on the faucet between your EHR system and the shell of your new data lake and start the data flowing, right?

TIP

Well, you can . . . but before you unload your entire EHR database into object storage such as Amazon Simple Storage Service (S3) or Microsoft Azure Data Lake Storage (ADLS), you really should give some thought to the major analytical uses of your data lake. If you're impatient and you want to start blasting away with data ingestion, don't worry — you'll get there soon enough. But even in this straightforward hospital example where you'll have only one primary source for your data lake — your new EHR system — you're better off starting with an analytical focus rather than a data ingestion focus.

Figure 10-5 takes you right into the data lake gold zone, where you'll be building and maintaining "packages" of curated data.

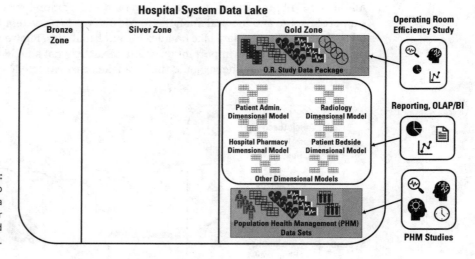

FIGURE 10-5: Setting up curated data packages in your data lake gold zone.

Earlier in this book, I provide a number of examples that discuss individual data lake components; some of those examples are hospital related. In the interest of continuity, you can continue down that medical data path into the data lake as a whole.

For example, you need to set up a data package in your gold zone to support an operating room efficiency study. Even if your hospital weren't implementing the new EHR system, you would still need to ingest, refine, enrich, and then curate surgical data from the legacy surgery management application. But now, you'll build the operating room study package with data ingested from the EHR system when it goes live.

TIP

Either way, you have a fantastic starting point for your data lake: a gold zone placeholder for your operating room study package and its data.

What else can you focus on in these earliest stages of your data lake? Well, you already decided that four of your current data mart dimensional models are worth retaining and moving into the data lake environment. You see then, also in Figure 10-5, additional placeholders in your gold zone for:

>> The patient administration dimensional model

>> The radiology dimensional model

>> The hospital pharmacy dimensional model

>> The patient bedside care dimensional model

Well, here's something interesting: No surgery management and operating room dimensional model shows up in Figure 10-5. In fact, when you look back at Figure 10-2, you see that the current surgery dimensional model didn't make the cut (surgery pun!).

TECHNICAL
STUFF

No worries! You know that surgery and operating room data will definitely be coming into the data lake because of the data package you'll create for the operating room efficiency study. You just won't be able to "forklift" anything from your current surgery data mart, even an empty database schema, into the data lake. You'll be starting over from scratch for reporting and BI related to surgery and operating room functionality — but that's probably a good thing!

You can certainly use your soon-to-be-retired surgery data mart's schema for reference as you create your new gold zone packaging for surgical data, above and beyond what you'll be loading separately into your operating room efficiency study data package.

As you get started with your data lake, reuse what you can, but don't feel restricted or constrained by what you have today. If today's analytical capabilities don't quite fit your needs or are brittle and problematic, leave them behind.

So, what else is going to be featured in your data lake? Population health management is a key capability of medical information systems and analytics. Certain health conditions and diseases are studied "as a population" over long periods of time to help medical professionals better understand a condition or disease, effectiveness of various treatments, and other "deep dive" aspects that can (you hope) lead to new treatment protocols and improve patient outcomes. Population health management (PHM) requires significant volumes of data to support complex analytics. Talk about a perfect match for a data lake, right?

PHM data sets will be built in the data lake gold zone alongside the dimensional models and the operating room study data package (refer to Figure 10-5).

Your hospital data lake will soon have more — many more! — packages of data under the management of the gold zone, all directly supporting your overall analytics continuum. For now, to keep things understandable, you can pause with these three groupings as you turn your attention to other parts of the data lake.

WARNING

You may be tempted to make some command decisions at this point for how these gold zone curated data sets will be stored and managed. Don't do it!

For example, consider the dimensional models that you're repurposing from your current data marts, as well as new dimensional models that you'll build for surgery and operating room analysis as well as many other families of hospital analytics:

>> Should those dimensional models be built inside the Swiss Army knife of data management, a tried-and-true relational database?

>> How about a columnar database to handle very large volumes and known data access patterns?

>> Or should the data be retained in object storage (such as S3 or ADLS) with the dimensionality provided by an "abstraction layer" such as Amazon Redshift Spectrum or Amazon Athena?

Figure 10-6 calls out the uncertainty factor of your data lake platforms, but rest assured that uncertainty is actually a good thing at this point!

You'll make these decisions soon enough. For now, as tempting as it may be to "get the technical stuff out of the way," keep your focus on the conceptual level until you have a solid, end-to-end perspective of your data lake. Don't paint yourself into a corner and limit your flexibility by making platform and technology decisions before you actually have to do so!

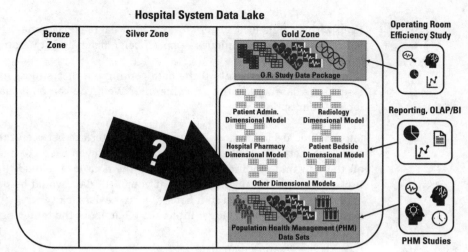

FIGURE 10-6:
Delaying platform
decisions until
you gain a
broader view of
your data lake.

Shifting Your Focus to Data Ingestion

With enough of a foothold in how your data lake will be used, you can now shift
your focus over to how data will make its way into the data lake. Figure 10-7
shows an extremely high-level view of what your overall hospital system environment will look like.

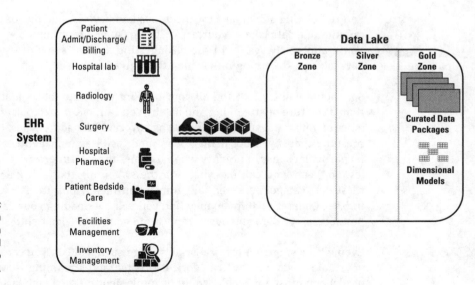

FIGURE 10-7:
Your EHR system
using both
streaming and
batch feeds into
your data lake.

Even with a single EHR system feeding your data lake, you may still use a combination of ingestion techniques — specifically, batch and streaming.

What a minute! Wouldn't all the data coming out of a single-source system be sent to the data lake in the same manner? Well, you can do it that way, but let's look at your options.

Suppose you decide to go with an all-batch interface between the EHR and your data lake. Let's say that every hour, or perhaps even every 30 minutes, you send all the new and modified EHR data into the data lake. Would that do the trick? Probably not, unfortunately. Some of your EHR data would be perfectly fine for analytical purposes if you sent batches into the data lake every half-hour or every hour, or maybe even at longer intervals. What about the following:

>> Facilities management data

>> Inventory management data

Even your patient administration data — admissions, discharges, and especially billing — can probably be satisfied with batch ingestion by the data lake.

But what about beside patient care? Surgery and operating room data? That CAT scan or MRI for a patient who is in severe discomfort and may have a serious medical issue?

You're building a data lake for the 2020s and beyond, and one of the key characteristics of a data lake — courtesy of its big data underpinnings — is data velocity. You'll almost always find yourself ingesting at least some of your data into the data lake via streaming rather than through a batch feed.

So, should you try to bring all your data into the data lake via streaming rather than a mixture of streaming and batch? You can, but if you look at the characteristics of your data, streaming might be "overkill" for some types. In this example, presume that inventory management and facilities management functions have no particular sense of urgency when it comes to real-time, lowest-latency analytics. So, yeah, you can piggyback on the streaming that you know you need for these data categories, essentially implementing a Kappa architecture (all streaming; see Chapter 5). But you may find yourself overloading your data streams with "unnecessary" data and overcomplicating your data lake architecture.

Even with a single enterprise-scale system such as EHR, you can absolutely split your data feeds into two categories — batch and streaming — with each being used when most applicable. You'll be implementing the Lambda architecture (see Chapter 5).

Breaking through the ingestion congestion

As soon as you start to focus on data ingestion, you can start placing some stakes in the ground for incoming data into your data lake bronze zone. Figure 10-8 shows how you dive way, way below the "streaming plus batch" highest-level placeholder for the interface between your EHR system and your hospital's data lake.

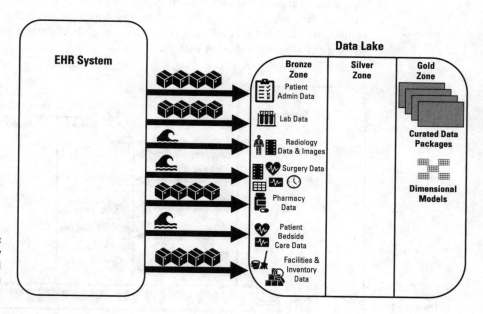

FIGURE 10-8:
Making key ingestion and bronze zone data set decisions.

As it turns out, of your eight major data sets, five will be ingested via batch, while three will be streamed into the data lake. (For drawing simplicity, facilities and inventory data — two separate data sets — are grouped together at the bottom of Figure 10-8, because both are batch oriented.)

So far, so good. But you still have a little bit of work ahead of you when it comes to your streaming data. For each streaming interface into the data lake, you have several options:

>> Stream the data into the bronze zone, but then also "unload" the data in the bronze zone, most likely into object storage such as S3 or ADLS.

>> Stream the data into, and then through, the bronze zone, and then unload the data into the silver zone.

>> Stream the data all the way through the silver zone, but then unload the data into the gold zone.

>> Stream the data all the way into the gold zone, but never unload the data into object storage; the stream itself functions as a data storage engine, as well as a transmission medium.

Figure 10-9 shows how, for patient bedside care data, you decide to stream the data all the way into the gold zone. Streaming analytics will then be applied against the patient bedside data to produce real-time patient care dashboards showing vital signs and other key data.

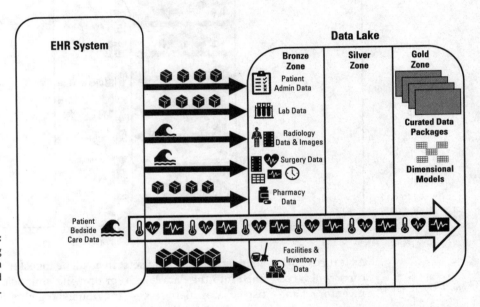

FIGURE 10-9: Streaming persistent data into the gold zone.

What about the rest of your streaming data? Figure 10-10 shows the decisions that you wisely made for your surgery data and your radiology data.

First, take a look at your surgical data. You already know that surgical data needs to be packaged up in some specific manner to support the machine learning models and other advanced analytics for the operating room efficiency study. You also know that even though you're not "forklifting" an existing dimensional model from one of your soon-to-be-retired data marts into the data lake, you'll be creating a new surgery and operating room dimensional modeling for BI, visualization, and online analytical processing (OLAP).

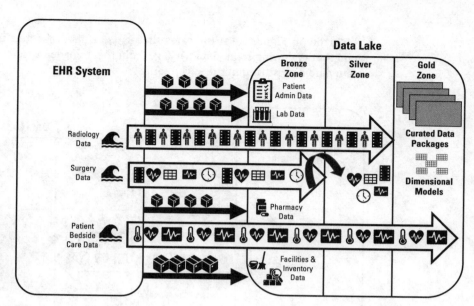

FIGURE 10-10:
Making different
architectural
decisions for
various data
streams.

You then decide to stream your surgery data into the bronze zone and then unload that data — but not into the bronze zone. Instead, the data stream will serve as storage for raw surgery data in the bronze zone. You'll refine and enrich the surgery data as you store it in the silver zone (probably in object storage such as S3 or ADLS, but you'll make that platform decision later).

You make a different decision for your radiology data, however. For now, you decide to carry the data stream all the way into the silver zone but leave that data in the stream for persistent storage. Maybe down the road you'll do something different with the radiology data, but for now, you elect the persistent stream option for the silver zone.

Cranking up the data refinery

REMEMBER

Your silver zone serves as your data lake's water treatment facility, turning raw and even dirty data into curated, well-organized, and ready-to-consume analytical data sets.

Figure 10-11 shows your silver zone at work — specifically, the first assignment you lay in its lap.

You've streamed surgical and operating room data into the silver zone, where you've unloaded the data. You've already determined that your data lake gold zone will contain a package of operating room data to support your hospital's efficiency study. Time to play matchmaker!

The arrow in Figure 10-11 indicates that as your data lake gets built out, you'll build that operating room data package from the unloaded surgical and operating room data now sitting in the silver zone.

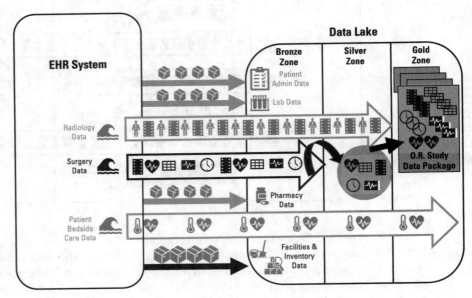

FIGURE 10-11:
Putting your
silver zone to
work.

Presto! With that decision, you now have your first end-to-end data pipeline for your data lake. What do you do next? Go define some more data pipelines!

Adding to your data pipelines

Figure 10-12 shows the initial set of end-to-end data pipelines that you've decided to build.

Sticking with your surgical and operating room data for a moment, take note in Figure 10-12 where that same set of silver zone operating room and surgical data that will be used to build the data package for the efficiency study will also be used to build a dimensional model for BI, OLAP, and visualization.

TIP

In fact, you'll probably be using surgical data in more than one dimensional model. Remember how, at the outset of this chapter, when you were surveying your hospital's current data marts, you took note that many of the data marts fed data to one another to support cross-functional BI and analytics? So, almost certainly, surgical and operating room data will be needed for more than just surgical analytics. But you can worry about those specific needs later. You've laid the groundwork by unloading refined and enriched surgical data into the silver zone, where's it's sitting there waiting.

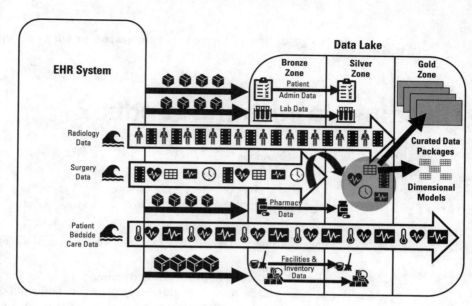

FIGURE 10-12: Adding data pipelines to your data lake buildout.

Taking a look at Figure 10-12 from top to bottom, you can see your data pipelines taking shape:

>> Patient administration data — admissions, discharges, and billing — is cleansed and now stored in the silver zone.

>> Laboratory data is also cleansed and stored in the silver zone. You may want to treat laboratory data in a special manner down the road, if you find that latency issues become an impediment. Right now, your lab data is transmitted by batch, but you can always change that to a streaming interface.

>> Radiology data is streamed into the silver zone and persisted in the data stream.

>> Surgery data is streamed into the data lake and unloaded into the silver zone, where so far you've identified two downstream hops into the gold zone (the operating room study package and the surgical and operating room dimensional model).

>> Pharmacy data is transmitted by batch into the bronze zone and then refined and enriched — also in batches — into the silver zone.

>> Patient bedside care data is streamed all the way into the gold zone, where it will be consumed by streaming analytics.

>> Facilities management and inventory management data is transmitted by batch and then cleansed before being stored in the silver zone.

So far, so good. Now you have only one component left to set up: the data lake sandbox.

Finishing Up with the Sandbox

REMEMBER

Your data lake sandbox is

>> An isolated area for discovery and exploratory analytics of the "tell us something interesting and important from all this data" variety

>> Your data lake development area, where you can specify, build, test, and refine new analytical models before putting them into production

Your hospital is already implementing streaming analytics for patient bedside care real-time dashboards. Now, suppose you want to build and deploy advanced streaming analytics that directly consume data from multiple incoming streams rather than from object storage or databases.

So far, you've identified three inbound data streams from your upcoming EHR application into your data lake:

>> Radiology data

>> Surgery and operating data

>> Patient bedside care data

As noted earlier in this chapter, you've decided (at least for now) to handle each of these three data streams differently, with different "unload points" — or, in the case of patient bedside care data, without unloading the data into object storage or a database.

Different paradigms for each of your data streams? No worries. As shown in Figure 10-13, you can "divert" each of the three data streams into the sandbox area where you can build and experiment with streaming analytics that consume data from all three streams in concert with one another.

TECHNICAL STUFF

You don't actually "divert" the data streams from their primary destinations into the sandbox, so you don't have to worry about interfering with mission-critical dashboards, analytics, and the resultant decisions and actions. Most streaming services allow multiple subscribers to a data stream. In this case, you would set up your sandbox as a subscriber to your three EHR-produced streams, in addition to the "core" portion of your data lake.

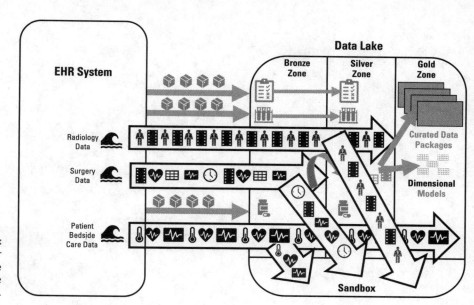

FIGURE 10-13: Bringing your data lake sandbox into the picture.

As shown in Figure 10-13, even the streaming data that is unloaded into storage remains in the streams for purposes of your sandbox development and experimentation efforts. Basically, you have near-total control over your data from the moment it hits your data lake until the data is served up to your users. You can mix-and-match as much as you want, using whatever technology services work for your purposes.

3
Evaporating the Data Lake into the Cloud

Chapter **11**

A Cloudy Day at the Data Lake

You won't encounter some mystical force of the universe that prevents you from building your data lake in your company's on-premises data center under the direct and total control of your internal IT staff. However, cloud computing and data lakes go together like peanut butter and jelly, so you'll almost certainly be thinking "The cloud! Of course!" as you pack up your data and head out on the highway toward the data lake.

Here's some good news: You don't need to be a cloud computing expert when it comes to your organization's data lake. However, you should understand a few cloud computing basics to keep your efforts on the right path.

TIP

If you want to soar high into the world of cloud computing, check out *Cloud Computing For Dummies*, 2nd Edition, by Daniel Kirsch and Judith Hurwitz (Wiley).

Rushing to the Cloud

If you walk into any IT organization today, you'll find teams whose jobs are primarily or solely dedicated to cloud computing. In many cases, those folks are focused on moving applications, databases, networking, and other computing assets out of their company's data center — where those assets are under the sole control of internal IT staff — to one or more cloud platforms.

So, what's this cloud computing frenzy all about anyway?

The pendulum swings back and forth

Long ago, when dinosaurs wrote COBOL and FORTRAN programs on gigantic mainframe computers, most organizations couldn't afford their own computers. Search the web for "how much did a mainframe cost in 1970," and you'll see that the price tag was north of $4 million! And that was in 1970 dollars — the price tag would be close to $30 million in today's money! (And don't even get me started on the puny computing power from 50+ years ago compared to today. . . .)

By the 1970s, though, almost every organization wanted to do at least some "data processing" for their back-office processes — accounting and payroll, inventory management, human resources, and so on. What a predicament, right?

The answer to the "we need to do it, but can't afford it" quandary was straight-forward: something called *timesharing.* Basically, large "computing service bureaus" purchased one or more mainframe computers and leased out space and computing power to smaller organizations (see the nearby sidebar.)

By the mid-'70s, however, *minicomputers* became popular. As you might guess from the name, a minicomputer was smaller than a mainframe. (Trivia: Minicomputers were sometimes more formally referred to as "midrange systems.") More important, minicomputers were far less expensive than mainframes, which meant that smaller companies and governmental agencies were able to purchase or lease in-house computers and bring some of those timeshared applications in-house.

Then, when "microcomputers" (PCs) came on the market and grew into powerful workstations, and when local area networks (LANs) and client/server computing became popular, all bets were off. Throughout the late '80s and into the '90s, pretty much every company made a concerted effort to bring the majority of its computing in-house.

Basically, the prevailing philosophy in the IT world became the exact opposite of today: "Let's take control and responsibility for our own computing resources."

As the saying goes, be careful what you wish for, because you might just get it.

CLOUD DATA LAKES IN THE DISCO ERA (SORT OF)

In the autumn of 1979, at the beginning of my senior year in college at Arizona State University (ASU), I landed a part-time computer programming job with the office of the Arizona attorney general (AG). My job involved consolidating and regularly refreshing data from many external federal and state agencies to provide online "one-stop information shopping" to support the office of the AG's investigations.

One problem, though: Mainframe computers were incredibly expensive, far beyond what a state government agency could typically afford back then. And in addition to the hardware and software expenses, a company or governmental agency would also need to pay for a couple full-time computer operators, who were integral to computer operations in those days.

The AG's office came up with a pretty nifty solution: Back then, ASU ran an old UNIVAC mainframe in its computer center for academic computing and some internal functions such as student admissions and tracking official grades. The AG's office leased space and computer resources on ASU's mainframe for its consolidated and cross-referenced investigation support data. To do our programming, we would sit at old-fashioned computer terminals in the AG's office in downtown Phoenix and connect to ASU's UNIVAC computer by telephone and modem. The AG office investigators would likewise dial into the ASU mainframe whenever they needed to access the consolidated investigation support data. All the data sat on ASU's UNIVAC on disks and old-style computer tapes, and all the code that I wrote and maintained likewise sat in the university's computer center, not at the AG's office.

Anyway, enough reminiscing from long, long ago. The point of this anecdote is that you can say I worked with a cloud data lake more than 40 years ago! Okay, it wasn't actually a data lake. Technically, it was more of a prehistoric data warehouse than even the data warehousing architecture that took hold in the early '90s. And yeah, that certainly wasn't cloud computing as we know it today. But that's my story, and I'm sticking to it!

Dealing with the challenges of on-premises hosting

Backups and recoveries. Software upgrades and patches. Capacity planning. Performance tuning. Network and systems security. Data center design and buildouts.

The list of responsibilities that came along with controlling our own computing resources grew and grew and grew. Before long, the basic operations management that came with then-modern computing was an incredible drain on most organizations' IT budgets. They needed to divert skilled IT staffers from application development, database design, and other "productive" activities to basic systems and network management and troubleshooting.

Well, that wasn't the best idea to bring computing resources in-house, was it?

The pendulum began to swing back in the other direction as organizations looked for a way to get out of the systems management and hosting business.

The case for the cloud

So, maybe timesharing wasn't such a bad idea after all. Even through the '90s and into the early 2000s, some organizations turned to hosting companies and service bureaus for at least some of their computing resource management. Was there a way to combine the external support of timesharing with modern, distributed computing, especially with all this Internet stuff making its way into application architecture? Absolutely!

TECHNICAL STUFF

Many people recognize Salesforce as the company that triggered the modern era of cloud computing. Salesforce's customer relationship management (CRM) software, unlike competitors such as Siebel, supported a software as a service (SaaS; discussed later in this chapter) model rather than on-premises software installation.

And the race to the cloud was on. In addition to offloading systems management responsibilities, organizations were driven by two key characteristics of modern cloud computing:

>> **Elasticity:** Cloud computing allows users to dynamically and (relatively) effortlessly add or subtract computing resources to match growing or shrinking workloads. You've probably heard something along the lines of "spinning up resources" such as database capacity and computing power.

   When you bring a new application online — or, in the context of this book, build a new data pipeline for your enterprise data lake — you can quickly add the right amount of resources without having to purchase new software and hardware, or install and configure your new components, or test and deploy that same software and hardware.

>> **Flexible pricing:** Flexible pricing and elasticity go hand in hand. The mantra of cloud computing is "pay only for what you use." When you add computing resources, your bill goes up. If you retire an application, your bill goes down. If you don't access data very frequently, your costs will be less than for an actively used database.

TIP

As you'll see with both Amazon Web Services (AWS) and Microsoft Azure, you can also control pricing by selecting various tiers of storage. You can put frequently accessed data where your storage cost is on the higher side but your access cost is low. If you have data lake content and you're not quite sure how often your users will access the data — or even if they'll access the data at all — you can drop that data into "archive-level" storage with very low storage costs. However, if and when you need to access that data from archive-level storage, your access costs will be on the higher side — not to mention response time will typically be in the hours range rather than blazingly fast.

Running through Some Cloud Computing Basics

Okay, you're sold. You've bought into the case for cloud computing. What do you need to know about cloud computing, especially in the context of data lakes?

Fortunately, you can get by with just a couple of key items:

» Public versus private versus hybrid clouds

» The various "as a service" alternatives

Public, private, and hybrid clouds

The first thing to take note of is that, regardless of technology, cloud computing comes in two primary flavors: a private cloud versus a public cloud.

In the spirit of actual clouds in the sky, think of a public cloud as the equivalent of a regularly scheduled airline flight, with perhaps 200 people aboard. Do all those people come from the same family or group or even know each other? Nope! As long as that flight still has available seats, anyone can make a reservation and fly from, say, Phoenix to Tacoma.

If you've got the bucks, though, you can splurge for a private flight. Forget owning or leasing your own plane for now, and think of calling up a service that offers flights aboard private planes and saying that you and two other people want to fly from Philadelphia to Atlanta and then to Los Angeles.

How about taking the analogy out of the skies and down to the water in the spirit of data lake analogies throughout this book? Suppose you go to Venice, Italy, and you want to travel among Venice's major islands. You can hop aboard a *vaporetto* (a public "waterbus" or ferry, capable of carrying hundreds of passengers at a cost of less than €10), or you can splurge for a water taxi that will carry only four or five people for maybe ten times the cost of a vaporetto (see Figure 11-1).

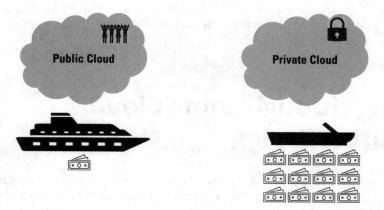

FIGURE 11-1: Public versus private clouds: a visual analogy.

With a public cloud, costs are distributed among those who make use of its computing resources, whereas with a private cloud, the costs are handled by a single company or perhaps a couple of companies working on a project together.

Why would you want to pay more — probably a lot more — for a private cloud? The answer is one word: privacy! Well, maybe one more word: guaranteed resources. A private cloud has all the advantages of cloud computing — offloaded systems management and administration, and elasticity of resources and pricing — and sort of feels like your own data center without all the hassle. Plus, if you have extra-sensitive data, you aren't sharing computing resources with other organizations and — in theory anyway — exposing your data to potential leakage.

So, does that mean with a public cloud your data is comingled with data from other companies? No! Cloud providers separate their customers' data and provide services for authorization and authentication. Still, the computing resources in a public cloud are shared among customers, which is why some companies opt for private clouds for ultrasensitive data and applications.

Do you have any options other than a private cloud or a public cloud for your computing in general and your data lake in particular? Sort of. The term *hybrid cloud* is overloaded with a couple of different meanings, including the following:

>> A combination of public cloud and private cloud services for your IT infrastructure

>> A combination of public cloud and on-premises data center services for your IT infrastructure

TECHNICAL STUFF

Actually, the two definitions of *hybrid cloud* are sort of the same, or at least overlapping. Some people consider an on-premises data center to be sort of a private cloud in the context that it's not "open to the public" for users outside the organization. Is an on-premises data center really a private cloud? Well, the answer depends on whether the data center provides the resource elasticity and pricing flexibility that are so important to the cloud computing paradigm. If you're talking about your organization's own data center, then it's probably a stretch to consider it to be a private cloud. If, however, you're referring to a third-party company that provides dedicated data center services, then sure, go ahead and call it a private cloud if you want. To-may-to, to-mah-to. . . .

Different "as a service" models

TIP

One of the best ways to think about cloud computing is as a service that your organization can access.

But exactly what type of service? As cloud computing has taken hold, three primary service models — or, more accurately, "as a service" models — have percolated to the top:

>> Software as a service (SaaS)

>> Infrastructure as a service (IaaS)

>> Platform as a service (PaaS)

TECHNICAL STUFF

You're probably going to be shocked — shocked! — to read that in addition to the big three of SaaS, IaaS, and PaaS, you may also come across the acronyms CaaS (for *container as a service*), FaaS (for *function as a service*), and even others such as AIaaS (for *artificial intelligence as a service*). Okay, you're not shocked. What you might call "aaS inflation" is sort of like how the original three Vs of big data have been expanded into a much longer list that includes almost any plausible word that begins with the letter V. Do yourself a favor: Unless you really want to get into the weeds of minor distinctions among numerous acronyms and phrases, just focus on the big three — SaaS, IaaS, and PaaS.

So, what are the similarities and distinctions among SaaS, IaaS, and PaaS?

Think of SaaS as a soup-to-nuts solution stack that assigns responsibility for everything — yes, everything! — to your cloud provider, including the following:

>> Application software

>> Your data

>> System software (operating systems, scheduling, runtime management)

>> Integration services such as middleware and application programming interfaces (APIs)

>> Databases and file systems

>> Processing power

>> Disks, persistent memory, and other storage

>> Networking and communications

TIP

If you've ever used Google Workspace (including Google Docs, Google Sheets, and Google Slides), you've tapped into SaaS. You have no insight into the computing resources that go into allowing you to create, update, or even just read any of these Google files, nor should you even have any interest in what's happening behind the scenes. You need to use software; someone (Google in this case) is making that software available to you through a plain old web browser; and that's a wrap!

On the other side of the cloud computing picture, IaaS requires about a 50/50 split in responsibilities between your organization and the cloud computing provider. As the name implies, you're making use of someone else's hardware infrastructure, which means that the cloud provider is responsible for servers, disks and other storage, virtualization services, and all the networking hardware (routers, bridges, gateways, and so on). Your organization, however, has responsibility for the following:

>> Application software

>> System software (operating systems, scheduling, runtime management)

>> Integration services such as middleware and APIs

>> Databases and file systems

Somewhere in the middle between SaaS and IaaS, you'll find PaaS. In this vernacular, a *platform* is not only all the hardware from IaaS, but also the systems software such as the operating system, job scheduling, and the middleware and APIs for integration. Your organization, however, will develop applications on a cloud computing "platform," and you're also responsible for managing your data that is stored within the platform's databases and file systems.

Figure 11-2 shows SaaS, PaaS, and IaaS side-by-side to give you a visual idea of the allocated responsibilities among the three. (You'll see some variations from one diagram to another if you do an image search for "SaaS vs. PaaS vs. IaaS," but for the most part, Figure 11-2 reflects the consensus.)

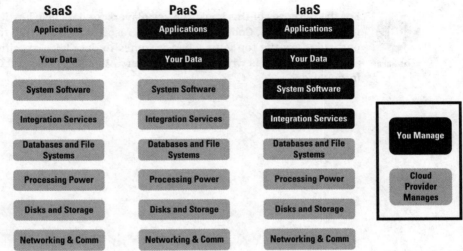

FIGURE 11-2: Allocation of responsibilities for SaaS, PaaS, and IaaS.

The Big Guys in the Cloud Computing Game

As you may suspect, a few companies rule the cloud computing landscape. The major global players in cloud computing are

>> Alibaba

>> Amazon (specifically the AWS business unit, as opposed to Amazon's retail business)

>> Google

>> IBM

>> Microsoft

You can also include Oracle in this list, even though its cloud revenue is expected to be "only" $1 billion by 2023, according to a 2020 study by RBC Capital Markets. Yeah, a billion dollars is small potatoes compared to Amazon's $21 billion for the *first half* of 2020 reported in the same RBC study. But still, a billion dollars is real money. . . .

You also have SAP to consider, especially for its HANA in-memory database and its latest enterprise systems flagship, S4/HANA.

REMEMBER

For the purposes of this book, the key players for data lake hosting and management are Amazon, Google, IBM, and Microsoft. And from that final four, two in particular are the top guns when it comes to data lake–specific services: AWS and Azure, which is why Chapter 12 covers AWS data lakes and Chapter 13 dives into Azure.

Chapter **12**

Building Data Lakes in Amazon Web Services

Building your data lake in Amazon Web Services (AWS) can sometimes feel like hacking your way through a jungle. (Get it? Amazon? A jungle?) You have dozens of services that you can stitch together for ingesting and then storing your data, as well as transforming and then moving your data along pipelines and then finally consuming data to drive decisions and actions.

Fortunately, you can follow some basic patterns with AWS that will help guide your pathway to the data lake if you elect to go down the AWS path.

The Elite Eight: Identifying the Essential Amazon Services

If you follow American college basketball, the term *March Madness* is familiar to you. The (supposedly) best 64 teams begin a tournament that ends up with that season's U.S. college basketball champion winning the final game.

Along the way, after the first couple of rounds are played, the subsequent rounds are given catchy nicknames, beginning with the "Sweet 16." Teams measure their success by making it to the "Final Four," but in between, you find the "Elite Eight."

You can apply that same nickname — the Elite Eight — to a collection of eight services that you'll likely combine to build your data lake in AWS. So, settle in for a survey of:

>> Amazon Simple Storage Service (S3)

>> AWS Glue

>> AWS Lake Formation

>> Amazon Kinesis Data Streams

>> Amazon Kinesis Data Firehose

>> Amazon Athena

>> Amazon Redshift

>> Amazon Redshift Spectrum

TECHNICAL STUFF

If you're one of those eagle-eyed folks who quickly spot patterns and anomalies, you may have noticed that in the preceding list, most of the services are preceded by *Amazon* but two are preceded by *AWS*. No, you're not looking at a sloppily created list of data lake–oriented services. For whatever reason, Amazon and AWS (the overall company and the business unit) name some of their cloud services with *Amazon* and others with *AWS*. For your purposes, think "distinction without a difference" — in other words, regardless of the official cloud service names, your focus is to pull together the right combination of services to build your organization's data lake.

Amazon S3

Amazon data lake architects and users find themselves frequently referring to Amazon S3, but they should periodically recall what *S3* stands for: Simple Storage Service. The full name describes exactly what S3 intends to fill as the epicenter of your AWS-based data lake: a simple service for data storage, with "simple" being relative to the many other database-type services available to you on AWS.

REMEMBER

One of the primary value propositions of a data lake is the ability to ingest, store, and manage the three major categories of data — structured, unstructured, and semi-structured — as "peers" without having to jump through hoops.

The Microsoft equivalent of S3 is Azure Data Lake Storage (ADLS), which I cover in Chapter 13.

The primary organizational structure of S3 is the *bucket*, which is just as it sounds: a container into which you put your data. Then, within each bucket, you store any number of *objects*. What's an object? Think of each object as a file containing whatever you want to store: data, free-format text, static images, audio, video . . . in other words, structured, unstructured, and semi-structured data (see Figure 12-1).

Amazon S3 Bucket

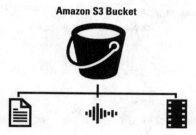

FIGURE 12-1:
The fundamental structure of Amazon S3.

Each object can be as large as 5 terabytes (TB), which gives you a lot of flexibility to store gigantic files — audio and video in particular — in S3 in your data lake.

TECHNICAL STUFF

Even though S3 doesn't natively support the concept of *folders* to organize your S3 objects within a bucket, you can sort of trick S3 into managing your objects in a logically grouped, "pseudo-folder" manner. Even better, you can use the Amazon S3 console (the way you create and manage objects within S3) to go along with the "yeah, S3 has folders" charade.

Suppose you're building a data lake for an insurance company, and you want to store JPG image files in S3 within your data lake bronze zone. You can specify folder names by city (PITTSBURGH, CLEVELAND, DETROIT, and so on), or by year and month (2021-AUGUST, 2021-SEPT, 2021-OCT, and so on), or even some combination of cities and months if that makes sense for you. The choice is yours.

S3 mimics a folder structure by placing the folder name between forward slashes (/) within the filename used for the object. Figure 12-2 shows how these "virtual" folders can give your S3 data a hierarchical structure that doesn't actually exist.

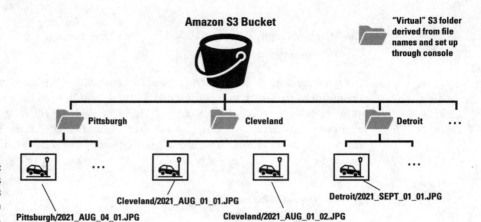

Amazon S3 Bucket

"Virtual" S3 folder derived from file names and set up through console

Pittsburgh   Cleveland   Detroit   ...

FIGURE 12-2:
Mimicking folders
in Amazon S3
through
filenames.

Cleveland/2021_AUG_01_01.JPG

Detroit/2021_SEPT_01_01.JPG

Pittsburgh/2021_AUG_04_01.JPG

Cleveland/2021_AUG_01_02.JPG

TIP

Within S3, you can also set up tiered storage for your data lake, based on factors such as:

>> Whether you have immediate, known analytical needs for your data

>> Whether your organization's users actually access and analyze specific data as time goes on

Chapter 6 has a quick discussion of S3 tiered storage for your data lake's silver zone.

And speaking of your data lake's silver zone, you can use Amazon S3 in your data lake's bronze zone, silver zone, or gold zone, or even in your data lake's sandbox. You can conceivably build your entire data lake on top of S3, with no other AWS data services such as Redshift in the picture (see Figure 12-3).

As you see later, services such as Athena and Redshift Spectrum give you access to S3-managed objects not only for data science, but also for the database-type access that is the foundation of classic business intelligence (BI).

TIP

You'll find hundreds of video presentations online that were recorded at various Amazon conferences and summits, giving examples of building AWS data lakes. You won't find too many that reference bronze, silver, and gold zones, however, at least when it comes to allocating S3 buckets across your data lake. You may, however, find references to moving data along a pipeline containing three different S3 buckets:

>> A landing bucket

>> A processed bucket

>> A published bucket

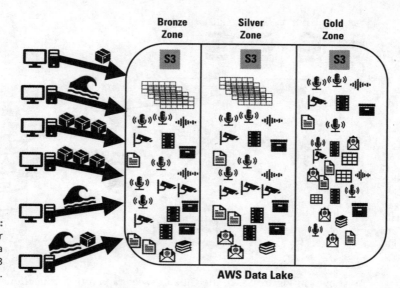

FIGURE 12-3:
Building your entire AWS data lake using only S3 for data storage.

Bronze Zone · Silver Zone · Gold Zone

AWS Data Lake

The landing bucket contains bronze zone data, the processed bucket contains silver zone data that you've refined and enriched, and the published bucket contains your curated packages of data.

AWS Glue

AWS Glue plays a critical role in most AWS data lakes. The Glue Data Catalog helps you organize and locate the mountains of data in your data lake.

TIP

Think of the Glue Data Catalog in this way: If you had an actual lake instead of a data lake, the Glue Data Catalog would contain a roster of every fish, every rock, every piece of discarded trash, everything in your lake. Even better, you would set up the Glue Data Catalog to update itself on a regular basis.

If you've ever worked with complex data sets spread out over dozens or even hundreds of files, you know that maintaining an up-to-date catalog is often an exercise in futility. No one would argue with the value of metadata, but keeping that metadata current? Yeah, right. . . .

Great news! Glue Data Catalog throws technology into the mix and "crawls" your data lake to keep its catalog up to date. Figure 12-4 shows Glue in action.

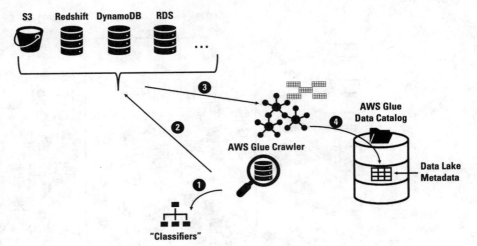

FIGURE 12-4:
Using Glue
Crawler and Glue
Data Catalog to
maintain
up-to-date data
lake metadata.

As shown in Figure 12-4, the Glue Crawler taps into a collection of "classifiers" that help it make sense of the various database and file formats you typically have in your data lake (Step 1). Armed with this information, Glue Crawler checks out your files stored within S3, along with the army of Amazon database services you can use in AWS (discussed later in this chapter): Redshift, DynamoDB, RDS, and others (Step 2).

TIP

Think of Glue Crawler in the same context as a search engine's crawlers, heading off to the far reaches of the Internet to find out what's on all those web pages. In this case, however, the "crawling" takes place in your data lake, not out there on the web.

Glue Crawler uses the information from its classifiers and infers the data structures and schemas from the data sets it accesses (Step 3). Finally, Glue Crawler writes the new information into the Glue Data Catalog (Step 4), and — presto! — your data lake is fully inventoried!

But wait, there's more!

Armed with all this up-to-date data lake catalog information, Glue can serve as the backbone of your extraction, transformation, and loading (ETL) across the data pipelines within your data lake. In fact, Glue works alongside AWS Lake Formation, discussed next.

AWS Lake Formation

AWS Lake Formation is a relative newcomer to Amazon's portfolio of data lake services. But Lake Formation can play an important role in constructing your overall data lake and your end-to-end pipelines.

Lake Formation works hand-in-hand with Glue, playing roles in:

>> Ingesting data into your data lake's bronze zone

>> Transforming incoming relational data into S3 bucket storage

>> Orchestrating the various steps along your data pipelines through your various data lake zones

>> Managing and governing access by users and IT staff to permissible areas of your data lake

REMEMBER

Lake Formation contains a mechanism known as a *blueprint* that you can use as the foundation of your data ingestion. You construct a blueprint to extract data from one or more sources and then land the incoming data into S3 buckets (see Figure 12-5).

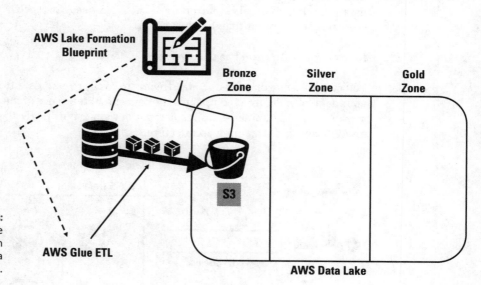

FIGURE 12-5: Using a Lake Formation blueprint for data lake ingestion.

TECHNICAL STUFF

You set up a Lake Formation blueprint to specify:

>> Both initial and incremental ETL jobs for first-time and refresh data ingestion, respectively

>> The specific source database columns that will be used to determine new or changed data for incremental ETL

>> The target S3 bucket for the incoming data

>> The file format (for example, JSON) into which incoming database data will be "unloaded" to be stored within S3

In this context, Lake Formation is like a typical ETL tool such as Informatica or IBM DataStage. If ETL is new to you, no worries: You can probably pick up the basics of Lake Formation data ingestion in an hour or two — it's that easy!

TIP

Lake Formation actually creates Glue jobs to do the data ingestion. You can take a look at the Glue workflow by switching from the Lake Formation console to the Glue console. In fact, you can even take a peek at the actual SQL statements that Glue generates to go after your source data. So, you can work with Lake Formation purely in a drag-and-drop, graphical manner and let the service "do its thing," or you can really get under the covers if you want.

Amazon Kinesis Data Streams

Glue and Lake Formation are powerful engines for batch ETL into and within your data lake. But data lakes are often about "the need for speed," which means streaming data rather than batch transfers.

No worries — Amazon has you covered!

You can use Amazon Kinesis Data Streams to, well, stream data from devices into your data lake. Figure 12-6 updates the conceptual reference architecture diagram streaming from Chapter 5 for hospital patient vital signs (refer to Figure 5-15) to an AWS-specific streaming architecture.

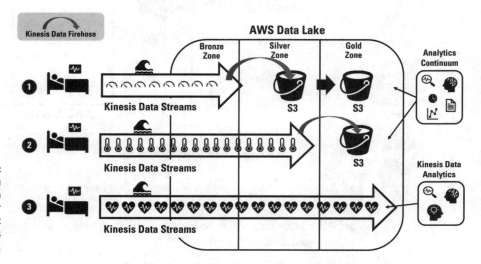

FIGURE 12-6: Using Amazon Kinesis Data Streams for hospital patient vital signs streaming.

In Figure 12-6, you can see that you have a lot of latitude when it comes to using Kinesis Data Streams to ingest data into your data lake. At the top of the diagram, one particular type of data — say, pulse rates and oxygen saturation levels — streams into the bronze zone, but then is "unloaded" into S3 in the silver zone after refinement and enrichment.

You use Kinesis Data Firehose in conjunction with Kinesis Data Streams to unload data from streaming input, as discussed in the next section.

The middle data stream containing a patient's temperature readings, however, makes its way into the silver zone without being unloaded. The temperature data is finally unloaded into an S3 bucket in the gold zone, where that data is directly consumable by various forms of analytics: BI and visualization, machine learning, and so on.

Finally, you have the bottom stream containing heart monitoring data, which is never unloaded into S3 or any other data store, at least in this scenario. So, how is the data used for analytics? Simple: Amazon Kinesis Data Analytics accesses data directly from a Kinesis stream.

Thinking about that third use case with the heart monitoring data that remains in the stream, you may be wondering, "How long does that data hang around if you don't explicitly store the data in S3 or some other data store?" Great question! The default retention for data in a Kinesis data stream is 24 hours, but you can configure the data to remain *persistent* (that is, not be dumped) for up to 8,760 hours. If you do the math, that's 365 days — an entire year (unless it's a leap year, in which case you're one day short).

You can adjust the retention period for a given data stream up and down as needed, but be careful: If you *decrease* the retention period, any data older than your new retention period *immediately* becomes inaccessible. Think of this sudden loss of stream-resident data the same as permanently deleting a file on your computer or exiting from Microsoft Word without saving your file. If that's what you meant to do, no problem. But if you deleted that file or didn't save your work by mistake, you won't be very happy!

Amazon Kinesis Data Firehose

You pair up Amazon Kinesis Data Firehose with Kinesis Data Streams to "unload" data out of a stream into a database or other data store within your data lake. Within the family of AWS, Kinesis Firehose allows you to store data into:

>> S3

>> Redshift

>> Amazon Elasticsearch Service (ES)

If you're using non–Amazon data services within your AWS data lake, you can use Kinesis Data Firehose to drop data into Datadog, MongoDB, Splunk, and other destinations. Check out Amazon's online Developer Guide for Kinesis Data Firehose to see which destinations are supported, as well to see the step-by-step instructions and tips for each data destination; you can find it at https:// docs.aws.amazon.com/firehose/latest/dev/what-is-this-service.html.

Amazon Athena

One of the biggest architectural choices you face when you're building a data lake is how many data services you should use throughout your data lake. Should you keep all your data, in all your zones, in object storage, which for AWS means S3? Or should you use relational databases, NoSQL databases, or other specialized data stores at various points?

And if you do decide to head down the homogeneous route with everything in object storage, what about classic BI and data visualization against your data lake? After all, your data lake should support the entire continuum of analytics, from descriptive analytics to predictive and discovery analytics, from rudimentary BI to machine learning and other "data science" analytics (see Chapter 2). Can you build your data lake to keep your storage architecture simple and still satisfy this entire portfolio of analytics?

REMEMBER

Absolutely! Amazon Athena is one of the services that you'll find on AWS that allows you to treat underlying S3 data as if you were accessing a database rather than an object store. Remember that S3 "objects" are actually files. Some of those files, such as JPG images, contain unstructured data, and you wouldn't even think about trying to run SQL queries against them.

Other files, though, contain semi-structured data that otherwise can be stored in a database. In fact, you may have brought a lot of that data in from external databases using Lake Formation Blueprints in which you converted database content into JSON or other files that are now stored within S3.

Remember how the Glue Crawler checked out S3 content and inferred a schema using classifiers and then stored that metadata in the Glue Data Catalog? AWS stores that metadata for more than just documentation purposes. Athena taps into the Glue Data Catalog and then can access S3 data using SQL, just as if the SQL were running against an actual database (see Figure 12-7).

Athena accesses the metadata from the Glue Data Catalog (Step 1) and issues a SQL query against "virtual" database tables that represent the underlying S3 data, as if that data were actually stored in a database (Step 2). The SQL is then converted to appropriate commands for whatever the file format actually is (Step 3), and then the result is sent back to Athena (Step 4).

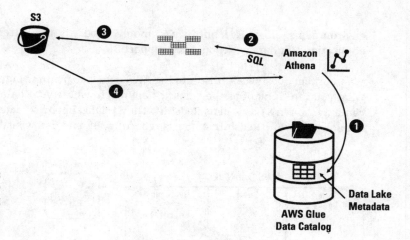

**TECHNICAL
STUFF**

Athena can access S3 buckets containing the following files:

>> Avro

>> CSV

>> JSON

>> ORC

>> Parquet

Amazon Redshift

Even before data lakes started catching on in the AWS world, many organizations were shifting their data warehousing to the cloud. And to nobody's surprise, many of those cloud-based data warehouses were built in AWS.

And that meant that Amazon Redshift became a very, very popular database.

Fast-forward just a little bit into the data lake era, and take the broader perspective of data lakes as an overall modernized environment to support analytics rather than just a monolithic object store. Putting all those pieces together brings you to one conclusion: Redshift is an important component to many AWS-based data lakes.

So, what is Redshift? The best way to think of Redshift is as a data warehouse-oriented, SQL-compliant database management system (DBMS). *Data warehouse-oriented* means that, unlike, say, SQL Server or Oracle, Redshift is not a "Swiss army knife" type of DBMS that is commonly used for transactional and analytical environments alike. Redshift is commonly used for the latter — analytical applications, or data warehouses to support BI.

Where, then, does Redshift fit into the AWS data lake picture? Figure 12-8 depicts what you can think of as the "classic" approach, where your data lake gold zone contains data in S3 as well as Redshift. The S3 data supports "data science" types of analytics, while Redshift supports reporting, BI, and data visualization.

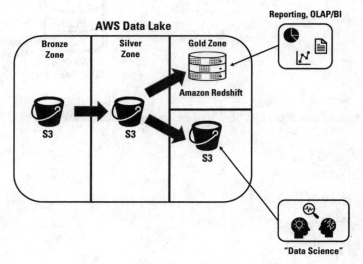

FIGURE 12-8:
Using Amazon Redshift in your data lake's gold zone.

Amazon Redshift Spectrum

Hang on a minute.

So, you definitely want to have the capability in your data lake to send SQL commands against your gold zone data (and possibly even "pre-curated" but still refined data in your silver zone). But it looks like you have two different approaches to consider. On the one hand, Amazon Athena gives you a relational "abstraction" on top of S3-resident, non-database data (refer to Figure 12-7). With Athena, you don't need to transfer any of your S3 data further along a data pipeline using Glue or any other ETL capability.

On the other hand, you can use ETL capabilities to convert S3 data in your silver zone into curated packages and store those packages in Redshift in your gold zone (refer to Figure 12-8).

Want to split the difference, sort of? Then say hello to Amazon Redshift Spectrum.

REMEMBER

Amazon Redshift and Amazon Redshift Spectrum are related, but they're not the same service nor should the names be used interchangeably.

In fact, Amazon Redshift Spectrum is far closer to Amazon Athena in how it works. Stop me if you've heard this before (like earlier in this chapter):

» Redshift Spectrum accesses metadata from the Glue Data Catalog.

» Your BI tool or your application issues SQL statements against a "virtual" set of database tables that, in turn, are mapped to underlying S3 data.

» Data in S3 is then accessed, and the result set is sent back to Redshift Spectrum.

» File formats in S3 that are supported include Avro, CSV, JSON, Parquet, and a bunch of others.

Yep, sure sounds a lot like Athena. So, why in the world does Amazon confuse the picture by offering two different "database abstraction services" within AWS?

Redshift Spectrum has *Redshift* in the service name for a reason. You must have a Redshift cluster operational within AWS to use Redshift Spectrum. Think of Redshift Spectrum as an extension of "core" Redshift, but it goes against external data rather than the underlying native storage.

Athena, on the other hand, is a stand-alone service that doesn't require Redshift anywhere in your AWS environment — in your data lake, or in a data warehouse, or as part of some other analytical application.

TECHNICAL STUFF

Beyond that fundamental difference, you'll come across a lot of back-and-forth "Which is better?" jawboning if you do some research on the two services. One school of thought holds that because you allocate AWS resources when you start to use Redshift, you have more control over processing power, memory, and other resources when you use Redshift Spectrum than with Athena.

TIP

Chances are, over time, Redshift Spectrum and Athena may jostle back and forth in the performance and capability game. For your purposes, here's a better rule of thumb:

» If you have "regular" Redshift in your data lake environment for any reason, such as migrating existing AWS-based data warehousing into your data lake, Redshift Spectrum is definitely worth a look for directly accessing your S3 data.

» If you have no intentions of using "regular" Redshift, you should probably stick with Athena for SQL access against your S3 data.

Looking at the Rest of the Amazon Data Lake Lineup

Beyond the eight services described in the previous section, Amazon offers more than 200 overall services on AWS. Many of those services are for AWS uses other than data lakes, and even with the rest, you won't necessarily make use of every single one for your organization's data lake. But it's worth a quick look at some of the others.

AWS Lambda

AWS Lambda allows you to build serverless applications. You can use Lambda to build operational applications — which would be outside the realm of your data lake — but you can also use Lambda to build analytical applications that directly make use of your data lake.

Whether you find Lambda interesting for your data lake will largely depend on the breadth of analytics your organization intends to deploy. If you'll be building analytical *applications* rather than directly accessing data by BI tools and machine learning engines, Lambda can well come into play.

WARNING

Don't confuse AWS Lambda with the Lambda architecture for data ingestion (see Chapter 5) that allows for separate batch and streaming data pipelines.

Amazon EMR

Amazon Elastic MapReduce (EMR) is a big data processing service that allows you to bring open-source tools such as Apache Flink, Apache HBase, Apache Hive, Apache Spark, Presto, and others into the AWS environment. You can think of EMR sort of as "Hadoop on AWS."

TIP

If you have "legacy data lake" capabilities from older Hadoop implementations, check out EMR to see if you can "lift and shift" that work into AWS.

Amazon SageMaker

Amazon SageMaker came onto the scenes in late 2017, and provides machine learning capabilities within the AWS environment. Given that a significant component to your organization's advanced analytics and "data science" portfolio will undoubtedly be machine learning, SageMaker will probably have a role with your curated data in your gold zone or in your data lake sandbox.

Amazon Aurora

Redshift isn't the only database you'll find in the AWS environment. Amazon also offers Aurora and Relational Database Service (RDS).

Aurora is a relational database management system (DBMS) that is compatible with both MySQL and PostgreSQL — so basically, a general purpose "Swiss army knife" database management system that you can use for transactional or analytical applications.

TIP

Whereas Redshift is more "data warehouse–like" in its architecture and usage, some organizations use Aurora for an *operational data store* (ODS) as part of their overall AWS data environment. For example, you can use Kinesis Data Streams and Kinesis Data Firehose to stream data out of S3 or Redshift in real time, along with operational data from another Aurora database, and unload that data into an Aurora database underneath some type of real-time analytical application.

Unlike with Redshift, you don't necessarily have to worry about supersized data volumes, because the classic ODS model retains only limited historical data (or perhaps no historical data at all).

So, Aurora probably won't be on the critical path for your AWS data lake, but you still can find it useful for niche applications.

Amazon DynamoDB

Amazon DynamoDB is yet another AWS database, but it uses a "key-value" structure architecture rather than either relational structures, which means you would classify DynamoDB as a NoSQL database.

If you have specific analytical applications that can benefit from a NoSQL database, and if you're definitely committed to the AWS environment, take a look at DynamoDB for part of your gold zone.

Even more AWS databases

Redshift, Aurora, DynamoDB. . . . Think that you're done with AWS databases? No way!

TIP

Check out `https://aws.amazon.com/products/databases` for an up-to-date list of AWS databases and their various use cases. If that link ever doesn't work, just do an Internet search for "AWS databases" and look for a search result near the top that reads something like "Databases on AWS."

WHY SO MANY AWS DATABASES?

For a long time, we got used to relational database management systems (RDBMSs) as sort of "Swiss army knives" of data management. That is, you can use an RDBMS such as Oracle Database, Microsoft SQL Server, IBM DB2, MySQL, and others underneath transactional applications or for data warehousing (analytical applications).

If you went back to the 1980s and even into the early and mid-1990s, however, RDBMSs were anything but an all-purpose, use-anywhere data management engine. If you were in the database field in those days (as I was), you were involved with old-fashioned pointer-based databases, object-oriented databases, knowledge management systems, "inverted file" databases, and other models.

Even though RDBMSs subsumed a lot of the capabilities of other database approaches, you often ran into special cases where those "Swiss army knives" just didn't do the job. Think about very large database (VLDB) situations where you had to turn to specialized RDBMSs such as Teradata or so-called "data warehousing appliances." Soon, columnar databases started showing up. And then niche players from the old days, such as geospatial databases or *temporal* (time-oriented) databases, also started making comebacks with new products and cloud-based services.

The bottom line: Data management has never really been a one-size-fits-all proposition, even though we sort of convinced ourselves otherwise with regard to RDBMSs. Amazon certainly seems to recognize the true state of data management. Its AWS workhorses such as Redshift and Aurora may comprise the lion's share of its customers' database usage, but niche applications require niche solutions, and Amazon seems to want to be there when the customers come knocking.

Building Data Pipelines in AWS

With a brief flyover of AWS cloud data lake services behind us (Get it? Flyover? Cloud?), it's time to take a brief look at how you would stitch these various services together for your organization's data lake. Figure 12-6 shows one example, but here's another one.

Suppose you work at a hospital and you're building an AWS data lake that needs to meet the following requirements:

>> Support for both streaming and batch data via the Lambda architecture (that is, separate pipelines for streaming versus batch)

>> Direct analytics against an inbound data stream

>> Unloading of inbound streaming data into the data lake's silver zone

>> Support for both object data and database-resident data in your data lake's gold zone

>> SQL access directly against object data (in addition to SQL access to the database)

>> An up-to-date catalog of the entire data lake contents

Great news! AWS has everything you need, as shown in Figure 12-9. In this figure, you see the following:

>> Kinesis Data Streams used to send patient vital signs directly into — and all the way through — the data lake, where that vital sign data is consumed directly by Kinesis Stream Analytics

>> Kinesis Data Firehose unloading the streaming data into S3 in the silver zone, in addition to the data passing through on its way to the streaming analytics engine

>> The combination of Kinesis Data Streams with the pairing of Lake Formation and Glue to support both streaming and batch data ingestion

>> S3 buckets as the sole storage engine for both the bronze and silver zones, which means that Lake Formation will unload any incoming relational data into JSON files in an S3 bucket in the bronze zone

>> Both S3 and Redshift in the gold zone

>> SQL access to S3 data using Redshift Spectrum, because the environment already includes Redshift (otherwise Athena would be used for SQL-to-S3 access)

» Support for the broad analytics continuum from BI and visualization through machine learning and even customized analytical applications

» The Glue Data Catalog crawling the S3 buckets and the gold zone Redshift database and then storing and maintaining the metadata

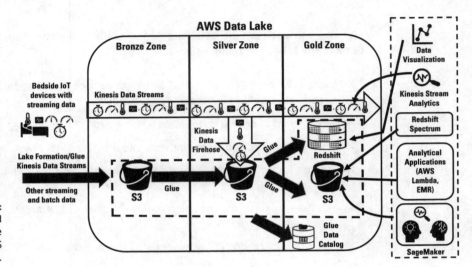

FIGURE 12-9:
An end-to-end hospital data lake built on AWS services.

Chapter **13**

Building Data Lakes in Microsoft Azure

I f you've decided to head down the Microsoft Azure path for your organization's data lake, you've got plenty of company. You know that market share data and other statistics can be all over the place when you do a little bit of Internet research, so you definitely need to check out a few different sources. In general, though, Microsoft Azure consistently shows up as one of the top two players in cloud computing overall, along with Amazon Web Services (AWS).

For example, a Q2 2020 survey from TechTarget (https://searchcloud computing.techtarget.com/opinion/How-can-AWS-Azure-and-GCP-increase-cloud-market-share) shows Microsoft Azure's overall cloud market share at 18 percent, not too far behind AWS, which is at 32 percent. However, according to their survey, the accompanying narrative also points out that Microsoft's cloud revenue growth rate was 43 percent, which means that

» Azure is increasingly being adopted by companies, governmental agencies, and not-for-profits.

» The many different Azure services are most likely being used more and more by existing customers.

WARNING

One of the top uses for Microsoft Azure is building data lakes. Keep in mind, though, that Azure is definitely not a "data lake in a box." Architecting your data lake in Azure takes a fair bit of knowledge to select appropriate services and to assemble them according to the reference architecture for your organization's particular needs and patterns. (See Chapter 4 for a discussion of data lake reference architectures.)

Setting Up the Big Picture in Azure

Microsoft Azure first came onto the scene in 2010 — coincidentally or not, right about the same time that the term *data lake* was coined, even though Azure functions as a cloud computing environment for more than just data lakes.

TECHNICAL STUFF

Microsoft originally named the cloud environment Windows Azure; it changed the name to Microsoft Azure in early 2014.

The Azure infrastructure

TECHNICAL STUFF

You should know a few big-picture things about Azure before venturing into the world of the platform's data lake services. However, a few short paragraphs can't possibly cover Azure in detail. If you really want to dig into the Microsoft Azure environment in detail, check out *Microsoft Azure For Dummies*, by Timothy Warner (Wiley).

Microsoft Azure supports both infrastructure as a service (IaaS) and platform as a service (PaaS) paradigms, whatever makes sense for your organization's specific cloud computing needs (see Chapter 11). I fill you in on a few of Azure's services in this chapter, such as Azure Data Lake Storage (ADLS) and Azure Data Factory (ADF). But if you really want to become an Azure expert, crank up the studying because Azure offers more than 600 different services for all sorts of computing needs.

Figure 13-1 shows the overall hierarchy of how the Azure cloud is organized.

The top of Azure's hierarchy is a geography — a specific market such as the United States, the United Kingdom, India, Canada, China, France, and so on. Then, within each geography, you find a number of regions. For example, within the United States geography, Microsoft provides the following regions:

>> Central U.S. (located in Iowa)

>> East U.S. (located in Virginia)

- » East U.S. 2 (also located in Virginia)

- » North Central U.S. (located in Illinois)

- » South Central U.S. (located in Texas)

- » West Central U.S. (located in Wyoming)

- » West U.S. (located in California)

- » West U.S. 2 (located in Washington)

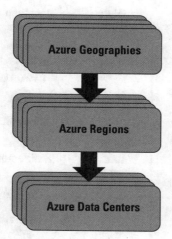

FIGURE 13-1:
Organization of
the Azure cloud.

TIP

Microsoft Azure's regions are constantly expanding. At the time Iam writing this, the United States geography and region list at https://azure.microsoft.com/en-us/global-infrastructure/geographies showed "Coming Soon" labels for an East U.S. 3 region (located in Georgia) and a West U.S. 3 region (located in Arizona). By the time you're reading this, those regions might already be up and running, and new regions might be coming soon.

You have control over the geography and region in which you set up any of your data lake–related or other services within Azure. So, if your company is regionally focused and operates solely within the Eastern United States, you can located all your services within East U.S. or East U.S. 2. If you have operations throughout the United States, you can spread your services to minimize overall data transmission. Or if you have a global company, you can divide your services among the regions that make the most sense for your organization's data topology.

Microsoft operates a number of data centers with each region. But that's where you stop selecting specific locations and rely on Microsoft to do the lifting for you. Microsoft will allocate your workloads as appropriate among the data centers within a region, so just sit back and relax and rely on their infrastructure experts to take good care of you.

The 50,000-foot view of Azure data lakes

Microsoft Azure services allow you to build the left-to-right pipelines that you see at the conceptual level in this book. Figure 13-2 shows a high-level, 50-foot view of how Azure services are linked together to build the framework for a data lake.

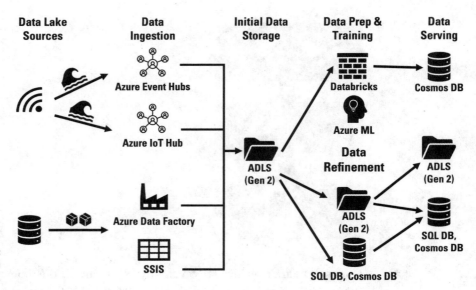

FIGURE 13-2: An Azure data lake framework.

REMEMBER

As you would expect from a modern data lake, services are available to support both streaming and batch data ingestion — in other words, the Lambda architecture (see Chapter 5).

With Microsoft Azure, you can use either Azure Event Hubs or Azure IoT Hub for streaming data ingestion, depending on your specific use cases. (And no, you don't see a typo with *Hubs* for events and *Hub* for IoT. Those are the actual Azure service names — one singular and the other plural.) On the batch side, you see the ADF and good old SQL Server Integration Services (SSIS), which you may already know from any work that you may have done with SQL Server data warehouses.

TIP

Regardless of the ingestion mechanism, data often winds up in ADLS — specifically, "Gen 2," or the second generation of ADLS. Think of this first persistent layer within an Azure data lake as the bronze zone, even though you may not see that exact term (or its equivalent, such as *raw zone*) on an Azure data lake reference architecture diagram. But regardless of terminology, you're definitely looking at ingesting and staging raw data for what comes next.

So, what *does* come next? Very often, in the Azure world, you'll see two different paths depending on whether a data pipeline is being built for "data science" versus classic business intelligence (BI) and data visualization. On the data science side, Azure Databricks and Azure ML (*ML* stands for "machine learning") are the workhorses, while on the BI and visualization side, you often refine and enrich data into Azure SQL Database or Azure Cosmos DB. Alternatively, you may keep ADLS data in ADLS, even after doing your refinement and enrichment.

Regardless, you're now in the silver zone, that "water treatment plant" portion of your data lake that takes in raw data and sends out ready-to-analyze data.

Finally, the equivalent of your gold zone is where data is served up to analytics in neatly curated packages. Cosmos DB and Azure SQL Database commonly show up again, though as with the silver zone, you conceivably can retain your curated data in ADLS object storage.

Confused? Overwhelmed? Don't be. The next section describes these key Azure data lake–oriented services — and a couple of others — one by one.

The Magnificent Seven, Azure Style

If you're a movie buff, you may have seen the 2016 movie *The Magnificent Seven*, starring Denzel Washington, Chris Pratt, and Ethan Hawke, among others. Or, if you're an older movie aficionado, you may know the original 1960 version of that film, with its all-star cast of Hollywood legends such as Yul Brynner, Eli Wallach, Steve McQueen, Charles Bronson, James Coburn, and Robert Vaughn.

Microsoft Azure has its own "Magnificent Seven" when it comes to building data lakes:

>> Azure Data Lake Storage

>> Azure Data Factory

>> Azure Databricks

>> Azure Event Hubs

>> Azure IoT Hub

>> Azure Cosmos DB

>> Azure ML

Azure Data Lake Storage Gen 2

ADLS is almost always the epicenter of an Azure data lake. Or, to be more precise, ADLS Gen 2 (the second generation) is almost always the epicenter of an Azure data lake.

Originally, Microsoft Azure gave you two different options for storing object data in the Azure cloud:

>> Azure blob storage

>> The first release or generation of ADLS

Azure blob storage and the first generation of ADLS each had their own advantages and disadvantages, which presented a bit of a quandary if you started off building an Azure data lake a few years back. Specifically, which of the two should you use for your bronze zone for incoming raw data?

BEWARE THE BLOB!

Actually, you shouldn't beware the blob, because blobs are one of your key assets when it comes to building a data lake. So, maybe a better title would be "Embrace the blob!"

In computerese, a blob is just like it sounds: a blob of data that's all lumped together, unlike the structure of, say, the data that you find in a relational database. Which means — drumroll, please — blob data is great for the heterogenous forms of data you typically find in a data lake: structured, semi-structured, and unstructured.

If you're really into computer trivia, legend holds that the term comes from the cheesy 1950s horror movie called — you guessed it — *The Blob*. Later, a *backronym* (an acronym that is subsequently created from a term already in use) surfaced, giving us the term *basic large object*. For good measure, an even more on-point backronym later showed up on the scene: *binary large object*.

Because you want to rapidly and easily store structured, semi-structured, and unstructured data within your data lake, blob storage is the perfect landing zone for incoming data. You can take in all sorts of files — CSV, JSON, MP4, PNG — and easily plop them right into your data lake in their as-is state. You can also ingest highly structured data from a database and "un-structure" the data into a file format such as JSON, if, say, you're building your entire data lake around object storage such as ADLS with no databases anywhere in the data lake. Later on, as you refine and enrich the data within your data lake's silver zone, you can dig into the details of your blob data as necessary.

Fortunately, the smart people at Microsoft took mercy on Azure data lake architects and developers and did the old "chocolate plus peanut butter" trick to come up with something new that was even better than either original form. Figure 13-3 shows the result.

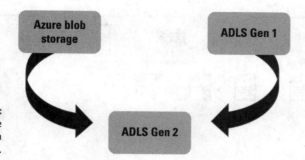

FIGURE 13-3:
ADLS Gen2, the best of both worlds.

TIP

You may still find older Azure data lakes that use "native" Azure blob storage or ADLS Gen 1. Any new Azure development, though, should use ADLS Gen 2. Even though ADLS Gen 2 is the service's official name because Gen 2 has supplanted Gen 1, most people just use the shorthand *ADLS* to refer to ADLS Gen 2. You have enough other acronyms and service names to keep straight in the Azure world, so dropping the "Gen 2" almost always makes sense in the interest of simplicity.

WARNING

Additionally, Microsoft has announced that its original ADLS (Gen 1) will be retired on February 29, 2024. (Happy Leap Day! In fact, you can put it this way: "All ADLS Gen 1 storage must leap to Gen 2 by that day!")

So, what exactly does a blob look like when it comes to your data lake? Just a whole bunch of bits and bytes all swirling around together like a bunch of amoebas? Fortunately, you have a wee bit more structure to your Azure blobs — and no, that's not a contradiction in terms. Figure 13-4 shows how ADLS (again, Gen 2) is built around a series of "file systems" that contain folders and files, the same folder/file paradigm that you almost certainly know from basic computer usage.

You see a couple of different structural models at work in Figure 13-4. The file system on the left side contains two folders. The leftmost of those folders contains two files, while the other folder contains only a single file.

The middle file system contains one folder that in turn contains two files. But it also has a file that isn't part of a folder. Then the file system on the right side contains two files but no folders.

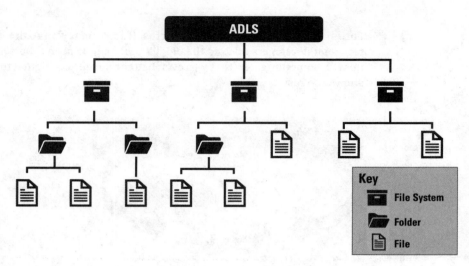

FIGURE 13-4:
ADLS containers, folders, and files.

Key

	File System
	Folder
	File

Basically, you can mix and match your folders and files at various levels in a hierarchy, in whatever manner makes sense for your data that you want to store in ADLS.

TECHNICAL STUFF

So, what kinds of files will you find within ADLS when you get down to that level? You may have CSV files for comma-separated data. And yes, these are the same CSV files that you may know from importing data into Microsoft Excel. You may have JSON files for data that follows the JavaScript Object Notation syntax. Or you can have MP4 files for moving images or PNG files for static images.

Just as with Amazon Simple Storage Service (S3), Azure gives you multiple tiers of storage for ADLS that you can mix and match based on your planned access frequency:

>> Hot

>> Cool (which you'll sometimes see in blogs and elsewhere online as "Cold")

>> Archive

Table 13-1 lists the characteristics of each of these ADLS tiers.

TABLE 13-1

ADLS Storage Tiers

Tier	Latency	Storage Cost	Access Cost
Hot	Fastest	Highest	Lowest
Cool	Pretty fast	Middle	Middle
Archive	Relatively slow (hours)	Lowest	Highest

TIP

If you have data that you've decided to keep in your data lake "just in case" but it has no immediate need for analytics, you can drop that data into ADLS Archive at first. If the data eventually turns out to be useful, make sure to "promote" the data out of Archive to keep your access costs down and to speed up the ultra-slow response time that Archive storage in Azure provides.

Azure Data Factory

Quick! When you hear the term *data factory*, what comes to mind? If you immediately envision a component that manufactures and produces data, then the Azure product management team did a pretty good job naming this particular service.

REMEMBER

The ADF is a key component of Azure data lake pipelines. In fact, *pipeline* is an official ADF term, not just an on-point description of an end-to-end data flow.

An ADF pipeline is composed of one or more "copy activities" that, well, copy data from a source to a destination. A destination for copied data is called a *sink*. Figure 13-5 shows a high-level ADF pipeline.

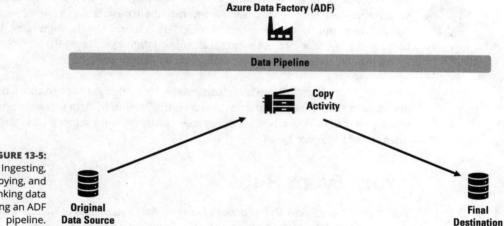

FIGURE 13-5:
Ingesting, copying, and sinking data along an ADF pipeline.

Pretty simple, huh? ADF fits very nicely into the extract, load, and transform (ELT) paradigm. You extract data — often a whole lot of data — from a source and then quickly plop that data into a new location without a lot of muss and fuss. The transformations will come later on within the bounds of the data lake, following the common big data ELT pattern (versus the ETL data warehousing pattern, where transformation occurs before "sinking" the data into its ultimate destination).

So, is ADF limited to accessing a single source and plopping that data directly into a single data sink? Absolutely not! You can string together multiple copy activities, against various databases and file types. For example, suppose you need to cross-reference and consolidate multiple data sources from your data lake bronze zone into "refined and combined" data in your silver zone, which in turn winds up in a data package in your gold zone. You can build a sequence of ADF copy activities to handle the entire end-to-end pipeline.

Azure Databricks

Despite its name, Azure Databricks is not actually a Microsoft product or service. Databricks is an entirely different company (www.databricks.com) that was founded in 2013 by some of the original Apache Spark developers. Databricks was very early to the Azure data lake party and has partnered with Microsoft for a while now. Here's how Microsoft puts it on its "What is Azure Databricks?" page (https://docs.microsoft.com/en-us/azure/databricks/scenarios/what-is-azure-databricks): "Azure Databricks is a data analytics platform optimized for the Microsoft Azure cloud services platform."

TECHNICAL STUFF

The Azure Databricks Workspace, which is based on Apache Spark, fits squarely in your Azure data lake silver zone. As you might surmise from the word *workspace*, Databricks supports collaboration among data scientists, data engineers, and end users using a variety of tools: programming languages (Java, Python, R, Scala), Spark SQL, or data visualization tools such as Matplotlib or D3.

From an Azure data lake architecture perspective, the best way to think of Databricks is in the "data preparation and training" realm of data science — in other words, your data lake silver zone but specifically for data science–oriented pipelines (refer to Figure 13-2).

Azure Event Hubs

You'll put Azure Event Hubs to work for your Azure data lake to handle streaming data — specifically (as Microsoft puts it) as a "big data streaming service" capable of handling billions of requests a day. If you want to stream data from devices such as a hospital's patient room vital sign monitoring machines, you can use Azure Event Hubs to handle the streaming.

REMEMBER

Pay particular attention to the word *hubs* in the service name. You can certainly use Azure Event Hubs for point-to-point data streaming, but you can also set up a "publish and subscribe" environment with multiple data producers and multiple data consumers, as shown in Figure 13-6.

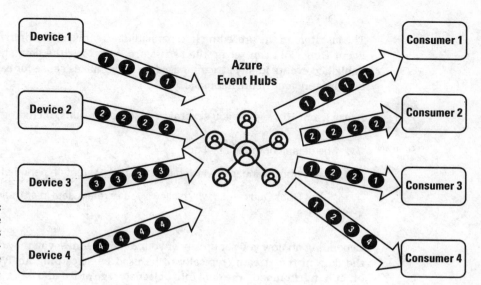

FIGURE 13-6:
Using Azure
Event Hubs
for a publish-
and-subscribe
model.

You see in Figure 13-6 four different devices, each of which produces its unique type of data. Each device publishes (streams) its data into Azure Event Hubs, which serves as a central collection point.

You also see four different consumers of the data, each of which "subscribes" to the data of interest from that same central collection point (Azure Event Hubs). Consumer 1 is only interested in the data produced by Device 1, while Consumer 2 is only interested in the data produced by Device 2. Consumer 3, however, needs data from both Devices 1 and 2, so you'll set up the "consumption stream" to direct data types 1 and 2 — but only those two types of data, not data types 3 and 4 — into Consumer 3.

Consumer 4, however, is greedy when it comes to data and wants data types 1, 2, 3, and 4 — all of it! No problem. You set up Consumer 4 to subscribe to all four types of data.

REMEMBER

Publish-and-subscribe basics are, well, pretty basic. Azure Event Hubs serves as more than just a "traffic cop" for incoming and outgoing data. When you're constructing your bronze, silver, and gold zones of your data lake, you have a variety of storage options for each:

>> Basic object storage (ADLS in the case of an Azure data lake)

>> Databases (Azure SQL Database and Azure Cosmos DB, as I explain later in this chapter)

>> "Specialized storage" such as Databricks

>> Persistent streams

The last item in the preceding list, persistent streams, comes into play with Azure Event Hubs. You can set up the *persistence* (how long the data stays around) for published events in any stream, based on what makes sense for each of your data pipelines in your Azure data lake.

Azure Event Hubs gives you several persistence options, including the following:

>> The default duration of 24 hours

>> "Event Hubs Standard," which has a maximum retention period of seven days

>> "Event Hubs Dedicated," which allows you to retain data in a stream for up to 90 days

Depending on how you set up any of your data pipelines, you may decide to persist the data in the stream (typically to be used by streaming analytics) or, on the other hand, "unload" the data into object storage or a database (see Chapter 4 and various examples in Chapters 5, 6, and 7). However, Azure Event Hubs gives you the best of both worlds with its "Event Hubs Capture" capability. You can persist data in a stream through its retention period, which will vary based on which of these durations you select, and then, upon "expiration," *automatically* send the data into ADLS before the data is removed from the stream.

Be forewarned, though, that you shouldn't think of or try to use a stream as *long-term* persistent storage. Microsoft does warn you that the larger your streams grow in terms of persisted data, the more you'll need to resort to tricks such as indexes to locate specific data in a reasonable time frame. Persisted stream data is great, as long as you don't push the envelope too far. So, make sure that as you're architecting your Azure data lake, you're doing a pretty good job mixing and matching ADLS and persisted streams as data flows into your data lake and then through your various zones.

Azure IoT Hub

Now, wait a minute. If Microsoft has Azure Event Hubs, what's the deal with Azure IoT Hub? IoT Hub is also (spoiler alert) a hub for streaming data. Do you need both for your Azure data lake? Is there any material difference between the two, or is this just another example of duplicate services or products from a single vendor that we all have to deal with?

One word sums up the most material difference between Azure Event Hubs and Azure IoT Hub: *bidirectional.* To be specific, Azure Event Hubs streams data in one direction from data producers to data consumers (or, as Microsoft puts it, "device-to-cloud messaging").

Azure IoT Hub, however, *also* allows data to be sent back to the same device that typically produces data. In Microsoft verbiage, that would be "cloud-to-device messaging" (see Figure 13-7).

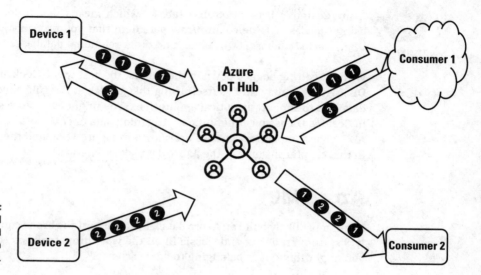

FIGURE 13-7:
Bidirectional messaging and streaming with Azure IoT Hub.

Aha! In Part 2 of this book, I offer an energy exploration company scenario in which a remote drilling well sends temperature and pressure readings, along with real-time video, into the data lake but also has a capability onsite to analyze the data and, if necessary, automatically shut down the drilling equipment if a problem is detected. I provide an Azure data lake version of that general scenario later in this chapter.

For now, though, the key point is that such an architecture requires your streaming data hub to be able to send data *back* to one or more devices that normally serve as data producers. In other words, you need bidirectional streaming, which falls squarely within the Azure IoT Hub realm, rather than Azure Event Hubs with its one-direction streaming.

Both Event Hubs and IoT Hub can be part of not only the same Azure data lake but even the same data pipeline. Stay tuned for examples!

TIP

Azure Cosmos DB

When most people think of *Microsoft* and *database* together, the first product that comes to mind is SQL Server. (Or, if you've been around for a while, you might think of Microsoft Access first.)

In the Azure world, SQL Server still has a role to play (stay tuned). However, Cosmos DB is sort of Microsoft's "big data database" and often plays a role in multi-component, Azure-based data lakes.

TECHNICAL STUFF

Azure Cosmos DB is a NoSQL database, which means that it doesn't store data using the classic table/column/row paradigm that you probably know from IBM DB2, Oracle Database, SQL Server, and other relational databases.

Without getting bogged down in the details, the best way to look at Azure Cosmos DB is that you may find yourself using this service in the gold zone of your Azure data lake to support analytical applications. You might even store silver zone data in Cosmos DB as you either unload streaming data or copy data out of ADLS using ADF. (These pipeline scenarios are shown in Figure 13-2, and they show up later in this chapter in some of the Azure data lake scenarios.)

Azure ML

You'll most likely build an Azure data lake to support the broad continuum of analytics, from reporting and classic BI all the way through advanced analytics that you might think of as belonging to "data science."

Within the world of data science, ML is crucial. Azure ML is usually paired with Azure Databricks and is used to train, automate, deploy, and then track and manage ML models.

TIP

If you're focused primarily on the data architecture and data engineering side of your organization's data lake, you don't need to know too much about the nuts and bolts of ML. You really just need to be aware that your data pipelines and overall architecture need to support more than just reporting, BI, and visualization when it comes to the analytics that will be delivered from your data lake. If, however, you do need to dig into mL, then you can check out both *Machine Learning For Dummies,* 2nd Edition, by John Paul Mueller and Luca Massaron (Wiley) for the roll-up-your-sleeves details, or *Data Science For Dummies,* 2nd Edition, by Lillian Pierson for a higher-level overview of the topic in the context of data science overall.

For your purposes, just remember this equation: Azure ML plus Azure Databricks equals a key capability of your Azure data lake.

Filling Out the Azure Data Lake Lineup

Every lineup of stars needs a cast of supporting characters. In the case of Azure data lakes, the "supporting characters" may actually be stars in their own right along any given data pipeline. Here's a brief overview of some of the other weapons in your data lake toolbox.

Azure Stream Analytics

In Part 2 of this book, I explain that one of the reasons to leave inbound data in a stream rather than "unload" the data into object storage or a database is to make use of stream analytics. As you can probably guess, stream analytics in general do exactly what the name implies: various types of analytics applied directly against an inbound stream, rather than against object storage or a database.

In the Azure world, Azure Stream Analytics operate directly against Azure Event Hubs or Azure IoT Hub (both of which I introduce earlier in the chapter and which show up again in later examples). You can also use Azure Stream Analytics against Apache Kafka streams if you've decided to head down the open-source route.

You might use Azure Stream Analytics to analyze

>> Hospital patient in-room vital signs

>> Data produced by autonomous vehicles

>> High-volume point-of-sale data from physical retail stores

>> Web traffic and transaction data

Microsoft Azure SQL Database

Good old SQL Server . . . sort of.

If you know SQL Server from developing applications or building a data warehouse, you're in luck. Azure SQL Database is basically the Azure cloud version of SQL Server. As with cloud computing services in general, you don't need to worry about most of the usual database management issues such as sizing or applying enough computing power to your data, or applying updates and patches to your on-premises database management system (DBMS) software.

If you need relational databases as part of your Azure data lake, you're definitely in luck. And if you've already worked with SQL Server, it's old home week.

In fact, you might even make use of the Azure SQL Database for more than just gold zone curated data. Figure 13-8 shows a pipeline with incoming relational data that you know for certain will be consumed by traditional BI.

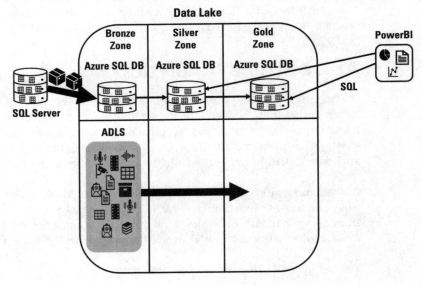

FIGURE 13-8:
Using Azure SQL Database in your Azure data lake.

Take note of a couple of points about Figure 13-8:

>> The data source labeled "SQL Server" can instead be "Azure SQL Database" if that source application were running in your organization's Azure cloud rather than your on-premises data center.

>> Even though the bronze, silver, and gold zones each show a separate database symbol in Figure 13-8, you can actually set up three separate schemas in the same overall database service (think in terms of a single SQL Server instance), one for each zone.

>> You'll probably run into folks who look at Figure 13-8 and say, "Those databases don't belong in a data lake! That's really a data warehouse!" Take a look at the beginning of Chapter 3 and the advice to stay above the fray when it comes to which storage engines do or don't "belong" in a data lake.

SQL Server Integration Services

If you've done some work in the SQL Server realm in the past, especially data warehousing work, then you likely know about other products that are part of the overall SQL Server family: the SSxS gang.

That's right: SQL Server Integration Services (SSIS) can be part of your overall end-to-end data lake architecture.

Within the Azure environment, you'll probably find yourself using ADF for batch data transmission. However, for on-premises applications running in your data center or perhaps at another data center, SSIS can come into play to send SQL Server data into Azure.

You can, in fact, run SSIS projects, packages, and workloads within Azure, which means that you can rehome any previously developed SSIS-based ETL without having to reinvent the wheel in ADF. So, if your organization has a mature SQL Server–based data warehouse that makes extensive use of the whole SSxS ecosystem, SSIS can well be an important part of your data lake, at least when it comes to structured relational data.

Azure Analysis Services

Another SSxS product you may have used for SQL Server data warehousing is SQL Server Analysis Services (SSAS). Microsoft built onto SSAS to develop the Azure version known as Azure Analysis Services.

If your data lake will support "cube-based" BI in addition to relational-based BI, you'll probably find yourself using Azure Analysis Services.

Power BI

At one time, the third member of the SSxS club was SQL Server Reporting Services (SSRS). A while back, however, Microsoft shifted away from SSRS to Power BI as its flagship BI tool for reporting and, more important, visualization.

Your data lake will almost certainly support reporting and visualization — that is, descriptive analytics. Even the outputs from ML are often delivered to end users in a visual manner. If you're headed down the Azure data lake path, Power BI will almost certainly be in the picture. And if you already know Power BI from past work with SQL Server data warehousing, you've already got one foot into the data lake.

Azure HDInsight

Back in the "prehistoric" days of data lakes when people talked more about "big data" than data lakes, Hadoop was the 800-pound gorilla. (Or, given the cute yellow elephant mascot for Hadoop, that should probably be "the 800-pound elephant.)

Most of the major systems vendors were actually a little late to the Hadoop party, and the early productization came out of companies such as Cloudera, Hortonworks, MapR, and Pivotal Software. Even as Microsoft invested heavily in Azure, it had an eye on Hadoop. Around 2015, Microsoft partnered with Hortonworks, one of those early Hadoop pioneers, to deploy a version of the Hortonworks Hadoop distribution in the Azure cloud. (Hortonworks subsequently merged with, and is now part of, Cloudera.)

TECHNICAL STUFF

"Original Hadoop" runs on top of the Hadoop Distributed File System (HDFS), though the component nature of Hadoop can support different underlying storage. With the Microsoft–Hortonworks partnership, they swapped out HDFS for Azure Data Lake Storage Gen 1 and branded the Azure Hadoop environment as HDInsight. You can run Hadoop applications and systems that used open-source services such as HBase and Hive (databases), MapReduce (distributed data processing), Oozie (scheduling), Pig (programming), Sqoop (for ETL), and other components. Later on, as Hadoop evolved, newer services emerged, such as YARN for resource scheduling and management under HDInsight.

Fast-forward to today. If your organization wants to build your data lake primarily using open-source services but still wants to make use of Microsoft Azure, you can use HDInsight to create clusters for Kafka, Spark, Storm, and all sorts of open-source software.

TIP

If your organization is still "into Hadoop" and also wants to take advantage of those 600-plus Azure services, HDInsight helps you bridge the gap as you build your data lake and data pipelines.

Assembling the Building Blocks

Azure definitely gives you a whole lot of services and tools that you can put to work for your data lake. How do you keep all of these options straight?

Suppose you work for an energy exploration company, and it's time to convert your conceptual end-to-end data lake architecture (see Figure 5-3 in Chapter 5) into an Azure data lake implementation. Or suppose you've been added to Ravi's, Chun's, and Timothy's team to rebuild an Azure-based data lake for a hospital (see Chapters 15 and 16). How do you pull together the appropriate Azure services for a given data lake use case?

TIP

Microsoft would like to lend you a helping hand, and you'd be well-advised to take them up on the offer. At `https://docs.microsoft.com/en-us/azure/architecture/browse`, Microsoft provides hundreds — yes, hundreds! — of Azure-centric data lake architectures for various pipeline use cases. (If Microsoft happens to change the link at some point in the future, just search the web for "browse Azure architecture Microsoft docs," and you'll find what you're looking for.)

Let's take a look at a few of these Azure data lake architectures so you can get an idea of the wealth of information available from the Azure data lake experts, right at your fingertips. Specifically, in this section, you see the following:

>> General Internet of Thing (IoT) analytics that you can apply to the patient bedside analytics use case

>> Predictive maintenance for IoT that you can apply to the remote drilling use case

>> Defect analysis and prevention

>> Transit company forecasting

General IoT analytics

Suppose you're a data lake consultant doing some architecture and implementation work for a hospital system. The chief medical officer from your client recently went to a conference where Ravi, Chun, and Timothy did a presentation about the patient bedside monitoring capabilities that they built at several of their own clients.

Your client has committed much of their IT infrastructure to the Azure cloud, including the start of a data lake. Now, they've asked you to put together an architecture for a patient bedside monitoring environment, using services within the Azure stack. Figure 13-9 shows what you've sketched out and what you'll be presenting later in the week.

The hospital has already installed a set of vital sign monitoring IoT-enabled devices in every patient room. Each of these devices produces streamed data that is consumable by either Azure IoT Hub or Azure Event Hubs. These data streams are then directly accessed and processed by Azure Stream Analytics, with the results fed directly into Power BI dashboards. These dashboards will show the status of any patient's vital signs, as well as produce alerts if any worrisome readings are detected.

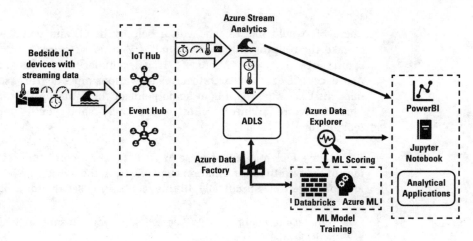

FIGURE 13-9:
Azure data lake architecture for IoT analytics.

At the same time, the streamed vital signs are also stored within ADLS in JSON files. The JSON files are then fed into Databricks using ADF. Once in Databricks, Azure ML uses ML to develop scoring models for patient conditions, which are then sent via Azure Data Explorer into Jupyter notebooks for collaborative data science work by the hospital's medical analysts.

Just as with the conceptual data lake architecture that Ravi's team put together for their clients, your Azure–centric architecture has

>> Both streaming and batch data feeds as appropriate

>> A combination of real-time data-driven insights and longer-term analytical work

>> Direct, real-time processing of streaming data alongside persisting that same data into data lake storage

Predictive maintenance for industrial IoT

Your data lake consulting work isn't only for hospital and healthcare clients; in fact, you do work for clients in different industries. However, the common thread for your particular client base is that you tend to focus on industrial IoT settings. After you've finished your patient bedside monitoring architecture and implementation, your next client is an energy exploration company that wants their existing Azure data lake to help predict when maintenance will be needed at their remote drilling sites.

The good news is that you've done similar work for energy companies in the past, even though this will be your first such effort with an Azure data lake. No worries!

In fact, you can leverage a lot of what you did for your hospital client, particularly when it comes to streaming data.

The one complicating factor with this client, however, is that they'll need to make use of *edge analytics* in their solution. Figure 13-10 shows what you come up with.

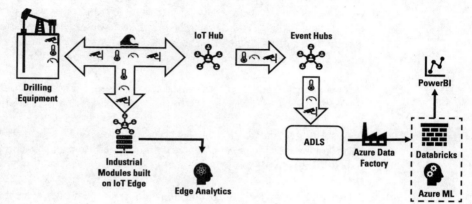

FIGURE 13-10: Azure data lake architecture for industrial IoT predictive maintenance.

The remote drilling equipment has sensors buried within the well that produce streaming data for temperature, pressure, and other readings. For purposes of the data lake, the drilling equipment might as well be a hospital patient's room because the streaming data is consumed and routed by Azure IoT Hub on its way into the data lake.

However, the complication is that the energy company wants to send a shutdown message to the equipment if the drilling equipment is in danger of failing. You don't want to assign that mission to the data lake for one main reason: Even with today's blazing-fast networks, why send data from a remote well into the cloud only to have a shutdown message sent back from the cloud? The idea behind edge analytics is to do some of your analytics at "the edge" of the enterprise — that is, where your operations are actually, physically taking place — rather than in your data centers or within a cloud service.

Once again, no worries! Vendors such as Microsoft are all over the idea of edge analytics. Even better, edge analytics and data lakes make a great team. As shown in Figure 13-10, the IoT Hub also routes the streaming sensor data to modules that do the analytics and determine if a particular combination of sensor readings, or perhaps a time sequence of one or more sensor readings, indicates a possible problem. The edge analytics will decide when a piece of equipment needs to be shut down. Because IoT Hub supports two-way streaming, a shutdown message can be produced that is then processed by the drilling equipment.

DATA LAKES AND BUSINESS PROCESSES

Back in the days when data warehouses ruled the land, you had a bit of a challenge when it came to working analytics into your business processes. Data warehouses and data marts were often "grafted" onto the tail end of an operational business process, which meant that the data-driven insights — that is, the BI produced from your data warehouse or data mart — usually fell into the "tell me what happened" category. There's nothing wrong with backward-looking data-driven insights, but they often surfaced too late in the process flow for you to interdict a problem or take advantage of an opportunity. If you diagrammed and documented the business process flows at a typical organization in any industry, or in a governmental agency, you would see a sequence along the lines of:

Operational business process → Operational business process → Operational business process → Operational business process → . . . → Analytical business process

The analytical business process would occur when you used Business Objects, Cognos, MicroStrategy, or some other BI tool to produce reports and visualizations out of your data warehouse or data mart.

A "better" paradigm for constructing modern business process flow is to interleave operational and analytical processes. In other words, at various points along a chain of business processes, you want to drive decisions and take actions that actually drive what occurs within the next operational business process. To support interleaved operational and analytical business processes, we turned to variations of traditional data warehousing such as *operational data stores* (ODSs) and *active data warehouses*, where the analytical data store was more than just the final stop for data along the process flow.

To make a long story short, ODSs and active data warehouses helped, but they didn't quite achieve the full breadth of interleaved business processes that many hoped they would.

Enter the data lake.

You can see with examples in this chapter for patient bedside monitoring and remote drilling equipment, the big data foundations of data lakes break through the traditional demarcation between operational and analytical business processes. Large volumes of various types of data can be transmitted and processed very rapidly — there are your three Vs for volume, variety, and velocity — which puts the data lake squarely in the middle of a modern business process flow when it makes sense.

But all that edge analytics stuff will be handled by someone else outside the data lake realm. You do need to be aware of what's going on, and you've accounted for what's happening at the drilling sites in your architecture. Your focus is the data lake, which means you'll pull in that streaming data. After the data is within the

Azure cloud, Azure Event Hubs takes over the streaming responsibility and routes the sensor data into ADLS.

You can tell from Figure 13-10 that ADLS serves as your data lake's bronze zone, and that's where ADF comes into the picture — as a gateway between your bronze zone and your silver zone. You'll build an ADF "copy activity" to pull the sensor data out of ADLS — let's say in JSON format — and drop the data into Databricks. Azure ML will go to work on the sensor data — conceptually the same as what you did with patient bedside vital sign data at your hospital client. Results are consumed and displayed on Power BI dashboards and visualizations for anyone who wants to see the big picture of what's going on at any of the energy company's drilling sites.

TIP

Even though the responsibility for detecting imminent problems and sending shutdown messages rests with the edge analytics, you still want to set up alerts within Power BI to let users know of imminent problems at any of your client's drilling sites.

Defect analysis and prevention

How about a simpler variation on the theme of predictive and preventive maintenance? Your next data lake client manufactures aircraft subsystems. They absolutely need to study their equipment's performance so they can stay on top of the maintenance schedules they send to the airlines and air freight company users of their systems. But unlike the remote drilling well scenario at your last client, they don't need to send shutdown messages or take direct interdictive actions for their equipment while in use. Piece of cake!

Figure 13-11 shows what you've come up with for an Azure-centric defect analysis data lake pipeline.

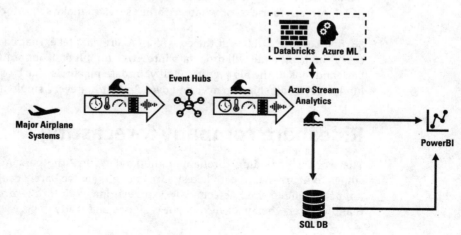

FIGURE 13-11: Azure data lake architecture for defect analysis and prevention.

Once again, streaming data is the way to go for the voluminous amounts of sensor data produced by the aircraft subsystems. You'll consume the streaming data using Azure Event Hubs, and then analyze the data directly in the stream using Azure Stream Analytics, which will connect to Power BI for dashboards and visualizations.

You'll also route the streaming data into Databricks, where Azure ML will do its machine learning to build new predictive models for your various equipment subsystems. And the streaming data will also land in curated data packages in Azure SQL Database, which will also feed dashboards and visualizations in Power BI.

Now take a good look at Figure 13-11. Notice anything missing? That's right: ADLS doesn't appear anywhere on the end-to-end data flow! But didn't you read earlier in this chapter that ADLS is the epicenter of an Azure-based data lake? That's right; you did.

REMEMBER

Now, wait a minute. How can ADLS be at the core of an Azure data lake but not be part of the data pipeline shown in Figure 13-11? Aha! That's because this particular data pipeline for defect analysis and prevention is exactly that: a single data pipeline, not an entire data lake.

A data lake is almost always an enterprise-wide proposition, serving many different users for many different business processes and functions within an overall organization. You'll build one or more data pipelines to support a given business process that needs to make use of the data lake: IoT predictive maintenance for a remote drilling well, or a hospital's in-room patient vital signs monitoring, or whatever some business process intends to accomplish.

Overall, though, you'll build numerous pipelines that, when taken together, will make up your data lake. Each data pipeline will be constructed from your overall toolbox of services. If you're working in the Azure environment, you'll pull in ADLS, ADF, Databricks, or whatever other services make sense for each pipeline.

So, just because ADLS is at the core of an Azure data lake, that doesn't mean that every single pipeline will drop data into ADLS or pull data out of ADLS. If you step back and look at the big picture of all your data pipelines side by side, then absolutely: ADLS will show up over and over . . . just not every single time.

Rideshare company forecasting

The word is spreading throughout the land: You're the person to call when it comes to Azure-based data lakes! Sure enough, you've barely caught your breath after finishing up your defect analysis prevention work for the aircraft equipment manufacturer when your next client is signed and ready to go.

A startup company wants to make a run at the big guys in the rideshare business. For now, they'll only be operating in your city, which is great for you: You've spent the past year on the road working on all those other Azure data lake projects, and you'd like a little time at home for a change.

Your client's top priority is to build a state-of-the-art, Azure-based environment to monitor and forecast shortages of available vehicles for their customers. Just like the major players in this market, they follow the "gig economy" model with contracted drivers working on their own schedules, which makes forecasting particularly tricky.

Figure 13-12 shows your Azure data lake architecture for this particular pipeline, and once again, streaming is front and center as data makes its way into the data lake.

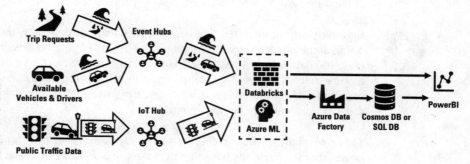

FIGURE 13-12: Azure data lake architecture for rideshare company forecasting.

TECHNICAL STUFF

Starting to detect a common theme? Batch data feeds certainly have their place along many data pipelines, but streaming data almost always plays a critical role. Think about the two major data ingestion alternatives I discuss in Chapter 5: Lambda and Kappa. Lambda supports both streaming and batch, while with the Kappa architecture, you "force" your batch data feeds into streaming. Notice that you don't see an architecture with the reverse — streaming data "forced" into batch and all ingestion done via batch feeds — as you would with traditional data warehousing.

Anyway, you once again use Azure Event Hubs to take in streaming data from two primary sources: trip requests booked by the company's main operational system and scheduling data that also comes from that same main operational system. But wait, you're not done yet! Your ML models for forecasting also need real-time traffic data. Fortunately, several years ago, your city invested in a new network of IoT sensors on all major streets. From real-time video to in-road speed sensors, a whole lot of data is continually produced for mapping applications and other users — including your client — who want to tap into what's happening on the roads.

You use Azure IoT Hub to consume the real-time traffic data, which — just like the data coming in through Azure Event Hubs — is streamed directly into Databricks, where your ML models do their thing. Power BI produces the real-time dashboards and delivers the alerts to your client's workload monitoring team. Based on what the Azure-based analytics are telling them, they can adjust pricing, flash out driver bonuses, and ply the other tricks of the ridesharing game to try to avoid a whole lot of unhappy customers.

To finish off the data pipeline, ADF will copy data out of Databricks into Azure Cosmos DB or Azure SQL Database (you still haven't decided which one to use yet) for additional dashboards and visualizations that include historical data.

One final thing to consider as you put your finishing touches on the architecture. This ride-sharing client — unlike your hospital client and your energy exploration client and most of your other data lake clients — is a pretty small company, at least for now. Would a data lake be overkill for them?

TIP

Definitely not! Remember, you're going to build their data lake in the Azure cloud, not in some on-premises data center. The beauty of cloud-based systems in general, and data lakes in particular, is that you can construct an end-to-end architecture that works for large companies and small companies alike. They'll be able to scale their computing resources higher or lower, whatever makes sense for the state of their company at any given time.

This ride-sharing client can start small, paying only for the storage and analytic power that they actually use but still make use of ADF, Databricks, Event Hubs, the IoT Hub, and all the rest of the Azure data lake stack. If they're successful in business and start expanding to different cities, they can scale up as necessary. You may need to make some adjustments to their analytics — you won't use streaming data from, say, Boston to forecast backlogs in Cleveland or offer on-the-spot driver bonuses in Pittsburgh.

But the data lake concept is in play for almost any company, of any size, especially with a cloud computing foundation.

4

Cleaning Up the Polluted Data Lake

IN THIS PART . . .

Navigate the rocky waters of a poorly constructed data lake.

Set the data lake rescue effort in motion.

Rearchitect your data lake for round 2.

Chapter **14**

Figuring Out If You Have a Data Swamp Instead of a Data Lake

Bad news: Your data lake is sinking, fast. Wait . . . how about this: Your data lake is taking on water?

Really bad metaphors aside, you have a big problem on your hands: Your data lake turned out to be nothing like what you expected it to be. Even worse, the data lake is nothing like the executives at your company envisioned when they approved the initiative and wrote the checks.

Now what?

The silver lining in that vicious thunderstorm shooting lightning bolts all around your data lake (finally, a metaphor that makes sense!) is that you really *can* turn things around. You start by putting aside pride of ownership and any sense of being defensive and start digging into the true health — or lack thereof — of your data lake.

Designing Your Report Card and Grading System

You need to grade the current state of your data lake on four key elements:

>> **Incoming raw data:** The newly ingested raw data that's housed in your bronze zone

>> **Data latency:** The velocity by which the raw data arrives, both streaming and batch oriented, and the resultant latency

>> **Data quality and governance:** Your overall data quality and governance, including master data and metadata

>> **Component architecture:** The component architecture of your data lake, which includes the various data services you're using

Figure 14-1 shows these four elements that you need to grade.

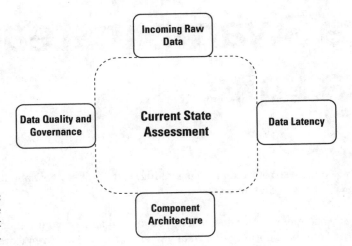

FIGURE 14-1:
Your data lake
four-element
scorecard.

**TECHNICAL
STUFF**

If the overall structure of the four-element model in Figure 14-1 looks familiar to you, you're not imagining things. The data lake grading system is based on the *balanced scorecard* evaluation model that companies and governmental agencies use to evaluate and score four key factors of their overall organizational performance. The original, first-generation balanced scorecard helped organizations avoid *financial myopia*, or a fixation on financial results at the expense of other key factors such as customer-related measures, their internal business processes, and overall learning and growth across their enterprise. You'll use a similarly structured model to achieve a similar goal: a balanced look at key factors of your data lake.

As you may suspect, you need to drill deeper than high-level evaluation factors to fully understand the health of your data lake. Figure 14-2 shows how each of your four main evaluation factors is further divided into the four elements that you'll score:

>> **Complexity index:** In general, how *unnecessarily* complex is the evaluation factor you're looking at right now? Your data lake is, of course, a complex enterprise-scale data environment that you built to support enterprise-scale analytics. But are there any parts of your data lake that are *too* complex and can be rearchitected or managed in a more streamlined manner?

>> **Compliance index:** You began your data lake with the best of intentions. You spent time matching up your real-world needs with various reference architecture patterns. You decided on specific products and services that you and your team can bolt together to turn your architectural concepts into reality.

Alas, somewhere along the long and winding road from concept to reality, your boat veered in a direction that you hadn't intended to take. Nobody made a conscious decision to ignore your architectural direction (or at least you don't believe that to be the case). But a little bit at a time, variations crept in, and eventually, your data lake implementation really ran aground from what should've happened.

You'll grade your major evaluation criteria on how closely they comply with your original data lake architecture. You need to know whether your original architecture wasn't as solid as you thought, or if indeed the fault lies in the implementation, not the architecture itself.

>> **Support index:** How much of a support burden is your bronze zone? How about your silver and gold zones? Your sandbox? Your streaming services for extract, load, and transform (ELT)?

How quickly and efficiently can requests for new data sets be met? Can data be quickly plopped over into the sandbox for quick-turnaround analytics, or does that process take an excruciatingly long time?

Your data lake won't be running on full autopilot. But at the same time, you may well have a situation on your hands where the support burden for one or more evaluation factors is impeding the data lake's ability to meet your organization's thirst for analytics.

>> **Tension index:** Maybe you find yourself ending your workdays screaming "Serenity now!" (from an old *Seinfeld* episode) as you struggle to contain your exasperation and frustration. Maybe you wind up in more than a few heated

discussions about some aspect of your data lake. Very possibly, elements of your data lake have become the "winter of your discontent" (apologies to both William Shakespeare and John Steinbeck) between your techies and business users or perhaps between those from different sides of IT.

TIP

Sometimes when you can't quite put your finger on exactly what's wrong, shifting your focus to the tension level about some aspect of your data lake tells you that you're definitely on the right path toward one or more problems and that you need to persevere with your detective work.

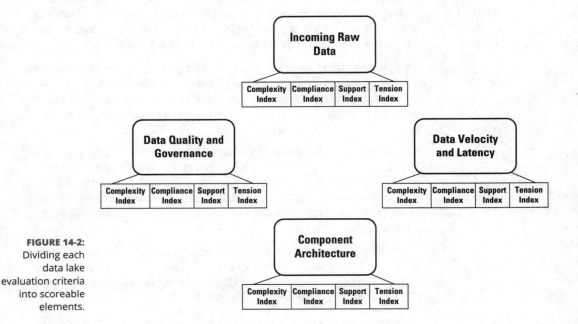

FIGURE 14-2:
Dividing each data lake evaluation criteria into scoreable elements.

Spread the word, far and wide throughout the land, that voting is now open!

You want input on the health of your data lake from as many people as possible, from all across IT, as well as the business users. Even if someone on the business side doesn't have a particularly strong insight into the nuts and bolts of your data lake, they still have valuable input to share about data quality, data latency, your metadata catalogs, and much more.

TIP

Use Qualtrics or any other survey software that your company lets you use. Send out your surveys through email or Slack or however you communicate in your organization. Stress the importance of participating in the survey, and don't make people spend any more than five to ten minutes offering their input.

Use a simple grading scale, like this:

>> 4 = Especially high; nearly perfect

>> 3 = Pretty darn good; just a few hiccups here and there

>> 2 = Mediocre; often painful and problematic but fortunately not a total disaster

>> 1 = Terrible; a total disaster; doesn't work as advertised; rotten; yuck (you get the idea)

You'll collect the survey results from your participants, tally up the scores for each of your evaluation categories, and then calculate a simple average.

REMEMBER

Using a 1-to-4 scale, designate an average score of 2.5 or less to signify a "hot spot" that bears further investigation and likely plays at least a partial role in your underperforming data lake.

Looking at the Raw Data Lockbox

Your data lake landscape begins with your bronze zone, the home for incoming raw data. You may be thinking, "How can we possibly mess up storing a bunch of raw data?" Hopefully, you'll never find out. But quite possibly, your data lake problems *begin* with your raw data.

WARNING

As shown in Figure 14-3, shut everything else out of your mind when you're digging deep into your raw data. Otherwise, your clarity will be adversely impacted by the muddied data lake waters. (Great metaphor!)

Ask yourself the following questions:

>> Do we have a single data store, such as Amazon Simple Storage Service (S3) or Microsoft Azure Data Lake Storage (ADLS), that we use for our bronze zone?

>> If we're using a single data store, is the data well organized and well managed within that environment?

>> If our bronze zone has more than one data store — for example Amazon S3 for semi-structured and unstructured data but a relational database for structured data — do we have well-defined rules of engagement for which data lands where?

>> Are all the data sets in our bronze zone fully cataloged, and are those catalogs current?

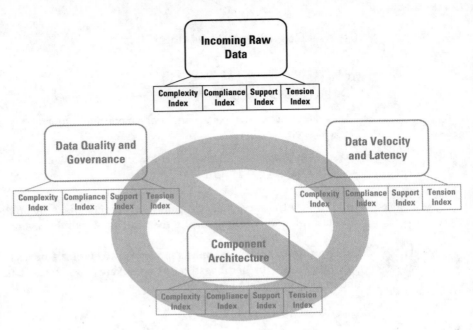

>> Are we running into performance issues or capacity issues in our bronze zone?

>> Do we have significant amounts of superfluous data in our bronze zone that we would never, ever use for analytics?

>> If users are accessing bronze zone data, are they fully aware that they're using raw data?

>> Are we able to rapidly honor requests to bring in new data sources or new data from existing sources?

You send out your surveys and get back the results that are shown in Figure 14-4.

What does Figure 14-4 tell you? First, the very fact that you have two hot spots out of the four categories that you evaluated isn't a very good sign. Apparently, your bronze zone is overly complex, as indicated by the fairly low average score of 1.8. Why is your bronze zone and its raw data overly complex? You don't know yet, but you'll figure out the reasons when you start digging. For now, you have your first smoking gun to follow.

And apparently, the bronze zone and your raw data are creating a great deal of angst across your organization —not something that you want to hear about what should just be a giant pool of ingested raw data. Hey, you expect tensions to flare for how curated data is used, or perhaps because not enough raw data is making its way through the data pipelines to become curated data in the first place. But tensions in the bronze zone? Noooooo!

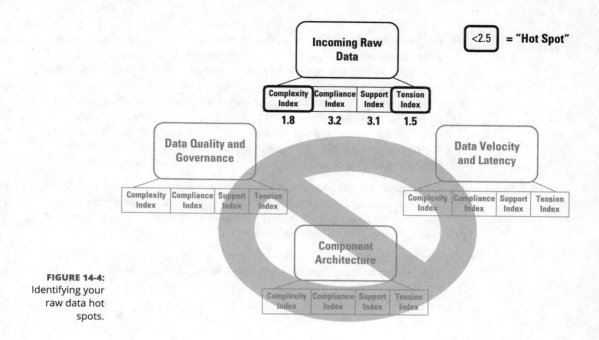

FIGURE 14-4: Identifying your raw data hot spots.

At this point you're ready to move on to score and analyze your next group of evaluation factors. But you already know that your data lake problems are beginning very early along your pipelines. You'll know more later, but quite possibly you'll be able to resolve some of your other issues by addressing these root causes, which will result in a positive impact that ripples down the line to your other areas.

Knowing What to Do When Your Data Lake Is Out of Order

When you move on to your second evaluation area — data quality and governance (see Figure 14-5) — you once again set aside the other categories for the time being. You'll have enough to consider just in this second area, including the following:

>> **Rudimentary data quality beyond the bronze zone:** In other words, is your data fundamentally error-free when available to users for their analytics? Note that data quality applies to your unstructured data, as well as your structured data. For example, if you have raw video in your bronze zone that is supposed to be enhanced and meta-tagged in your silver zone, but what you actually have is another copy of the same exact raw data, then your data cleansing and refinement has fallen down on the job.

>> **Data consistency:** For example, you have two copies of some piece of data stored in different data packages in your gold zone. Each copy is correct, but one copy is "stale" and represents a previous state of that data that has been superseded. For example, suppose you have multimedia employee data stored in two or more gold zone packages. Each employee profile includes a photograph. However, for one of your company's employees, one of the photographs is older and out of date, while the other is the most current one. Even though this problem may seem minor, it can be indicative of a larger data consistency problem.

>> **Cataloging:** Beyond your bronze zone, is your data fully cataloged and easily accessible to your business users and data lake team alike? How robust is your user-facing metadata? Does the metadata come with full explanations of business rules? How is your data lineage?

>> **Master data management:** Does your master data hold up throughout your data lake? Is an "active customer" the same across all components? Across all data packages in your gold zone?

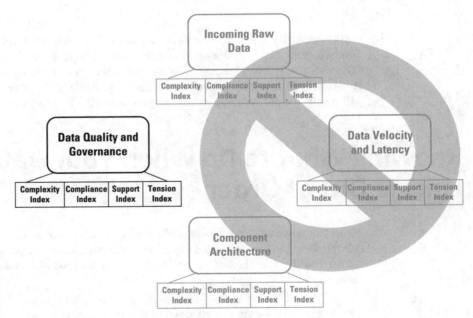

FIGURE 14-5:
Diving deep into your data lake's quality and governance.

Figure 14-6 shows the results of this portion of your survey and you absolutely cringe when you see the results! Imagine the feeling you would have if you were in the middle of a lake in your small boat, and suddenly you spotted a tsunami straight out of an apocalyptic movie headed straight for you? Yeah, that feeling!

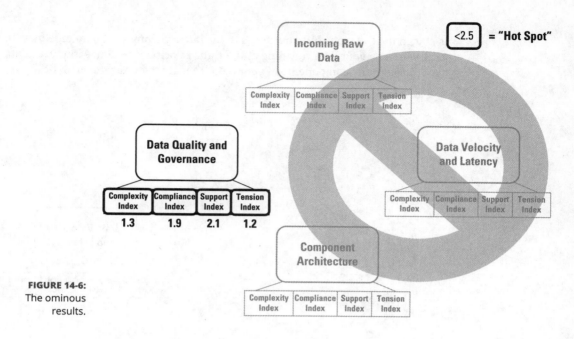

FIGURE 14-6:
The ominous
results.

You stare at your survey results and digest the bad news:

>> Whatever data quality and governance capabilities you *do* have are, apparently, too complex — or at least your users view them as such.

>> Maybe because of that complexity, not much of your data lake is in compliance with master data, metadata catalogs, or pretty much anything else.

>> Your business users are probably the ones reporting that support requests for data quality, inconsistencies, master data questions, and catalog inquiries aren't exactly setting land-speed records for response time.

>> Not surprisingly, tensions are running high over all these factors — even higher than for your bronze zone raw data problems (see the preceding section)!

Too Fast, Too Slow, Just Right: Dealing with Data Lake Velocity and Latency

Wow! Isn't anything going right with your data lake? So far, the story isn't a pretty one. Nonetheless, you persevere in your hot-spot analysis (not that you really have much choice).

As shown in 14-7, you shift your focus to the latency along your data pipelines. In other words, is your data traveling at the right velocity as it comes into your data lake? Through the components of your data lake? Into your users' analytics?

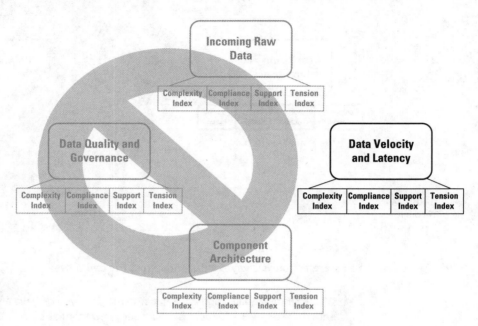

FIGURE 14-7:
Grading your data velocity and latency.

REMEMBER

At the highest level, you have two different families of data velocity for your data lake:

>> Streaming data

>> Batch data

You'll further subdivide each velocity category. Some of your streaming data feeds will be real-time in nature, while others may still be streaming but have a slight time lag to them. Likewise, some of your batch feeds will be spaced out — perhaps at the end of each day — while others might be "rapid batch," such as every 10 to 15 minutes.

Your overall data lake architecture will almost certainly have a mix-and-match collection of data feeds along your various pipelines. But do you have the right mix? Do you have the right velocity for each group of data from its point of origination to its final destination? Does data from one group get synthesized and combined with data from another group in a timely manner to create a unified data package for your analytics?

You, and everyone else who is participating in your "find the hot spots" survey need to examine all your data flows and ask yourself:

>> Is the data moving fast enough along the pipeline?

>> Is any data moving too fast along a pipeline? In other words, are you streaming data that really can be transferred in a batch-oriented manner?

>> Are users having to deal with stale data that arrives too late to interdict a problem or identify and then take advantage of a sudden opportunity?

Figure 14-8 shows the results of scoring your data lake's velocity and resultant latency (finally, you have some good news!). Three of your four scores are above a grade of 3. Your tension index is still below 3, but at least it's above the 2.5 watermark (great metaphor!) that indicates trouble. Quite possibly, tensions along the velocity and latency front are a ripple effect from the tensions elsewhere in your data lake portfolio.

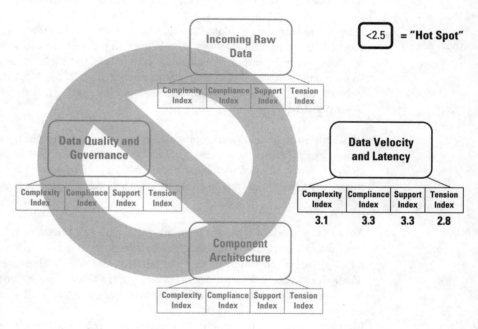

FIGURE 14-8:
Good news on the data velocity and latency front.

Dividing the Work in Your Component Architecture

If your data lake resides solely in, say, Amazon S3 buckets, then by default, your component architecture is a-okay. In other words, you've settled on the simplest, single-component topology possible, and data moving along your pipelines isn't traveling from one platform to another.

REMEMBER

More likely, though, your data lake is made up of multiple components. The many reference architecture options described in Chapter 4 present you with a variety of multi-component data lake architectures, and Chapters 12 and 13 for Amazon Web Services and Microsoft Azure, respectively, move those conceptual architectures into the implementation world.

But how well have you bolted those components together? Does data flow smoothly from, say, S3 into Amazon Redshift? From ADLS into Databricks?

How many component platforms do you actually have? In an Amazon Web Services (AWS) environment, does it look like you ran a contest to see how many data services you can actually use? Does your data lake make use of S3, Redshift, DynamoDB, Aurora, Relational Database Service (RDS), Neptune, Timestream (whew, take a breath), Quantum Ledger Database (QLDB), Keyspaces, and DocumentDB?

You built your data lake in a phased, iterative, and incremental manner, one or more data pipelines at a time, guided by known and probable analytical needs. Quite possibly, at a given phase, a previously unused data service wound up debuting in your data lake for the first time. Do you have a problem? Perhaps, but not definitely.

Now that your data lake has been built out, you can take a step back and look at your overall component architecture to see if, perhaps, your team has scattered data a little bit too widely. If so, then perhaps you need to do some rationalization of all those databases and data services you're using, just as you did with your legacy data marts when you set out on your data lake adventure.

Figure 14-9 shows the results of your survey when it comes to your component architecture.

Groan . . . back to bad news. Well, first a little touch of good news. Even if you're using a fair number of data services, you seem to have them in good shape, architecturally. Your compliance score is 3.6, which is pretty darn good. You appear to be using data services correctly, for the right purposes.

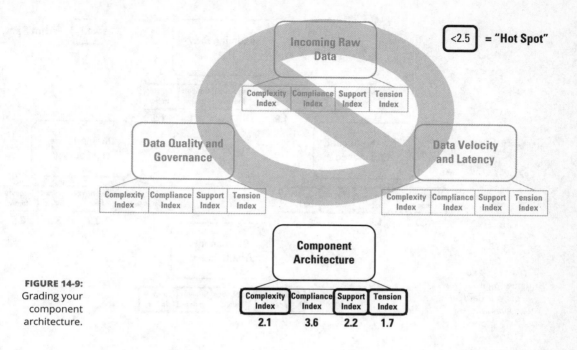

FIGURE 14-9:
Grading your
component
architecture.

However, your complexity score (2.1) is a fairly low. Can you be using too many data services? Possibly, because the support index score is also low. And once again, tensions are flaring with a score of 1.7.

Tallying Your Scores and Analyzing the Results

Figure 14-10 brings together all your individual category scores for each of your evaluation categories.

So, you and your team take in the big picture and have at least a little bit of encouraging news but also some crystal clear signs that you have some big-time data lake pollution cleanup ahead of you. Here's a summary:

>> On the positive side, your extract, transform, load (ETL), and ELT capabilities appear to be in good shape. Data is moving along your pipelines at more or less the right velocity. You most likely don't have any major overhaul work ahead of you for your streaming or batch services.

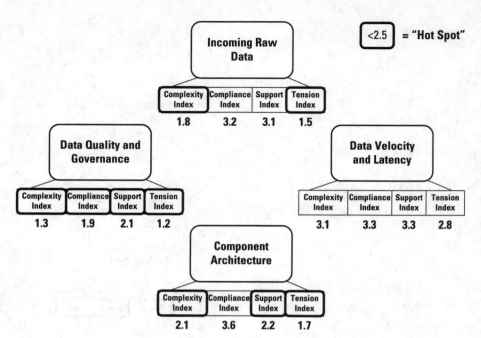

FIGURE 14-10:
Bringing together all of your data lake evaluation scores.

>> Your biggest area of concern is data quality and governance. Coupled with the low score for the complexity of your component architecture, your data lake seems to have problems with quality, metadata catalogs, and master data that can be caused or worsened by having to provide those capabilities across a number of different components.

>> You don't know why yet, but your bronze zone also scored fairly low on complexity. Quite possibly, problems that begin there are rippling through into other components, as well as the governance of all those pieces.

>> Tensions are running high, but they're likely a direct result of these other problems and can conceivably be tamped down by solving these issues.

Your data lake is limping along, but you have a plan to get things back on track!

Chapter **15**

Defining Your Data Lake Remediation Strategy

Suppose you're lucky enough to get in on the ground floor of your organization's data lake. (Or would that be "get in on the lake bottom"?) You and your colleagues may do all the work on your own, or you may get some outside assistance from expert-level data lake consultants.

Now suppose your data lake runs into trouble, and you need to turn your poorly performing data dump or data swamp back in the direction that you originally envisioned for all your efforts. You might also seek assistance from outside experts — which is where Ravi's company enters the picture for this chapter.

Ravi, Chun, and Timothy all work for a boutique consulting firm in the northeastern United States that specializes in data lakes for hospital systems and other medical organizations. Ravi founded the company more than a decade ago, back when the idea of data lakes was first becoming popular as a way to bring structure and discipline to big data solutions.

One of the specialty areas of Ravi's firm is helping clients who have already gone far down the data lake path but have little to show for their efforts and their investment. Clients who have more of a data swamp than a solidly architected data lake turn to Ravi's firm to help define a remediation strategy.

Ravi and the others in the firm do a lot of speaking at regional conferences and events, and these speaking gigs often bring in new business. Last week, Ravi gave a presentation in Philadelphia on how to turn a data dump into a well-functioning data lake. Sure enough, two days later, Ravi received an email inquiry from a sub-urban Philadelphia hospital that has the exact situation that Ravi described in his presentation. The next day, Ravi, Chun, and Timothy all met with the prospective client, and before the day was out, they had a new consulting engagement, which is where this chapter's tale begins.

Setting Your Key Objectives

You always begin by establishing specific key objectives for a data lake remediation engagement. Sometimes the objectives will vary slightly, but for the most part, you can use a "starter kit" similar to the one that Ravi's firm created a long time ago, and which they apply to each new data lake remediation engagement.

This new project is no different. By the end of the first day of the engagement, the white board in the conference room that Ravi's team will use as the "war room" has a list that is preceded by a giant DO NOT ERASE warning. This list of key objectives will remain in place for the whole engagement as a daily reminder of what the team intends to accomplish for their hospital client. It contains the following items:

>> Rationalize and improve the data lake without a total rebuild.

>> Fully address identified data lake shortcomings and hot spots.

>> Lay the groundwork for future data lake enhancements through a solid rearchitecting.

>> Stop data mart propagation, especially data marts that are still being created because of data lake issues.

>> Broaden the analytics continuum that uses the data lake.

>> Unify key enterprise analytics onto one logical platform.

Going back to square one

Ravi, Chun, and Timothy have an especially challenging job because the client hospital system already has its data lake up and running. Unlike a "greenfield clean slate" engagement, where the client doesn't yet have an operational data lake, Ravi and his team need to work in a grounded-in-reality manner and take stock of what they're dealing with.

Figure 15-1 shows the hospital's current operational applications.

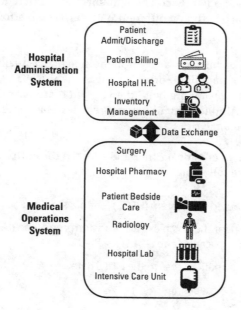

FIGURE 15-1: The current hospital operational applications.

Many of Ravi's clients have an integrated, enterprise-wide electronic health records (EHR) system in place, while others have gone down the best-of-breed path with a portfolio of individual-function applications for patient care, the hospital laboratory, radiology, patient admissions and discharges, and the many other functions that take place in a medical setting.

As it turns out, this new client fits neither of the standard patterns when it comes to its operational applications. Long ago, the hospital's IT staff worked with outside software developers and consulting firms and custom-developed two applications:

>> An application for nonmedical, administrative functions such as patient admissions and discharges, billing, human resources (HR), and inventory management

>> An application for all the medical operations and functions: surgery, pharmacy, patient bedside care, radiology, the hospital lab, and the intensive care unit (ICU)

The two applications regularly share data back and forth. Patient data is sent from the administration application into the medical operations system, while key medical information needed for patient records and billing is sent back from the medical operations system to the administration system. All these data transfers take place in hourly batch transfers. For the most part, these two systems act independently from each other. Each is maintained by a different team from the IT organization, and each is run on different hardware and platforms in the hospital's data center.

When it comes to reporting and analytics, the hospital actually was an early adopter of the data lake paradigm, or at least it thought it was. Way back in the early 2010s, as big data was taking hold, the IT team that maintains the hospital administration system implemented an on-premises Hadoop environment for administrative-focused analytics.

The team worked with an outside partner and adopted the entire Hadoop stack of that time, including the following:

>> The Hadoop Distributed File System (HDFS) for data storage and management

>> Open-source Sqoop for the batch extract, transform, and load (ETL) between the administration application and HDFS

>> MapReduce programmatic access to the HDFS data

>> Apache Oozie for job scheduling

>> Apache Hive and the Hive Query Language (HQL) for rudimentary database-type queries

Three years later, however, the IT team that supports the medical operations system went down a different path. They implemented a batch ETL feed of their data into the Amazon Web Services (AWS) cloud environment, batch-transferring clinical data into Amazon Simple Storage Service (S3) buckets.

Figure 15-2 shows both the Hadoop and AWS peer solutions for the hospital's analytics.

Even though the two teams went down different paths for their analytical data, both teams agreed on one principle (unfortunately): To their way of thinking, the Hadoop and AWS solutions were solely for "data science" — machine learning and other advanced analytics. None of the strategists or architects believed in analytics being a broad continuum that not only included predictive and discovery analytics, but also encompassed descriptive analytics (classic business intelligence, or BI). The key decision makers all (unfortunately) were in agreement that classic reporting, BI, and visualization was an entirely separate discipline than machine learning, data mining, and other advanced analytics.

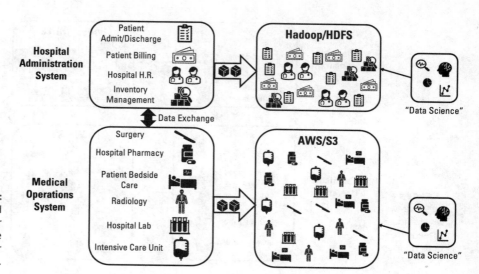

FIGURE 15-2: Peer analytical solutions, one for administrative data and one for medical data.

Therefore, a third IT team implemented batch ETL feeds from both the Hadoop and AWS environments into an on-premises SQL Server database to support much of the hospital's necessary descriptive analytics: reporting, BI, and rudimentary data visualization. Essentially, both the Hadoop and AWS systems are doing double-duty:

>> Supporting advanced analytics

>> Serving as supersized staging areas that feed a downstream data warehouse

Figure 15-3 completes the end-to-end picture of the hospital's main operational and analytical components.

But wait, there's more! Ravi's team also learns that in addition to the Hadoop and AWS components and the "official" downstream data warehouse (all shown in Figure 15-3), the hospital's data center is still filled with about two dozen other independent data marts for specific functions such as:

>> Hospital lab reporting and visualization

>> Radiology reporting and visualization

>> Intensive care unit (ICU) patient tracking

>> Patient room management

In fact, two of these smaller-scale data marts just went live last month to address data visualization needs that weren't easily met by any of the main analytical components (Hadoop, AWS, or the SQL Server data warehouse).

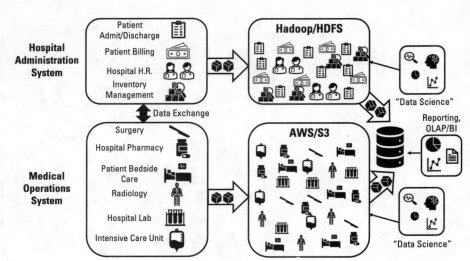

FIGURE 15-3: A downstream data warehouse taking feeds from both Hadoop and AWS.

Don't worry — you've seen enough cluttered diagrams so far, so I'll spare you one more. Just use your imagination to overlay about two dozen additional data marts onto Figure 15-3, and you'll have a pretty good idea of the mess that Ravi's team is going to try to fix without having to throw everything away.

Determining your enterprise analytics goals

All the preceding points fall under the first four items on the list in the team's war room, from rationalizing and improving the data lake without a total rebuild through stopping data mart propagation. By now, you know that data lakes aren't just about data; they're also every bit as much about the analytics that they support. The fifth and sixth items on Ravi's list — broadening the analytics continuum that uses the data lake, and unifying key enterprise analytics onto one logical platform — are equally important.

You can see from Figures 15-2 and 15-3 that the hospital has anything but a unified logical platform. They use their data lake only for "data science" rather than the full continuum that also includes BI, reporting, and rudimentary visualization. So, as Ravi, Chun, and Timothy proceed, they'll absolutely keep an eye on the analytics side every bit as much as the data side.

Doing Your Gap Analysis

When you have an idea of what you're dealing with, you need to start digging into the problem areas in the current data lake. Ravi's team is totally on board with this idea. They take their standard Qualtrics survey that addresses key evaluation areas (see Chapter 14), do a little bit of customization for this hospital's environment, and send it to the list of stakeholders and others that their project's sponsor has provided to them. A few days later, all the results are back, and they're even worse than anticipated!

Figure 15-4 shows the ominous results.

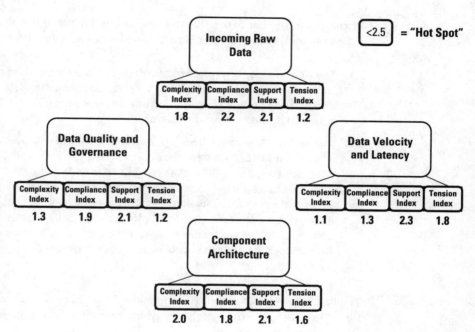

FIGURE 15-4:
The current state survey results.

Notice how for each of the four assessment categories — raw data, quality and governance, velocity and latency, and component architecture — and then for each of the four measurements within each category (complexity, compliance, support, and tension), *every single measurement has graded out as a hot spot!*

When the project sponsor first contacted Ravi after his presentation, she declared that the hospital had more of a data swamp than a data lake. Everything that Ravi, Chun, and Timothy learned during their initial research seemed to confirm this worrisome assessment. Now, with the survey results in, nobody has any doubt at all. Call it a data swamp, or call it a data dump, or call it anything else: The hospital definitely has a mess on its hands!

Identifying shortfalls and hot spots

Ravi, Chun, and Timothy go to work. They spend the next week reviewing architecture diagrams, talking to hospital staffers from both the IT and the operational sides, and doing their consulting thing that they do so well. By the end of that next week, the whiteboards in their war room are getting pretty full with the lists of shortfalls and the details of the data lake hot spots.

At the top of the list is the fact that the hospital actually has two data lakes (at least in name), even if neither is really architected as a data lake should be:

>> The older Hadoop environment has more than a decade's worth of administrative data all piled up in HDFS. Only a small amount of this data is either unstructured or semi-structured; mostly, it's structured data that has made its way from the administration system into HDFS.

>> Over in AWS, Ravi's team finds a more evenly balanced data portfolio of images and videos, notes and medical charts, and accompanying structured data. However, the so-called data lake in AWS is really just a single collection of numerous S3 buckets. A solidly architected data lake has formally defined zones that form the foundation of critical data pipelines. This hospital's AWS environment, unfortunately, has no concept — officially or otherwise — of bronze, silver, and gold zones for raw, refined, and curated data, respectively. Neither does the Hadoop environment. Data refinement and enrichment are haphazard at best.

The batch transfers between Hadoop and AWS often result in problematic delays for attempts at real-time analytics, where literally seconds might make the difference in patient outcomes.

Additional issues are noted and logged. Figure 15-5 highlights the major issues found by Ravi's team and parcels out those issues into the four major assessment categories.

Prioritizing issues and shortfalls

What should Ravi, Chun, and Timothy tackle first? By prioritizing the issues and shortfalls, they can help filter through masses of information that they've collected so far and set the stage for their data lake recovery strategy.

Ravi's team meets with their project sponsors and, after a two-hour meeting, they have a plan in place (or at least the prioritization of what to tackle first). The prioritized list, shown in Table 15-1, takes its place under another DO NOT ERASE label in the team's war room.

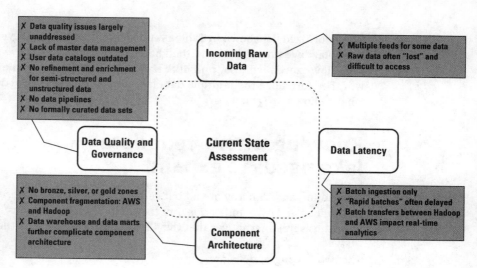

FIGURE 15-5:
Cataloging and
assigning data
lake issues.

Incoming Raw
Data

X Data quality issues largely
  unaddressed
X Lack of master data management
X User data catalogs outdated
X No refinement and enrichment
  for semi-structured and
  unstructured data
X No data pipelines
X No formally curated data sets

X Multiple feeds for some data
X Raw data often "lost" and
  difficult to access

Data Quality and
Governance

Current State
Assessment

Data Latency

X No bronze, silver, or gold zones
X Component fragmentation: AWS
  and Hadoop
X Data warehouse and data marts
  further complicate component
  architecture

X Batch ingestion only
X "Rapid batches" often delayed
X Batch transfers between Hadoop
  and AWS impact real-time
  analytics

Component
Architecture

TABLE 15-1

Data Lake Remediation Priorities

Priority	Tasks
1	Unify the Hadoop and AWS data lake components onto a single platform.
2	Formalize bronze, silver, and gold zones into the data lake.
3	Re-platform the downstream data warehouse and bring it under the control of the data lake environment.
4	Migrate data mart capabilities into the data lake and stop data mart proliferation.
5	Introduce streaming data flows where appropriate.
6	Formalize master data management (MDM).
7	Unify classic BI and advanced analytics under a unified analytical framework.
8	Increase usage and acceptance of the data lake through a broadened analytics portfolio.

Identifying Resolutions

When you have your prioritized list of remediation tasks in order, you need to devise exactly how you'll make each of those tasks real and actionable rather than just a string of words.

The prioritized list shown in Table 15-1 certainly looks good to everyone involved. Now, Ravi's team needs to add the "how" factor to each of those prioritized task sets. How exactly will they unify the Hadoop and AWS sides of the data lake? How will they formalize the multiple data lake zones? How will they do all the rest of what's shown in Table 15-1?

Knowing where your data lake needs to expand

Ravi, Chun, and Timothy are all but certain where they're headed with regard to the Hadoop and AWS unification. But they still do what good consultants do: Come up with several alternatives that they'll evaluate against each other.

The two leading options are:

>> Move the existing hospital administration data from Hadoop into AWS, redirect the data flows from the hospital administration system into AWS, and retire the on-premises Hadoop.

>> Do the exact opposite: Redirect everything into Hadoop, and retire the AWS component.

Can the hospital re-platform both components onto a totally different cloud platform? Perhaps, but from what Ravi and his team can tell, the IT staff at this hospital is overworked supporting their two custom-developed applications (hospital administration and medical operations). Tossing both of the cloud data lake platforms and starting over from scratch would be much more of a new data lake initiative than a remediation effort.

So, for the moment, Ravi's team stops at the preceding two options: Either expand the AWS side or expand the Hadoop side to now include the other. And now — drumroll, please — they need to make a decision.

Hadoop-based data lakes have, for the most part, gone out of style, especially on-premises Hadoop, as is the case with this hospital. As I explain in Part 3, cloud computing and data lakes go together like fish and chips. AWS is one of the leading cloud-based data lake platforms, and a major portion of the hospital's existing data lake is already in AWS.

Ravi sketches a two-phase platform migration effort on the war room's whiteboard, as shown in Figure 15-6.

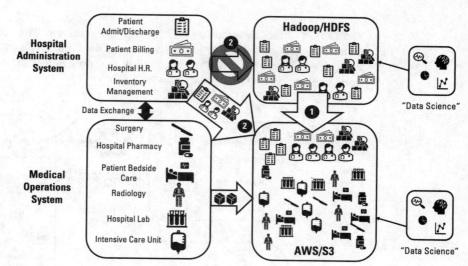

FIGURE 15-6:

FIGURE 15-6:
A two-step
process to
migrate the
hospital's entire
data lake
onto AWS.

First, the hospital needs to transfer its HDFS data into AWS (specifically, into S3 buckets). Ravi knows that several options exist. But given that the Hadoop sort-of data lake has been operational for more than a decade, a *lot* of data is sitting in HDFS right now.

**TECHNICAL
STUFF**

Ravi decides that the hospital should use the AWS Snowball Edge data migration service to unload the HDFS data and get all that data up into S3 buckets under AWS control. Snowball Edge is a physical device (think of it as a super-super-supersized jump drive) that will be shipped to the hospital. The IT staff will copy the HDFS data onto the device and then ship the device to AWS, where the administration data will be loaded into S3 buckets in the hospital's AWS data lake.

Getting the existing HDFS data into AWS is only the beginning. The way things are set up right now, the batch transfer between the hospital administration application and the HDFS side of the data lake. Step 2 (which needs to occur in parallel with Step 1, transferring your HDFS data into AWS) is to cut over that feed from the hospital administration application into HDFS, as shown in Figure 15-6.

If you're looking at that new data feed on Figure 15-6 between the hospital administration application and the AWS environment and wondering, "So, what sort of data feed? Batch or streaming?," then congratulations — you're on top of the whole data lake architecture business! Whereas the soon-to-be-decommissioned feed between the hospital administration application and on-premises HDFS was solely a batch interface, by no means is the hospital stuck with maintaining that batch-only paradigm. In fact, one of the problems that Ravi's team has picked up on is a latency issue between when a patient is admitted to the hospital and when that patient's basic information is available not only for analytics, but even for medical operations (lab testing, radiology, and in-room care).

Figure 15-7 shows the solution that Ravi's team proposes. The hospital administration application will write patient admission data into an Apache Kafka stream, and the admission data will be consumed in real time by both the medical operations application and the S3 data lake.

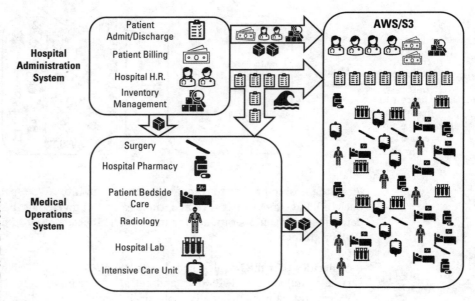

FIGURE 15-7: Introducing streaming to benefit both the medical operations application and the data lake.

TECHNICAL STUFF

Should the hospital cut over any of its other data interchange flows from batch to streaming? Perhaps, but for now, Ravi's immediate focus is to ensure that the patient admission information makes it into the hospital operations application and the data lake in real time. As Ravi, Chun, and Timothy dig deeper into the analytical usage of the data lake, they may uncover specific needs where other data transfers should be done via Kafka or perhaps even some other streaming service. For now, though, they'll move the hospital from a totally batch transfer architecture to a Lambda architecture, with both batch and streaming.

That takes care of the top priority and even priority item number 5 from Table 15-1 (introducing streaming data flows where appropriate). Now onto the next few items from the prioritized list.

Repairing the data lake boat docks

Even with the Hadoop environment retired and all the analytical data now residing inside of AWS and specifically within S3 buckets, the hospital's data lake is still more of a data swamp. In Figure 15-7, you see a whole lot of data in the data lake, but not much order or discipline.

Fortunately, the first step for Ravi's team is simple, as shown in Figure 15-8.

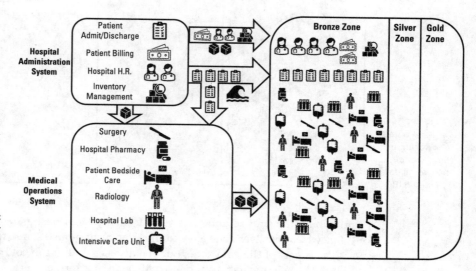

FIGURE 15-8: Adding shells for the silver and gold zones.

The beauty of a data lake is that even when you have a total mess on your hands as Ravi's hospital client does, you can sort of wave your magic data wand and declare that, henceforth, the cluttered, chaotic existing data will be categorized as the bronze zone, filled with raw data.

Wait a minute, though: Not all of that existing S3 data is raw, right? Some of it has probably been enriched and refined and perhaps even curated. Yep, you're exactly right. The hospital's data lake has certainly been used for analytics for a while now. The problem, though, is that nobody can easily determine which buckets of data have been refined and enhanced, or even curated, versus which buckets contain raw and possibly erroneous data.

TIP

Because Ravi and his team are working with an existing data lake rather than building one from scratch, the best thing to do is declare that all existing data is considered to be part of the raw zone. Later, as they define and build out the data pipelines, they can "promote" any of the existing data into either the silver or gold zone as necessary. But rather than get bogged down with heavy-duty data profiling, they can move on to the other pressing items on their list, such as what to do about the existing data warehouse.

Figure 15-9 gives you the answer to the data warehouse quandary.

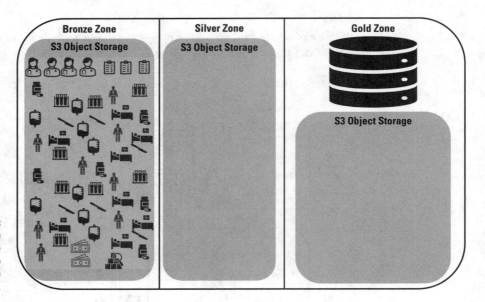

FIGURE 15-9:
Adding a data warehouse component into the overall data lake architecture.

Notice how the bronze zone has now formally been designated as residing in S3. Likewise, the silver zone is — for now, anyway — also slated to be platformed in S3, as is part of the gold zone. But you also see within the gold zone a database symbol. The existing data warehouse will be re-platformed here, as will the existing standalone data marts that keep popping up.

TECHNICAL STUFF

For now, Ravi's team defers the specific database platform decision for the gold zone. They can conceivably port the existing on-premises SQL Server data warehouse into the AWS environment. They might decide to rebuild the data warehouse in one of the AWS databases such as Amazon Redshift or Amazon Aurora. They might even decide to use a third-party database environment such as Yellowbrick. That decision will come soon enough, but the important stepping stone has been laid, and the data lake is starting to look a lot better, at least on paper.

Before moving on to the analytical side of the hospital's data lake, Ravi's team has one remaining prioritized item to tackle: MDM. Figure 15-10 shows the proposed solution to help the hospital client finally realize some apples-to-apples MDM.

The MDM engine will be housed within the silver zone of the data lake, which makes sense. Back in the bronze zone, raw data is, well, raw. The whole idea behind the bronze zone is rapid ingestion and voluminous housing of data, with little need for governance functions such as data quality and even rudimentary transformations.

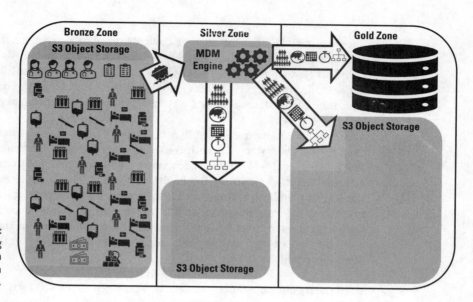

FIGURE 15-10:
Placing master data management in your silver zone.

Over in the gold zone, the idea is to take data that is already refined and enriched and build high-quality data sets that are closely aligned with high-impact analytical needs.

That leaves the silver zone, which is absolutely perfect! Refining and enriching data involves transformations. A key aspect of MDM is applying necessary transformations to data types and sizes, data values and permissible encodings, and data-oriented business rules in the quest for apples-to-apples data unification. What better place to house an MDM engine?

REMEMBER

Ravi, Chun, and Timothy have been down this road before, though, and they realize that lots of folks just don't get the importance of MDM or even the idea. So, as part of their recommendation package, they pull together a couple of key examples that directly apply to this hospital.

Patient data originates in the hospital administration system when a patient is admitted to the hospital. However, the master patient record over in the medical operations system is very different from the original source in the administration system. The batch transfer between the two systems takes care of the necessary translations and transformations between those two operational applications. However, both formats for patient data have been fed into the data lake.

Until now, the different formats weren't an issue, because the HDFS side of the data lake handled patient administration analytics while the AWS side handled analytics related to the hospital lab, the hospital pharmacy, surgery, and other medical functions.

The good news is that the current downstream data warehouse had to unify the different patient record formats because the warehouse took feeds from both on-premises Hadoop and AWS. So, Ravi can point to what happens in the data warehouse environment as a perfect example of what MDM should be doing in the data lake, long before data makes its way into any sort of curated data packages.

TECHNICAL STUFF

Another good example of MDM in action relates to the disease classification codes used in the two systems. The International Statistical Classification of Diseases and Related Health Problems codes, more commonly referred to as ICD codes, are a formal taxonomy used in the healthcare realm. The hospital recently adopted the ICD-11 standard, and the patient administration system, which includes billing, converted from the previous ICD-10 standard. However, the support team for the medical operations system was several months behind in their ICD-related work because of high-priority maintenance and enhancements that had already been scheduled.

Until the medical operations system was changed over to ICD-11, the batch transfer jobs between the two systems needed to translate ICD-10 codes to ICD-11 whenever necessary. Over in the data lake and then in the data warehouse, problems occasionally arose with apples-to-oranges issues between the two standards.

If necessary, Ravi is fully prepared to go down the tutorial path for MDM for any doubters. For now, though, he can check off yet another prioritized item on the data lake remediation list.

Linking analytics to data lake improvements

The final two items on Ravi's prioritized list follow directly from the unification of the data lake itself. Currently, the hospital experiences an unfortunate bifurcation between classic BI and visualization — which make use of the downstream data warehouse — and the "data science" advanced analytics.

Now, though, the downstream data warehouse has been tagged for incorporation into the overall data lake environment. Essentially, the hospital has no choice but to unify its analytics portfolio against the data warehouse. The Hadoop side of the data lake is going away, which means that any "data science" that uses hospital administration data will now be pointed against AWS data.

TIP

Ravi, Chun, and Timothy have all been around long enough to realize that no matter how strongly they advocate the data lake concept in a broad, all-inclusive sense, at least a few stubborn stakeholders will insist that a data lake is for data science, a data warehouse is for BI, and never the twain shall meet.

Ravi asks Chun to draw an "alternative architecture" picture that they can pull out if — or when — any controversy arises with regard to their recommendations. Chun draws the diagram that you see in Figure 15-11.

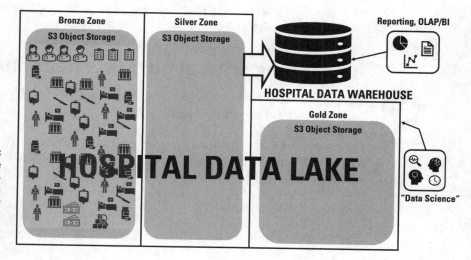

FIGURE 15-11: Addressing the data warehouse–versus–data lake controversy without impeding your overall architecture.

And then there was one.

REMEMBER

All that remains on Ravi's conference room whiteboard list is the final item: driving acceptance and usage of the data lake through a broadened analytics portfolio. Ravi, Chun, and Timothy are all in agreement on this one, based on their experience and successes with previous clients: Build well-architected data pipelines from the raw data into the data lake gold zone and all the way through to high-value, high-impact analytics.

What's that you say? Easier said than done? Maybe, but constructing data pipelines out of a data swamp is definitely doable! In fact, Chapter 16 lays it all out for you.

Establishing Timelines

Take a good look at the large body of work that you've laid out for your remediation plans. Wow! Feeling a little bit overwhelmed? Don't be. As soon as you allocate those tasks to your overall timeline, your pulse rate will drop back into the normal range, and you'll be ready to keep moving on your remediation efforts.

Ravi's team is now in the home stretch, at least as far as their strategy and planning work is concerned. Certainly, actually doing the remediation work will be a time-consuming effort. Ravi doesn't know yet if the hospital will engage his firm to assist with the work or if they'll do it on their own using their internal IT resources. Regardless, one of the final strategy steps for Ravi's team is to establish the timelines for that remediation work, whenever it begins.

Identifying critical business deadlines

REMEMBER

Any program or project plan needs to take into consideration any critical business deadlines that can impact the body of work.

For example, if the hospital were planning to dump its two legacy applications — hospital administration and medical operations — and replace them with a new EHR system, the EHR work would need to be factored into any data lake remediation schedules. Or, if major upgrade work on one of those applications were scheduled, Ravi would likewise need to consider the overall scheduling.

Fortunately, at least for data lake remediation efforts, the hospital isn't quite ready to head down the EHR path quite yet, though the new chief medical officer has been advocating that direction ever since she started her job six months earlier.

Sometimes you need to work around business deadlines or mandates, not just technology-related ones. A while back, when the United States implemented the Affordable Care Act (ACA), hospitals and healthcare organizations all across the country needed to factor ACA-related mandates into ongoing work — including big data initiatives that can be thought of as first-generation data lakes.

For now, though, Ravi can prepare his schedules without worrying too much about major systems initiatives or mandates that would cut into the body of work that needs to be done.

Sequencing your upcoming data lake repairs

Figure 15-12 shows the first-draft sequencing and timeline that Ravi's team has prepared for the data lake remediation work.

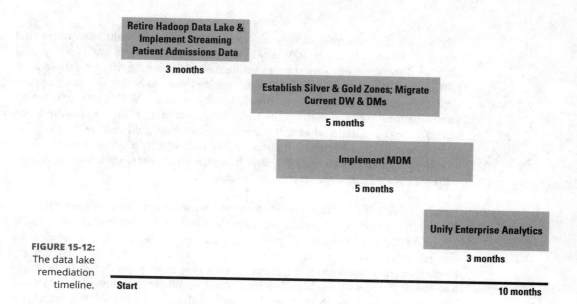

FIGURE 15-12:
The data lake
remediation
timeline.

To nobody's surprise, the sequencing of work closely follows the prioritization that Ravi's team had previously laid out. Leading off and batting first, the Hadoop data lake component will be retired, and the feed from the hospital administration system will be cut over to the AWS component. At the same time, part of the data ingestion — patient admission data, specifically — will be reimplemented as a streaming interface instead of continuing as a batch feed.

And as shown in Figure 15-7, that streaming feed — tentatively implemented in Apache Kafka — will also stream that same patient admission data into the medical operations application, replacing the batch transmission there as well.

The next body of work will go a long way toward turning the hospital's data swamp into a well-architected data lake, at least from a structural perspective. The silver and gold zones will be established, and the current SQL Server data warehouse will be subsumed into the new data lake gold zone. At the same time, the data marts that continue to pop up will likewise be subsumed into the gold zone.

Actually accomplishing this work takes more than just drawing a line on a diagram, of course. After Ravi's remediation plan is accepted, either his team or the hospital's internal staff will flesh out the project plans for this body of work. Ravi is confident, however, based on similar work that his team has done at previous clients, that his proposed timelines are realistic.

If you find yourself in a similar situation where you're trying to establish high-level timelines, do what Ravi did: Fall back on your own experiences in comparable situations and base your estimates off of what actually transpired on those projects.

TIP

When the silver and gold zone work begins after about a month to ensure that adequate progress is made, additional work on MDM will begin and run in parallel. The silver zone enrichment and refinement will lean heavily on MDM capabilities, and the downstream gold zone curated data packages likewise require apples-to-apples master data across key subject areas. With these two workstreams running in parallel, by the time the remediation effort enters the home stretch, the raw data in what will become the data lake gold zone will be accompanied by well-architected companion zones that will help bring about the level of analytical maturity that the hospital has been after ever since it started flirting with big data and first-generation data lakes.

Finally, to finish out the overall ten-month remediation work, efforts will shift toward the analytics side. Quite possibly, the same toolset portfolio that the hospital uses today will remain in place. Or, perhaps, the hospital might replace its current BI and visualization tools with new ones. It may implement packaged predictive analytics for medical settings, or it may send a number of its business and medical users to machine learning training. Whatever takes place, Ravi has allotted three months to these preliminary analytics efforts that will largely be oriented toward unification of what today are still fragmented efforts across the hospital's enterprise.

So, what's left? The data pipeline buildouts, that's what. The whole idea behind Ravi's remediation plans are to use the ten-month schedule to establish a "beachhead" with this next-generation data lake and the accompanying analytics. Presuming success in this endeavor, the hospital can then "break out of the beachhead" and begin to build the high-impact data pipelines that I show you in Chapter 16.

Looking for dependency and resource clashes

EHR implementation and upgrades, governmental healthcare mandates, a merger with another hospital. . . . All of these, and more, need to be factored into the remediation schedule, as described in "Sequencing your upcoming data lake repairs," earlier in this chapter.

The hospital also needs to pay attention to possible resource clashes. Cutting over hospital administration system data feed to AWS from Hadoop and implementing streaming for patient admissions data certainly makes sense in isolation. But who will do the work? What skills are required? Are people with the right skills to do the work already in the organization? And, here's the big question: If so, do they have the bandwidth to accomplish the work?

All the usual project management and resourcing best practices come into play here. Whether you're a program and project management traditionalist who uses Microsoft Project or an equivalent tool or you're more of an agile project management person, you need to be aware of resource loading, dependencies, and all the rest of the body of work that a program or project manager must do.

TIP

If you're more of a "big picture" data lake architect and strategist and you don't really like to get bogged down in details, don't despair. Bring a skilled project manager onto the team at the right time to work out all the details. Somebody has to do it!

Defining Your Critical Success Factors

When it comes to your data lake remediation, you can just hope for the best when you get your plans all set — the "put your faith in the data lake gods" approach.

WARNING

Don't do it! Remember that you're doing your best to rescue a data lake initiative that somehow went off the rails.

You need to get your ducks in a row and write down the things that absolutely, positively must be in place to strengthen the likelihood of data lake success this time around. In other words, you need to decide on the *critical success factors* for your data lake remediation effort.

Ravi's team pulls their presentation together. They socialize their recommendations with key stakeholders and make a few adjustments here and there. Finally, the big day arrives, and they begin to walk through their remediation plan and the rationale behind their specific recommendations.

They finish with a flourish, and the session opens for questions. One of the, ahem, crankier directors from IT narrows his eyes and offers this little tidbit: "When the previous IT regime started this data lake, they had all these grandiose ideas for what it would do, and it wound up a total mess. If we decide to go with your remediation plan, how can we tell if it's been successful or not?"

What does "success" mean?

Ravi has the perfect answer to this loaded question. In fact, he already made a back-pocket PowerPoint slide in case the question came up. Table 15-2 shows what Ravi's "How do we define success?" slide looks like.

TABLE 15-2

Defining Data Lake Remediation Success

Priority	Success Criteria
1	The on-premises Hadoop data lake is retired; all data is in the AWS environment.
2	There are formally established data lake zones for raw, refined/enriched, and curated data.
3	The data warehouse is re-platformed and under data lake control.
4	Independent data marts are retired; no new ones are being created.
5	Batch data flows are accompanied by streaming data where appropriate.
6	A full MDM initiative is underway.
7	A rationalized and unified enterprise analytics framework has been implemented.
8	The groundwork has been laid for the rapid buildout of data pipelines to directly support high-impact analytics.

If the items in Table 15-2 look familiar to you, they also probably look familiar to many of those gathered for Ravi's team's presentation. Near the beginning of the engagement, Ravi had enough foresight to achieve consensus of the prioritized body of work that the remediation plan needed to accomplish and that needed to be factored into the proposed body of work and the architectural recommendations.

Now, all Ravi has to do is slightly reword each of his prioritized objectives, and —presto! — he has a ready-to-use list of critical success factors for the data lake remediation!

TIP

Ideally, you want your success criteria to align with measurable *key performance indicators* (KPIs) along your timeline, if possible. For example, your top-priority item — retiring your on-premises Hadoop environment — would be tagged with "100 percent" for the completion of that effort. If you're dividing your Hadoop retirement into several phases of work, you might designate the completion of Phase 1 as being successful if 50 percent or more of the data in Hadoop has been transferred into AWS.

If you really want to get fancy, you can determine financial metrics for your return on investment (ROI) on your infrastructure costs, IT personnel costs, or other expenses associated with your data lake. For example, retiring Hadoop should save you $200,000 next year, based on infrastructure and personnel savings. One year following completion of the Hadoop retirement, you'll be able to see if your expected savings were actually met and if success was truly achieved.

As Ravi explains it to the gathered audience, if the hospital accomplishes each and every one of the items on this list by the end of the ten-month engagement and then begins rapidly building out and deploying new data pipelines within this new data framework, it absolutely will have successfully remediated its data lake and will be fully justified in declaring victory!

What must be in place to enable success?

Ravi, Chun, and Timothy are good consultants, which means they're fully aware that data lake success is about more than just technology and architecture.

TIP

The age-old trio of technology, human and organizational factors, and work processes (see Figure 15-13) rears its head yet again. Ravi's team has covered the technology side: platforms, data integration and interoperability, tools and services, and more. But what about methodology? What about program and project management? Does this hospital resolve controversies and disagreements in a timely manner? How are requirements collected, prioritized, and scheduled?

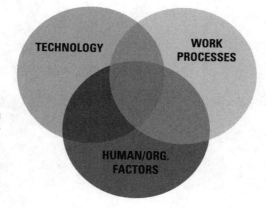

FIGURE 15-13:
The inevitable trio of technology, human and organizational factors, and work processes.

On the human and organizational factors side of the equation, additional questions arise:

>> Does the hospital have the skills in place to accomplish the body of work?

>> If the hospital goes outside for consulting assistance, how does it ensure that it's paying for qualified resources?

>> How does the hospital deal with resistance to change or even outright project sabotage?

>> What are the respective roles of business and IT when it comes to data and analytics?

REMEMBER

Whether you're building a data lake from scratch or turning a data swamp into a well-functioning data lake, make sure that you're paying attention to more than just technology and architecture. The success of your efforts depend on your having a broad enough view of what it takes to be successful.

» Improving data already in your data lake

» Bringing existing data lake content out of semiretirement

» Continuing the success story with newly ingested data

Chapter **16**

Refilling Your Data Lake

I n Chapter 15, I introduce Ravi, Chun, and Timothy, three consultants who have put together a hospital's data lake remediation strategy. Ravi (the founder of the small boutique consultancy) and his team did such a great job defining their client's fixing-the-data-lake strategy that the hospital asked them to stay on as advisers while the internal IT team carried out the remediation strategy over the next ten months.

Now, it's time for the finishing touches.

With the hospital's data lake freshly restructured and partially reconstructed, the next stage is to start really making use of "Data Lake 2.0" and not look back. Fortunately, Ravi, Chun, and Timothy have been down this road more than a few times, and they're ready to keep going when their client contact asks if they'd like to continue working on the data lake turnaround effort.

The Three S's: Setting the Stage for Success

The initial work of your data lake remediation effort (see Chapter 15) primarily focuses on two key bodies of work:

>> "Stopping the bleeding" (talk about a great analogy for a hospital data lake!) in the current environment by identifying and then correcting the most problematic areas that have made the data lake all but useless

>> Pivoting from whatever state the data lake was in before the remediation effort began to a well-architected "Data Lake 2.0" in preparation for moving forward

The ten months of work that came out of Ravi's team's remediation strategy has accomplished these two items. Now, with the framework in place for finally turning the hospital's data lake into what it was originally envisioned to accomplish, it's time to start building and filling end-to-end data pipelines, each of which results in high-value, high-impact analytics.

Ravi knows from experience that these new data pipelines will fit three different patterns:

>> Refining and enriching raw data that is already in the data lake but is underutilized.

>> Making better use of data lake objects and content that are already refined and enriched but are also currently underutilized

>> Rapidly ingesting new data and feeding it through data pipelines to prove out the "need for speed" characteristic of modern data lakes

All these patterns are critical to instilling confidence in the environment's new viability in the stakeholders and others who had all but given up on the hospital's data lake.

Refining and Enriching Existing Raw Data

One of the best places to start when you're trying to turn a data swamp into a solidly architected, well-functioning data lake is with, well, the swamp itself. In other words, take a look at data that is already stored within the data lake but that:

>> Is still in raw form, yet to be refined, enriched, or curated

>> Can be pulled together along newly constructed data pipelines into high-value analytics in a reasonably short period of time

Starting slowly

Ravi presents a short list of analytical functionality to the engagement sponsors, who huddle amongst themselves and decide that an operating room efficiency study would be a great starting point. Ravi smiles. When he gets back to the project "war room" (just an ordinary conference room), he informs Chun and Timothy that they can dust off the work they did on their previous engagement when they built another hospital's data lake from scratch, including the curated data and accompanying analytics for operating room efficiency.

Figure 16-1 shows the current state of this hospital's operational systems and the data lake that Ravi's team will start with.

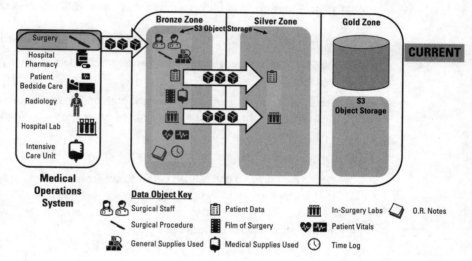

FIGURE 16-1: The starting point for the operating room efficiency study.

In Figure 16-1, you can see that, of the hospital's two main operational applications — the hospital administration system and the medical operations system — only the latter is applicable for this initial data lake remediation build-out. Better yet, the hospital's original "Data Lake 1.0," which existed before the remediation effort, already contains a wealth of data from the surgery and operating room management module within the medical operations system.

Unfortunately, that surgery-related data lake content is, for the most part, only in raw form within the current data lake. The exceptions are as follows:

>> **Surgery patients' demographic and health information:** This information is refined upon batch ingestion via classic extraction, transformation, and loading (ETL) capabilities. Originally, the hospital's data lake didn't have a silver

zone (see Chapter 15), but when Ravi's team rearchitected the data lake, all the refined surgery patient data was categorized within the silver zone, while the raw patient data was housed within the bronze zone.

>> **Hospital lab data related to surgeries:** This data has been treated in the same manner as the surgery patients' demographic and health information: refined upon ingestion, and now split between the bronze zone for raw lab data and the silver zone for refined and enhanced lab data.

Ravi divides the work between Chun and Timothy. Chun, who is highly experienced with machine learning and other aspects of data science, takes the models that the team had previously built and deployed elsewhere and does some minor adjustments based on this hospital's specifics. Meanwhile, Timothy — the team's data guru — designs and builds a new set of batch ETL routines that will

>> "Round up" the relevant surgery-related raw data in the bronze zone.

>> Do the necessary transformations to apply master data management (MDM) rules.

>> Enrich the semi-structured data (patient vitals and surgery notes) and unstructured data (the digital recordings of surgeries) via text mining and image mining.

>> Invoke the ETL between the bronze and silver zones.

>> Group the enriched and refined data into gold zone curated data packages that will be consumed by Chun's analytics.

Figure 16-2 shows what Timothy has planned.

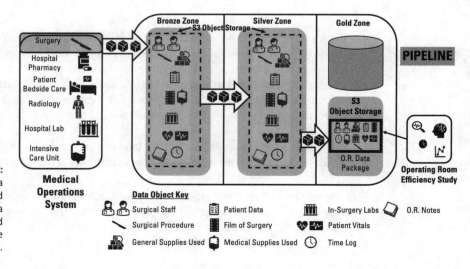

FIGURE 16-2: The first data pipeline to feed existing raw data into a curated gold zone package.

TECHNICAL STUFF

Timothy decides to retain copies of the enriched and refined surgery and operating room data in the silver zone in addition to the curated and packaged copies in the gold zone for one important reason: The surgery-related data will eventually be used by far more than just Chun's operating room efficiency study, which requires the data to be packaged in a specific manner. This way, other analytical uses — from classic business intelligence and rudimentary visualization to predictive and discovery analytics — can tap into this new pool of refined and enriched surgery-related data that's sitting there waiting, patiently, in the silver zone to support more and more analytics over time.

Adding more complexity

So, what's next? Again, Ravi reaches into his bag of tried-and-true hospital analytics, and sure enough, the hospital's stakeholders go wild over the idea of a real-time patient care dashboard that also supports advanced in-room patient analytics. One problem, though: In the hospital's "Data Lake 1.0," all data transmissions are done via batch processing, and the real-time patient care dashboard really needs streaming data.

TECHNICAL STUFF

No worries — Ravi's team already recommended that the new and improved version of the data lake follow the Lambda architecture, with both batch and streaming data feeds along the pipelines (see Chapter 15).

Still, Ravi knows that they'll need to unwind some of the existing data flows. Figure 16-3 shows the current state where patient bedside care data is fed via batch ETL into what is now the data lake's bronze zone.

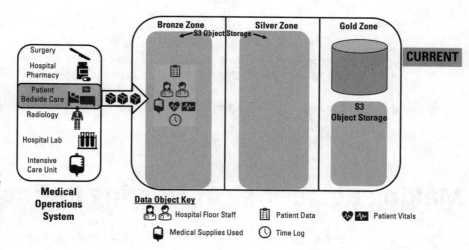

FIGURE 16-3: Batch ETL of patient bedside data in the current hospital data lake.

Whenever Ravi's team has implemented real-time dashboards with hospital clients in the past, they've built a streaming pipeline directly from the data source(s) into the streaming analytics with which the users interface. Ravi has Timothy do the necessary data profiling for what would be produced by the medical operations system. They'll need to do some minor transformations to some of the data along the streaming pipeline but again, nothing to worry about: Apache Kafka, the open-source streaming service they'll use, supports transformations directly against streamed data. So, they won't need to "unload" the data into the bronze and silver zones; the persistent data stream itself will serve as the gold zone storage layer for the patient bedside data.

Figure 16-4 shows the end result of this next buildout of the hospital's new and improved data lake architecture.

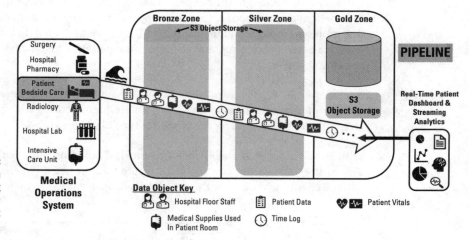

FIGURE 16-4: Streaming data and streaming analytics for the real-time patient dashboard.

Ravi secures approval from the client to proceed with the first two remediation-driven enhancements that will tap into existing data lake content: the surgery efficiency study and the real-time patient dashboard. Several weeks go by, and Ravi unveils the new capabilities to the stakeholders, who are thrilled.

Onward and upward!

Making Better Use of Existing Refined Data

Your data lake might have a whole lot of data that has been ingested and then enriched and refined.

And then it just sat there, lonely and unused.

Take a good look around your data lake that's undergoing remediation. Chances are, you'll find a whole lot of data that made it into what is now your silver zone — that is, the data was refined and enriched — but somehow never made its way into any analytics. Consequently, your data lake might have some of that proverbial low-hanging fruit there for the picking. Start making use of your underutilized data, and good things will probably happen!

Even though the hospital's data lake contained some refined and enriched data before Ravi's team began their remediation work, that refined data was all intermingled with raw data. Now, though, the refined and enriched data has been "repositioned" into the new silver zone. As Ravi maps out the next round of data lake–driven analytics, he decides that it's time to tap into some of that underutilized silver zone data.

Feeling adventurous, Ravi decides to tackle the emergency room data that is managed by the medical operations system.

If your eyes are particularly sharp and your memory is firing on all cylinders, you may be thinking to yourself, "Wait a minute . . . in Chapter 15, when Ravi's team began their work, the medical operations system didn't have an emergency room module." You're correct! To avoid overcomplicating the diagrams and the accompanying narrative, only a subset of what you would expect to find in real-world hospital management applications is being used at various points — enough to demonstrate the power of a data lake but not so much as to make following the examples an exercise in futility. Now, though, it's time for a really good emergency room application, so that's why you're seeing the emergency room data for the first time.

Figure 16-5 shows how the hospital's original data lake processed emergency room data (and actually did a pretty good job), even though they didn't really use that data for analytical purposes.

The raw emergency room data resides in the newly designated bronze zone, while the refined and enriched emergency room data has been repositioned into what is now the silver zone.

So, what should the hospital do, analytics-wise, with the emergency room data? One of the subject matter experts (SMEs) who serves on the data lake improvement steering committee has a great idea: Cross-reference and analyze everything that happens in the emergency room for patients who first show up there but wind up needing to be admitted to the hospital.

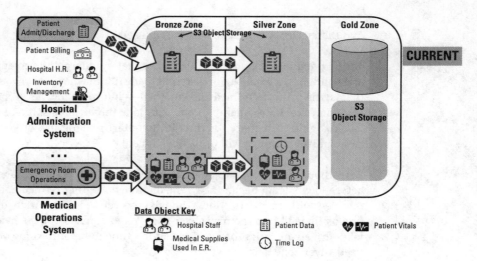

FIGURE 16-5:
Emergency room data fed through the bronze zone into the silver zone.

Fortunately, the other half of this analytical equation also lies in the new silver zone. Patient admissions and discharge information from the hospital administration system is already being brought into the data lake and refined, with the refined versions of the data already stored in what is now the silver zone.

Better yet, the discharge information contains a full log of everything that happened to a patient while under in-patient care:

>> The doctors, nurses, and other hospital staff who saw the patient

>> Every lab test and the results

>> Any X-rays or other imaging done by radiology

>> All meds prescribed and administered

Basically, the patient discharge record is one-stop shopping for everything related to a patient's stay in the hospital, and it's already in the data lake silver zone, right there for the taking!

Ravi, Chun, and Timothy put their heads together and come up with a great end-to-end solution for the analytics that the hospital would like to implement. Still, there's one complication: The emergency room data is already in the silver zone via batch transfers, but the analytics would be better served by real-time streaming data.

Ravi proposes a two-step solution to the project's sponsor and the stakeholders, and they agree. In the first phase, as shown in Figure 16-6, they simply tap into and then extend the existing batch-oriented data pipelines, carrying both the emergency room data and the patient discharge data into the gold zone. Then, when the data is in the gold zone, they store the integrated and cross-referenced data not in the Amazon Simple Storage Service (S3) object store but in the Yellowbrick database designated as the official database storage vehicle for the data lake's gold zone, alongside object storage.

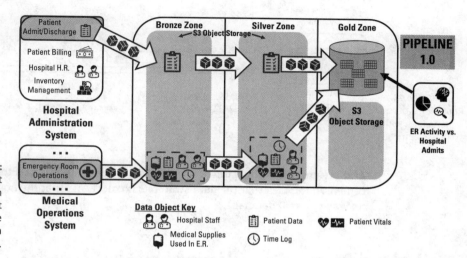

FIGURE 16-6: Building the first emergency room and inpatient cross-reference with batch data pipelines.

TIP

The idea, Ravi explains, is to initially focus on the analytical side rather than trying to do too much at once, including replacing silver zone data and the start of that pipeline that's already in place. Then, after the first phase has been successfully accomplished and the analytics have been tweaked, they can move on to Phase 2.

So, what exactly is Phase 2? Figure 16-7 shows how the batch-oriented pipeline for the emergency room data is replaced with a streaming flow of data, again using Apache Kafka as they did for the patient bedside data.

In fact, streaming presents a perfect opportunity to unveil another item from Ravi's team's bag of data lake improvement tricks: split-streaming data to two different destinations. In Figure 16-7, you can see how the primary path of the emergency room data leads straight to a real-time emergency room dashboard, mimicking what they already implemented for the patient bedside care dashboard (refer to Figure 16-4). However, the streaming emergency room data is also directed to the Yellowbrick database along with the patient discharge data, which is still being fed in batches, at least for the time being.

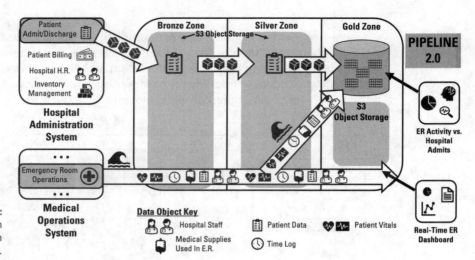

And presto! When this latest body of work is completed, Ravi's team has further cemented the idea that the data swamp is no more and that the hospital is well on its way to a real data lake.

Building New Pipelines with Newly Ingested Raw Data

Your data lake revitalization efforts will largely focus on sprucing up what you already have in the way of data, but you are by no means constrained to that existing content. You'll almost certainly start looking for new data sources, and that's exactly what has happened with Ravi's client.

The hospital's IT team has caught data lake fever! They're now hard at work corralling raw and refined data and building new data pipelines for new dashboards, great-looking visualizations, machine learning, and all sorts of "data science" functionality. The only thing lacking in the work that Ravi's team and the hospital IT staff have accomplished is that, so far, no new sources of data have been brought into the data lake picture.

Before Ravi's team says their farewells, they want to lay the groundwork with a proof-of-concept that will demonstrate to their client that, when the opportunity arises, new data can be quickly ingested and sent along a newly constructed data pipeline, resulting in even more high-value, high-impact analytics. Ravi asks Chun to do a little bit of looking around, and the perfect opportunity quickly surfaces.

The hospital recently implemented a mobile app that allows patients to schedule, modify, or cancel appointments; look up their own medical records; check billing and insurance information; and communicate via messaging with hospital medical staff. The app pulls data from both the hospital administration and the medical operations systems for billing and insurance, appointments, labs, and other medical information. However, the messaging component is unique to the app; no data store of the messages, or any associated metadata about the messages, exists anywhere other than in the app's underlying database.

One of the hospital's project stakeholders was recently at a conference, where someone presented a paper about the relationship between patient-to-hospital messaging and patient outcomes. Factors such as the following were all theorized to have relevancy with a patient's overall health and the outcomes from medical treatment:

>> Frequency of overall patient messaging

>> Relative percentages of messages that patients initiate versus those initiated by hospital staff

>> Tone and clarity of messages

>> How many messages were about health-related matters versus administrative topics such as appointments or billing

Was this the case at this hospital? A study that brought together patient messages and patient health histories and outcomes can certainly shed some light on the topic. Should there prove to be a relationship, the hospital can then apply predictive analytics to patient messages themselves and attempt to interdict major health issues.

Figure 16-8 shows the current state of the data lake, where patient admissions and discharge data is already ingested into what is now the data lake bronze zone and is carried through into the silver zone with a little bit of refinement and enrichment. But right now, messages from the app have no connection to the data lake.

The first thing that Ravi's team does is build a feed from the app into the data lake bronze zone. As shown in Figure 16-9, they decide to use a simple batch interface rather than head down the streaming path. The analytics performed against the messages will be part of long-term studies, so real-time data feeds via streaming would be overkill for the app's messages.

The patient discharge information that is already in the silver zone contains everything that the hospital's analysts and data scientists will need to determine patient outcomes, so that part of the picture is already taken care of.

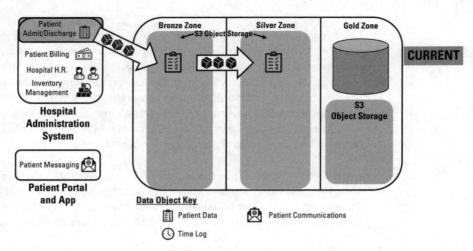

FIGURE 16-8:
The starting point for analyzing message content versus patient outcomes.

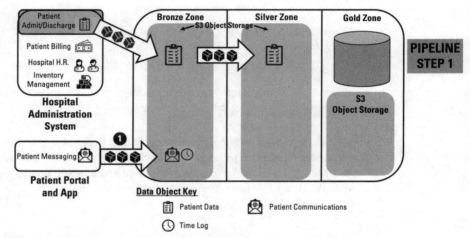

FIGURE 16-9:
Building a batch interface between the app and the data lake for messages.

Next, Ravi's team gets busy building text mining capabilities into the silver zone enrichment and refinement for the inbound messages. Each message will be analyzed and then augmented with a set of structured data that will include

>> Identifying information about the patient

>> Whether the message is medically related versus administrative

>> The severity level of any medical conditions being referred to in the message

>> The timeliness of the message versus when the medical condition first caused concern or when whatever the message's subject first surfaced

>> Any associated sentiment on the part of the patient

Now, though, Ravi's team makes a critical decision. The message itself is unchanged from when it was first ingested into the data lake, even after the text mining is completed. Do they really need to keep a copy of the raw message without the augmented information and then another copy with the augmented information? Not really.

REMEMBER

Ravi knows that a good model for semi-structured data such as these messages, as well as unstructured data, is to "reposition" or "promote" that data from the bronze zone into the silver zone when the enrichment and refinement is completed. In other words, as shown in Figure 16-10, the message begins in the bronze zone, but after it undergoes text mining, the message and the newly determined amplifying data is considered to be part of the silver zone.

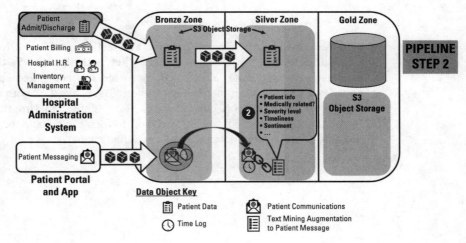

FIGURE 16-10: Enriching semi-structured data and then repositioning the data into the silver zone.

The third and final step along the new data pipeline is to do yet one more repositioning or "promotion" of the message data, this time from the silver zone into the gold zone. Chun and Timothy have created a new curated data package for the machine learning analytics that Chun has developed. The enriched message is now colocated along with patient outcome data pulled from the patient discharge record in the gold zone, as shown in Figure 16-11.

REMEMBER

Notice that, unlike the messages, the patient outcome is actually copied via batch feeds from the silver zone into the curated data package in the gold zone. Why the difference? The patient discharge data in the silver zone is already being used directly by other analytics, as well as being fed along other data pipelines into different curated data packages in the gold zone. Therefore, patient discharge data needs to remain in its enriched and refined form in the silver zone because it has other uses and contributes to other data pipelines.

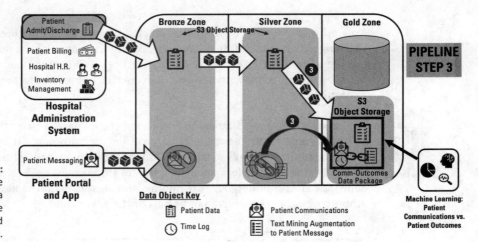

FIGURE 16-11: Completing the curated data package and the associated analytics.

Two more weeks go by for development and testing, and Ravi unveils these latest capabilities to the project's stakeholders. They're thrilled! Ravi's team has done it again: a successful data lake remediation that has continued past the strategy phase (see Chapter 15) into actually refilling "Data Lake 2.0" with new content via new pipelines, to support new analytics. Ravi, Chun, and Timothy pack up their materials, say their goodbyes, and head off to their next challenge, leaving behind not only a rejuvenated data lake but a satisfied client.

5
Making Trips to the Data Lake a Tradition

» Assessing your current state

» Solidifying your data lake vision

» Defining your data lake architecture

» Specifying your kickoff activities

» Sailing past your initial data lake release toward future expansion

Chapter **17**

Checking Your GPS: The Data Lake Road Map

How do you get to the data lake? A LAKE.

No, that's not a riddle, and I'm not just repeating part of the question to stall for time. A LAKE refers to a five-phase data lake methodology consisting of (check out the first letter of each phase listed below):

» **A**ssessment

» **L**ofty vision

» **A**rchitecture

» **K**ickoff activities

» **E**xpansion

If you follow the phased activities laid out in A LAKE, you can help take your company from wherever you stand today with your data and analytics to widespread delivery of high-impact, high-value data-driven insights throughout your organization.

Getting an Overhead View of the Road to the Data Lake

Your data lake road map is built on a five-phase approach. You're trying to achieve very specific objectives with each phase, as shown in Table 17-1.

TABLE 17-1   **Your Five-Phase A LAKE Data Lake Road Map**

Phase	Objective
Assessment	To clearly understand your current state of enterprise analytical data and identify "hot spots" that you need to address with your data lake
Lofty vision	To paint a compelling picture for how your data lake will deliver your next generation of analytics
Architecture	To determine how all the pieces of your data lake will fit together
Kickoff activities	To achieve early success to generate even more excitement about your data lake
Expansion	To progressively build out your data lake capabilities in a phased, iterative manner

Each phase is described in detail in this chapter, but you should take note of a key element of A LAKE from the big picture perspective. As you build your organization's data lake road map, you'll frequently circle back to one or more earlier points on your timeline to make sure that you haven't gone off-track. If you were driving to a brand-new lake resort hundreds of miles away, the last thing in the world you'd want is to faithfully follow your map and somehow wind up in the middle of the desert because that's where your map led you.

Table 17-2 describes how A LAKE helps you stay on course.

TABLE 17-2 **A LAKE Confirmation Loopbacks**

Phase	Confirmation
Assessment	Confirm collected information about data and analytics in your current state, especially hot spots you'll need to address.
Lofty vision	Confirm that your data lake vision addresses hot spots and doesn't take away or diminish current analytical capabilities.
Architecture	Confirm that your conceptual data lake architecture supports your vision and addresses current hot spots, and then confirm that the implementation architecture is aligned with the conceptual architecture.
Kickoff activities	Confirm that your initially selected data lake capabilities address current hot spots, is aligned with your data lake vision, and is fully compliant with your data lake architecture without workarounds.
Expansion	Confirm that each phase addresses current hot spots, remains aligned with your data lake vision, is fully compliant with your data lake architecture, and builds upon deliverables from previously delivered capabilities.

Assessing Your Current State of Data and Analytics

You've likely heard some variation of a wise saying from poet Maya Angelou: "If you don't know where you've come from, you don't know where you're going."

You know enough about data lakes to have a general idea of what you and your organization want to achieve and why a data lake is worth your time and resources (see Chapter 2). However, you need to start by digging very deep into every nook and cranny of your organization's analytics landscape today, along with all your data that supports those analytics. If you clearly and fully understand the good, the bad, and the ugly about your current state, then you can make sure that you address all of today's shortcomings — and also make sure that you keep the good stuff rolling along, even if you'll be modernizing the underlying technology.

WARNING

The very last thing you want to do when building a data lake is inadvertently take a few steps backward in some department's analytical capabilities that they have today. Sure, you might modernize your data architecture, but if you take away some department's most crucial data-driven insights that they use almost daily as a consequence of that modernization, you'll have some very unhappy people to deal with!

Figure 17-1 shows the two parallel paths your current-state analysis will take: one track for your enterprise analytics and another for your enterprise data. You also see at a high level the major topics that you need to address for each.

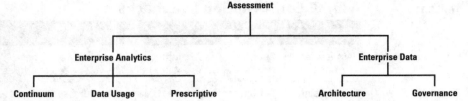

FIGURE 17-1:
Dividing your
current-state
assessment into
data and
analytics.

You need to do more than just survey your current state. You need to assign some type of a score to many important factors that signify the health of your analytics and data. Taken together, these scores will tell you what is and is not working today.

TIP

You can use any scoring model you want. If your organization requires using a standardized scale where 1 = terrible and 10 = fantastic, no problem. Or maybe they tell you to follow a green/yellow/red color-based rating system. Or, you can use Harvey balls (see Figure 17-2) with an empty circle signifying "none" or "poor," a filled-in circle signifying "full" or "high" or "great," and various slices along the way indicating different in-between scores. You can even stick with a simple, three-level high/average/low grading system, indicating the overall state of capabilities for each of the items that you're scoring. Whatever works for you is fine, as long as you're keeping score.

FIGURE 17-2:
Harvey balls for
scoring.

Snorkeling through your enterprise analytics

Does your company have an existing portfolio of analytics? Absolutely! But do today's analytics consist primarily of rudimentary, after-the-fact reports? Do your current data warehouses and data marts produce tons of analytics but somehow key decisions are made more on experience or even hunches than data-driven insights? Are you able to easily mine mountains of data in search of elusive patterns that can then drive decisions and actions?

Figure 17-3 shows how you'll divide your current-state assessment of your company's analytics into three sets of activities:

>> Your current analytics continuum, from rudimentary reporting to the most sophisticated machine learning and artificial intelligence

>> How well your analytics make use of different types of data

>> Your organization's ability to turn data-driven insights into decisions and then subsequent actions

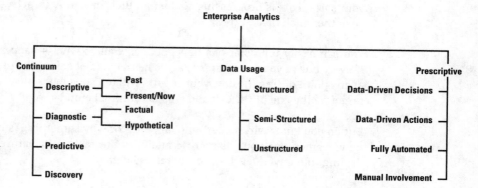

FIGURE 17-3:
FIGURE 17-3:
Parallel paths of your analytics assessment.

Scoring your analytics continuum

How good a job does your organization do with descriptive analytics? Are folks at all levels of your company, in many different organizations — finance, human resources, supply chain, sales, and so on — able to pull up tabular reports, graphs, or visualizations that tell them what happened last quarter versus the same quarter last year?

Also, what about data-driven insights into what's happening right now? Can your IT support staff effortlessly check into how many help-desk tickets were resolved so far today, and then drill into patterns that can indicate serious issues swimming under the surface? Can your logistics team pull up map-based visualizations that show exactly where every single inbound component is at this very moment and how that component is being transported (by rail? by ship? by truck? in the air?), and then identify possible issues with meeting manufacturing schedules or customer demand?

TIP

Spend a fair bit of time studying your current data warehouses and data marts and how those environments are accessed using business intelligence products such as Business Objects, Microsoft Power BI, MicroStrategy, and Tableau. The combination of classic data warehousing and business intelligence forms the backbone of your enterprise descriptive analytics.

Knowing what happened and also what's happening right now is important. But do you know why? You need to score how well your organization does with *diagnostic analytics* in concert with your descriptive analytics.

Suppose that you're a sales manager with a company that sells industrial equipment to large and medium-size manufacturers, and much of your entire workday is tapping, swiping, and pinching the screen on your iPad. No, you're not tweeting or watching the latest funny animal videos or checking out your favorite sports team's scores and stats. You use your iPad to analyze customer activity, to see how your sales team is progressing against all their quarterly targets, and for numerous other analytical purposes.

You can easily tell what has happened, as well as what's happening right now. If every one of your account managers has a quota of sales calls to make each day, at any point during the day, your reports will tell you who is on track to meet their target by the end of the day and who is running behind.

But do you know why something happened or why something is happening right now? Sometimes your diagnostic analytics are factual in nature, obtainable by drilling into lower-level or closely related data:

>> Your team didn't meet their collective revenue target last month, even though 15 of your account managers exceeded their personal targets. Why? Because five account managers fell way, way short and dragged down your entire team's performance.

>> Steve, one of your account managers, falls short of his sales call targets almost every day. You can study his call log and see that he usually spends almost twice as long on each phone call as the rest of your team does for a cold call. Basically, Steve is running out of available time, and he simply can't meet his call number targets.

But can your current diagnostic analytics go beyond cold, hard facts and present you with hypotheses about why something happened or is happening? Can it be that sales dropped off last quarter in certain regions for weather-related reasons?

Or, on the flip side, you know that sales doubled in a couple of your territories, but even after digging into your reports, nothing jumps out as a definitive reason. You don't want to look that proverbial gift horse in the mouth, but can you turn your analytical power loose on data from inside and outside your enterprise to come up with one or more data-driven hypotheses for that magnificent sales performance?

Diagnostic analytics can be tricky. Sometimes the "why it happened" factor is almost a by-product of your descriptive analytics, obtainable by drilling into your reports and visualizations. This family of diagnostic analytics deals in facts and is essentially a follow-up set of descriptive analytics that you use to reinforce your initial descriptive findings. Other times, though, your diagnostic efforts need more analytical oomph from machine learning or other advanced analytics to try to produce some hypotheses rather than additional facts.

REMEMBER

You absolutely, positively need your data lake to be able to support the full range of diagnostic analytics. By understanding how well you do (or don't) deliver those capabilities with today's environment, you'll have a baseline to work with.

You probably do a decent job at predictive analytics, like the following:

>> What customers most likely want to purchase a new product that you're introducing next quarter?

>> What is the optimal pricing for that new product, based on market and competition factors?

>> What is the likely impact on your sales and market share by a new competitor muscling their way onto your turf?

Still, you need to do the grunt work and score your organization for its breadth and depth of predictive analytics. Is it only the sales and marketing organizations that make widespread usage of these techniques, or do you find similarly eager adoption over in supply chain, human resources, and other organizations?

Finally, do you regularly turn your analytical power loose on gigantic piles of data with an open-ended mission of "go find interesting and important things that we need to know about"? How well does your organization do discovery analytics?

Grading your breadth of data usage

In parallel with studying and scoring your organization's analytics continuum, you also want to get a handle on the types of data that your organization uses for your analytics.

Almost certainly you use *structured data* — numbers, shorter character strings such as names and job titles, and dates — in your analytics. But do you also perform analytics on *semi-structured data,* such as tweets, blogs, and emails? What about *unstructured data,* such as videos, audio files, and images?

REMEMBER

Right now, you're not assessing and scoring your data architecture for those three classes of data. You have a separate track for data architecture and governance. At this point, you just want to determine if you even use semi-structured and unstructured data as part of your analytics. Sure, your organization captures and stores videos and images, but do you actually perform analytics, or do you just store the unstructured data as-is for anyone who wants to pull up an image or video file to take a look later on?

Writing data-driven prescriptions

Using analytics to produce tons of data-driven insights is fantastic. But does your organization drive those insights into data-driven decisions and then subsequent actions? Sometimes? All the time? Rarely?

No matter how robust your analytical tools and data architecture seem to be, your organization may suffer from "insight leakage" along the path from the data-driven insights to the actions that they are intended to steer. Your well-architected data lake can definitely help you address this problem, but first, you need to get a good idea of how prescriptive your current analytics are (or aren't).

As you survey different departments and their respective usage of analytics, take stock of how well they use data and analytics to drive both decisions and — even more important — actions. When you do find success stories, you should also document whether that insight-through-action chain is done in a "lights out" fully automated manner or in a semi-automated, semi-manual manner.

Receiving your final grades

Figure 17-4 shows a sample analytics scorecard that you might come up with after you've finished diving deep into your company's analytics.

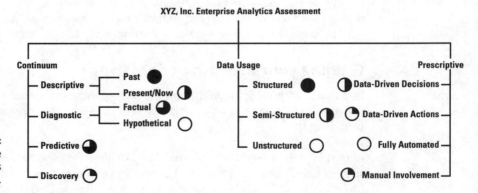

FIGURE 17-4: A sample analytics scorecard.

So, what does the scorecard tell you? First, the good news:

>> The solid Harvey balls for past-facing descriptive analytics using structured data tell you that your data warehouses and data marts are probably fairly mature (you'll find out on the data architecture portion of your assessment). At the very least, they're definitely well used.

>> The mostly filled Harvey ball for factual diagnostic analytics seconds the positive assessment of your data warehousing and business intelligence. Your users are able to drill down into reports and visualizations to see root causes at lower levels of granularity.

>> Another mostly filled Harvey ball for predictive analytics indicates that for well-defined use cases, your folks are able to build models and ask questions of the "tell us what is likely to happen" variety.

Now, the bad news:

>> *Discovery analytics* (turning your computing power loose on data with a somewhat open-ended mission) aren't very prevalent in your company.

>> Your organization does almost no analytics on unstructured data. You can have some really important insights buried in videos and images, but right now they aren't accessible, either on their own or as a follow-on step to accompany your structured data analysis.

>> When it comes to the all-important "last mile" of driving decisions and actions from your analytics, your folks are leaving a lot on the table. "Insight leakage" is prevalent throughout your organization.

It's still early in the game when it comes to preparing your data lake road map, but a couple of key points should jump out at you:

>> Whatever you do, you absolutely can't take any backward steps when it comes to your descriptive analytics using structured data that's mostly delivered through business intelligence tools on top of your data warehouses and data marts.

>> Your organization isn't totally out of the game with more advanced analytics — after all, you do a pretty good job with predictive analytics — but you definitely need to step up your game, and you'll need your data lake to play an important role.

>> The icing on your data lake cake (awkward metaphor alert!) is helping to drive those data-driven insights into downstream decisions and actions. You probably already knew this wasn't exactly a strength in your organization, but now you have this shortcoming painfully documented right there in front of everyone. As you plan, architect, and build your data lake, you definitely need to keep that "last mile" of data-driven decisions and subsequent actions at the forefront!

You also need to document the state of analytics for each major organization within your company, not just at the enterprise level. So, you'll prepare individual scorecards just like your enterprise-level one for finance, supply chain, marketing, sales, human resources, and other organizations.

REMEMBER

After you have your nice little collection of scorecards, you can identify the "hot spots" that are the most critical areas to fix as your data lake is built. If you use Harvey balls, look for the empty and almost-empty circles. If you use a numeric scale, find your 1s and 2s. With a green/yellow/red system, all your reds will jump out at you.

Diving deep into your data architecture and governance

Because your analytics don't materialize out of thin air, you also need to put on your scuba gear and dive deep into your data across your enterprise. You need to focus on both data architecture and data governance.

Just as with your enterprise analytics, your data architecture and governance decompose into key areas that you'll need to evaluate and score. Figure 17-5 shows the parallel paths that you'll take for architecture and governance and the areas within each.

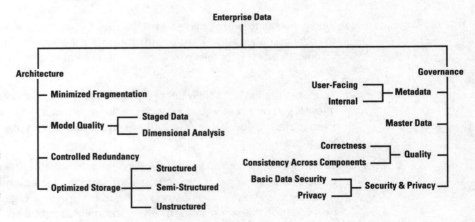

FIGURE 17-5:
Your data architecture and governance parallel paths.

Scoring your analytical data landscape

Take a good look around your data warehouses, data marts, big data environments, *spreadmarts* (your spreadsheets that have taken on an official mission of supporting Power BI, Tableau, or other analytical tools), and any other analytical data stores that you have. Now, score your analytical data landscape on the following evaluation criteria:

>> How fragmented is your analytical data? Do you have a centralized enterprise data warehouse (EDW) as the epicenter of your environment and only a few extraneous data marts here and there? Or, is your analytical data scattered all over the place in hundreds or even thousands of nonintegrated data marts?

>> Do your databases have some really first-rate data models? Or, on the other end of the spectrum, are your data models the database equivalent of holding together an old car with baling wire and chewing gum?

>> When you do have duplicated data across your data marts, do you have control over that redundancy through well-architected data interchange? Make sure you document if your data is proliferating wildly like something out of a horror movie and nobody can tell which version of any particular piece of data is the current and correct one.

>> Are you efficiently making use of your databases for your structured data? How about any big data environments or file systems for your semi-structured and unstructured data?

REMEMBER

Your current data environment will be replaced in part, or maybe even totally, by your new data lake. By understanding today's hot spots and problem areas, you can make extra-sure that your data lake addresses those issues.

Checking off the rules and regulations

Storing lots and lots of data is one thing. Building some pretty sweet data warehouses and data marts is another. But how well has your organization stayed on top of keeping all that data in smooth running order?

Data governance is every bit as important as data architecture. Of course, your data lake will be well governed. But what about today's data? As with your data architecture, identifying today's problem areas can help you laser-focus on specific aspects of data governance to address for your data lake.

Start tallying up your scores for the following:

>> **Metadata, both user-facing and internal:** Do your users have complete, up-to-date catalogs that steer them to the right data in the right place? Do the catalogs tell them what key pieces of data actually mean, along with any business rules that they need to be aware of? Beyond your users, do you have metadata that gives you critical statistics about your database performance or how much data was moved in each of your extract, transform, and load (ETL) feeds into your data warehouses and data marts?

>> **Master data that helps keep your most critical data subject areas in synch throughout your enterprise:** Does *customer* or *employee* or *product* mean the same in all your data warehouses and data marts? Can you easily pull together customer data from multiple places and merge it for combined analytics? Or do you have to jump through hoops to bring together all that customer data because of different data structures and different business rules?

>> **Data quality, in several contexts:** Have you washed away data errors coming from your source systems before you present data to users for analytics? Also, are multiple copies of the same data free of timing issues and other consistency-related problems across multiple data marts and other analytical data stores?

>> **Are your data warehouses and data marts secured, or did you essentially build a one-stop-shopping environment for hackers and intruders?** Are Social Security numbers, tax ID numbers, and other personally identifiable information protected? Does your analytical data fully adhere to policies and laws such as the Health Insurance Portability and Accountability Act (HIPAA)?

Tallying up the score

Ta-da! You've done the digging and the hard work and taken a good, long look at your current analytical data architecture and how well all that data is governed. Figure 17-6 shows your scorecard for your company's data architecture and governance that will accompany the one you built for your analytics.

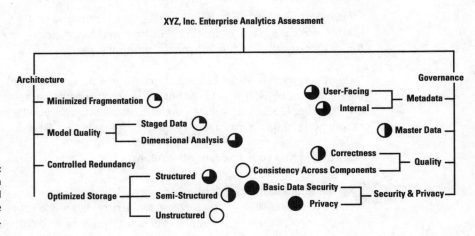

FIGURE 17-6:
A sample data architecture and governance scorecard.

What does this scorecard tell you? Again, you can start with the good news:

>> The mostly solid Harvey balls for your dimensional data model quality and the storage of your structured data tell you that your data warehouses and data marts are, for the most part, pretty solid.

>> Both your user-facing and internal metadata are pretty solid. Make sure that you maintain that level of data understanding as you build out your data lake!

>> You've done a great job at data security and data privacy. Good work!

Of course, you have some bad news:

>> Your data marts and data warehouses might be well structured, but you have way too many of them, as indicated by the low grade for minimizing fragmentation.

>> Curiously, even though your structured data for dimensional analysis is well organized and well managed, your staged data that is collected and then feeds your dimensional models (for example, your cubes and your star schemas) doesn't score very highly. Apparently, your staged data is far more fragmented and disorganized than it should be, and it's hindering your data pipelines from source systems through analytics. The silver lining, though, is that in your data lake, you can definitely bring technology such as Amazon Simple Storage Service (S3) or Microsoft Azure Data Lake Solution (ADLS) to the party to improve your data staging.

>> Your data quality is so-so. Basic data correctness can definitely be improved, as indicated by the half-filled Harvey ball. But you should be far more worried about the lowest possible score (the empty Harvey ball) for data consistency across your components. This ultra-low score means that not only do you have far too many data components (as you already identified), but also those data marts and data warehouses are all out of sync with each other and can't easily be brought together if needed. So, yeah, your data models in each of perhaps hundreds of data marts are pretty solid, but each data mart is an island to itself. Not good!

Putting Together a Lofty Vision

Now that you know the good, the bad, and the really bad about your current analytical data, you can start to paint the picture of a significantly better tomorrow.

You should use two techniques to build your lofty vision for your data lake:

>> Press releases

>> Day-in-the-life scenario diagrams

Hot off the presses, straight from the lake: Writing a press release

TIP

Quite possibly, you'll be building your data lake on the Amazon Web Services (AWS) platform. But even if you opt for Azure or some other platform, you can still take advantage of one of Amazon's secret weapons: the press release.

No, not the kind of press releases that Amazon issues to the public for quarterly earnings or other significant business milestones. Amazon uses press releases as a critical weapon in the early stages of its internal products or, on the AWS side of Amazon's business, for client consulting engagements.

Amazon's philosophy is that a good project or product should "work backward" and begin with a customer's view of a particular end state — for example, a well-built and fully deployed data lake — and then carry that vision backward into the nuts and bolts of how to realize that vision.

One of your first activities is to write an actual press release that peeks into the future and powerfully describes the business value that will be delivered at the completion of your data lake initiative. Think of the press release exercise this way: You do a little bit of time traveling, check out the superb work that you and your team did, and then shout out to the world how fantastic your data lake is. And then, for your grand finale, you send that press release back in time to the present day, to help sell your data lake and get everybody on board!

You can vary the format of your press release as you see fit, but in general, your press release should

>> Have a straightforward title that shouts, "Success!"

>> Be set in the future — not necessarily immediately after your data lake goes live, but a little bit later, when your data lake is being widely used and delivering significant business value.

>> Avoid future tense (such as "The data lake will enable supply chain users to . . ."). Instead, describe the data lake as a fait accompli.

- » Begin the narrative with a sweeping, powerful summary of your data lake that can stand on its own if someone didn't read past the first paragraph.

- » Describe what problems your company has today and how the data lake solved them.

- » Throw in a quote or two as you would find in a real press release.

- » End with some sort of grand finale.

Here's a press release example that you can leverage for your own initiative:

XYZ, Inc. Enters New Era of High-Value Analytics With State-of-the-Art Data Lake

XYZ, Inc., an industry-leading global specialty goods retailer, announced today that its recently constructed enterprise data lake has taken the company into a new era of delivering data-driven insights to make critical business decisions and take actions. XYZ's data lake provides infinitely scalable, logically centralized, and tightly integrated management for all forms of data. XYZ users in finance, supply chain, human resources, and other organizations now have one-stop shopping for critical business data, including images, videos, and audio files. XYZ has deployed a new generation of analytical tools to take advantage of the data lake and provide executives, mid-tier managers, and line employees with broad, unprecedented levels of data-driven insights into every aspect of their day-to-day jobs, as well as special situations that require sophisticated data and analytical support.

"We've always had sophisticated, cutting-edge analytics for our online business," XYZ CEO Robert R. Roberts noted. "But our physical stores have always lagged behind due to numerous aging data marts and other environments that were still in place. These data marts didn't talk to one another, which meant that, far too often, we didn't have the 360-degree view of critical areas of our business that we needed to make data-driven decisions and then take action."

The data lake provides "packages" of integrated data to users for well-defined, predictable needs. "We need to carefully analyze traffic flow and customer activity in our stores," Mr. Roberts continued. "In the past, even though we had surveillance cameras throughout our stores, our analysts can only call up entire video streams and watch them, end to end, trying to spot activity or patterns of interest. The sheer volume of video we stored made it impossible for our analysts to do anything other than spot checks. Now, all video surveillance is first preprocessed through an intelligence engine. The data lake tags a video with supplemental information such as who individual customers are, as identified through facial recognition. Any important and interesting activities are highlighted and proactively pointed to our analysts."

Mr. Roberts gave an example. "Suppose that a customer spends a little bit of time in one department and picks up a few items but doesn't purchase any of them.

The customer leaves and goes to another department but returns to that first department ten minutes later, picks up those same items again and appears to be interested. Still, the customer doesn't make a purchase. We can theorize that the customer is interested in those items, but something is holding her back. Maybe it's the price, in which case we can email or text the customer a coupon for 15 percent off those particular items that we think she's interested in."

Roberts continued, "We're piloting a program where we have artificial intelligence do video analysis and decision-making in real time, without human intervention. Now a coupon can be texted to the customer while she's still in the store and ideally still in the department. We've been running this pilot for two months, and already we've seen 21 percent of targeted customers purchase one or more of the couponed items on the spot."

Before XYZ deployed its data lake, analytics were primarily used to determine what happened in the past. Now, not only are integrated analytics being used for predictions and forecasts, but the analytics are also being used in an actionable manner, to definitively drive decisions and actions.

"Our new data lake is one of the best technology investments XYZ, Inc. has ever made," Robert R. Roberts proclaimed. "From this point forward, we're in an entirely new era of analytics leading us to new heights in data-driven decisions and actions."

TIP

Make sure that your press release hits a good many of those hot-spot problem areas that you identified during your assessment. Convince everyone who reads your press release that your data lake is the answer to their data and analytics headaches.

Designing a slick sales brochure

You know what they say: "The devil's in the details." They also say, "A picture's worth a thousand words." Whoever "they" actually are, "they" are right!

Your press release is a great start to painting the picture of a lofty vision for your data lake. You need to go a step farther and, well, actually paint a picture! Actually, you need to paint a *lot* of pictures.

Figure 17-7 shows a comparative day in the life for Helen, a claims analyst at an insurance company. Let's assume that Helen is responsible for first-level processing of auto and property insurance claims. Today, when Helen receives a new claim, she needs to access the following:

>> The primary customer information database that contains all the structured data about a customer — biographic and demographic, claims history, policy payment history, and so on

>> A separate vehicle master database

>> A master database of industry standard repair costs for both vehicles and buildings

>> A repository of videos that customers take themselves that document damages, as well as videos taken by the company's claims adjusters and third-party claims adjusters

>> A different repository filled with still images, also of damages and also taken by both customers and adjusters

>> Yet another repository that stores the audio files from all "tell us what happened" telephone interviews with customers

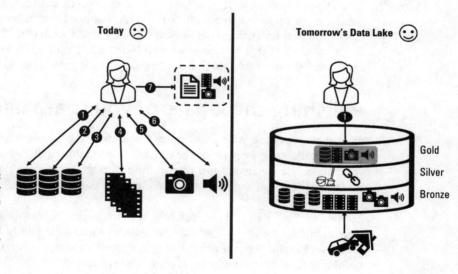

FIGURE 17-7: Analyzing every scrap of data about an insurance customer: today versus tomorrow.

Helen needs to access six different databases and repositories to find the information she needs. Then she needs to juggle all those results on her computer or iPad, because she doesn't have a single portal that takes her into all those databases.

After the data lake is built, though, Helen's life — at least at work — gets a whole lot better. She no longer has to make six different requests to various databases and repositories; the data lake does the hard work for Helen, bringing all the raw information into its bronze zone. The silver zone does the data cleansing and integration and prepares "packages" of consolidated information about a customer's claim that are popped into the gold zone.

Best of all, that package of integrated data about a new claim is waiting for Helen without her having to specifically request it. Why? Because when the incident is reported to the insurance company's claims system, the claims system automatically triggers the data lake to begin building the package of data that will be relevant to that claim.

You need to build dozens of these comparative day-in-the-life drawings to show the difference between today's pre–data lake world and what will be possible after your data lake is built and deployed. Because your data lake is an enterprise-wide endeavor, make sure that you include compelling scenarios from every corner of your company — finance, human resources, sales, marketing, customer support, and so on.

REMEMBER

Just as with your press release, your day-in-the-life scenarios need to address the hot-spot shortcomings that you identified when you graded today's analytics and data at your company. If your usage of unstructured data for analytics scored poorly, come up with some really strong, high-impact scenarios where unstructured data plays a critical role in some department's analytics. If today's data is fragmented all over the place — as with Helen's in Figure 17-7 — then definitely emphasize the one-stop shopping of the data lake's gold zone.

Polishing the lenses of your data lake vision

After you've written your press release and created a couple dozen day-in-the-life diagrams, take a pause for the cause. Lay everything out in front of you. Read your press release again, and then thumb through your collection of diagrams, paying particular attention to the "Tomorrow's Data Lake" side.

Are you excited? Can you see clearly how much better your work life will be after your data lake comes to life? Do you feel the same as if you're driving to your favorite lake, and you make that last turn around a mountain bend, and there it is, unfolding right in front of you, as far as the eye can see?

WARNING

If you don't have a warm, fuzzy feeling about your data lake after spending some time with your press release and your diagrams, something is wrong! Maybe you don't really have a compelling business case to invest lots of time and money in a data lake.

Hopefully, that's not the case. Odds are, if your press release and portfolio of day-in-the-life diagrams just aren't doing it for you, then you need to go back to the drawing board and take a fresh look at what your data lake will do. Preview what you have with even more people around your company than you've done so far. Go back to people you've already interviewed and really try to pull out some compelling scenarios from them that are directly tied to your data lake.

When you're ready, you can move ahead to the architecture phase to start specifying what you're going to build. But until you know for certain how your data lake is going to be used, keep cycling through the vision-related activities.

Building Your Data Lake Architecture

Your lofty vision is a business-focused, high-level portrait of your data lake. You can't implement a lofty vision, though. After you've solidified that vision, you need to start filling in the blanks through two key deliverables:

>> Your conceptual architecture

>> Your implementation architecture

Conceptual architecture

You start working on your conceptual architecture by surveying the reference architectures available to you (see Chapter 4) and finding one or more that appear to fit the particulars of your organization.

Suppose that your company built and deployed a state-of-the-art data warehouse two years ago. At all levels of your company and throughout organizations (such as finance, marketing, supply chain, and sales) users absolutely love the data warehouse. Thousands of employees are clicking away with Power BI or Tableau to access the data warehouse's contents and help drive their decisions and actions. The data warehouse has been an absolute success!

Guess what? Your data warehouse isn't going anywhere, or at least it *shouldn't* be going anywhere. Maybe over time, some of your data warehousing capabilities will migrate into the data lake, but for now, they should remain in place.

REMEMBER

Your conceptual architecture needs to be grounded in the reality of your organization.

Figure 17-8 shows one of the conceptual architectures that preserves the critical role of your relatively new data warehouse. Notice how your new data lake and your existing data warehouse act as peers to one another. Each has its own set of data feeds from relevant source applications, with each data feed designed to meet specific analytical needs.

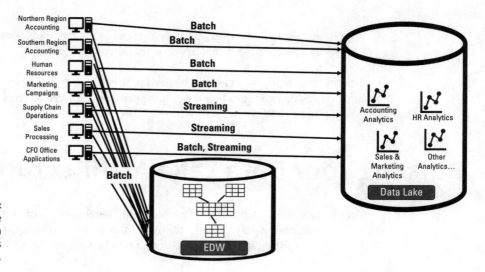

FIGURE 17-8:
Your data lake and data warehouse as peers.

For your data lake, accounting and human resources data, along with some of the application data from your chief financial officer (CFO), makes its way into the data lake in batches because of the relatively slower pace of these types of analytics. Supply chain data, sales data, and some of your CFO data is useful for lower-latency analytics and is streamed into the bronze zone (raw zone) of your data lake.

Some, or even much, of the same data is already making its way into your EDW, and it will continue to do so. Essentially, you've implemented a split-feed architecture, where the data lake and data warehouse will continue to serve as peers to each other.

Alternatively, you may decide to have your existing batch feeds into your EDW do double-duty. Figure 17-9 shows an alternative split-feed architecture where the batch data coming into your EDW's staging area continues on to the data lake, replacing most of the separate batch feeds into the data lake that are depicted in Figure 17-8. If you find any data in your accounting, human resources, or other applications that aren't being fed into your EDW but that may be of value in your data lake, you can still send that data directly into the data lake. The dashed lines in Figure 17-9 show the possible supplemental data feeds into the data lake to augment those coming via the data warehouse.

What will come into the data lake directly from your source applications? Any data that should be streamed and isn't already flowing in a real-time or near-real-time manner into your EDW.

You have complete control over your conceptual architecture. Sit down with your fellow data lake architects and planners and brainstorm the scenarios that will help you choose which of the two alternatives shown in Figures 17-8 and 17-9 (or perhaps some other alternative) makes the most sense for retaining your data warehouse.

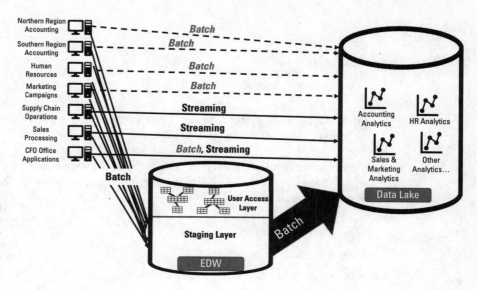

FIGURE 17-9:
Your data warehouse feeding certain data into your data lake.

On the other hand, your existing data warehouses and data marts may have scored very low during your assessment activities. Consequently, you have no desire to maintain any of them. Check out your reference architecture portfolio and see which one or more seem to fit your particular organization's landscape.

Implementation architecture

You build on your lofty vision through your conceptual architecture, but you're still not done with your architecture work. Sooner or later, that conceptual picture of your data lake needs to be translated into specific products and services.

TECHNICAL STUFF

Suppose your company has gone all-in on AWS. Unless you come up with a powerful, compelling reason that your data lake shouldn't be built in AWS, guess what? Your data lake will be built in AWS! That means that your AWS-based implementation architecture will feature some or many of the following components and services:

- » S3
- » Amazon Redshift and/or Redshift Spectrum
- » AWS Lake Formation
- » AWS Glue
- » Amazon Kinesis
- » AWS Lambda

>> Amazon EMR

>> Amazon Aurora

>> Amazon DynamoDB

And maybe even more! Chapter 12 describes these services and how they fit together into an AWS-based data lake.

On the other hand, suppose your company has embraced the Azure platform for its cloud-based applications. In that case, your implementation architecture will include some or all of the following:

>> Azure Data Factory

>> Azure Data Lake Storage (ADLS)

>> Azure Databricks

>> Azure SQL Data Warehouse

Chapter 13 takes you through the world of Azure data lakes.

Beyond the worlds of AWS and Azure, you may decide you'll be pouring water — make that data — into your data lake through open-source services or through services and products from smaller vendors (or maybe even a combination of both). Whatever you decide, your implementation architecture is the final stop as you turn your data lake vision into a blueprint to guide your buildout (see Figure 17-10).

FIGURE 17-10:
Progressively turning your data lake vision into a solid blueprint.

Deciding on Your Kickoff Activities

Many years ago, the old-time comedy team of Abbott and Costello did a famous routine called "Who's on First?" When it comes to your data lake, you need to ask and answer a similar question: "What's first?"

Your data lake is an enterprise-scale undertaking, which means that you'll be iteratively and incrementally building out your data lake over several years, in formally defined phases. But where should you start?

TIP

Take a look back at your press release (see "Hot off the presses, straight from the lake: Writing a press release," earlier in this chapter). What were the two or three hard-hitting data lake capabilities that you included to describe how wonderful your data lake turned out? Start there, and see if those capabilities are ones that should be first out of the gate.

Your kickoff phase can be as short as four to six weeks, or you can conceivably be working on that first release of your data lake for three or four months. The amount of time you spend isn't the most important factor in deciding where you want to begin — though you do want to choose capabilities that won't take you too long (say, six months or even longer) to complete.

TIP

Because your data lake is an enterprise-scale endeavor, your kickoff release should include capabilities from different organizations to emphasize the breadth of the data lake. Maybe you decide to bring in data to deliver one set of predictive analytics related to sales and also bring in other data that will deliver discovery analytics for your supply chain folks. You probably don't want to go with more than two areas for this kickoff release; you want to hit a home run on this first go-round and then build from those successes.

You also should combine streaming and batch data feeds into the data lake for this first set of deliverables. Your data lake will be ingesting data using both of these paradigms, so you want to demonstrate as early as possible the power of data lakes and how they differ from the data warehouses and data marts that your users are probably most familiar with.

Also, make sure that you check back with the current-state assessment that you did for your organization's data and analytics. Try to address at least three or four current-state hot spots with your kickoff deliverables. If you're doing little or nothing with analytics on semi-structured or unstructured data, then maybe you want to ingest tweets, videos, and images and do some really cool analysis on that content. If your current user-facing metadata is totally lacking, then accompany your analytics with head-turning cataloging to help users navigate your data lake. Sell the improvements!

WARNING

Your kickoff release shouldn't be a throwaway prototype! You need to prove not only the business value of your data lake through the analytics that you deliver, but also the architectural viability of your architecture. You're not mocking up pretend sets of data or mimicking streaming data ingestion via behind-the-scenes tricks or anything along those lines. True, you're continuing your data lake sales pitch to your organization's business users and executives. But you also need to see if the implementation architecture that you've come up with, and the products and services that you've selected, are truly what you expect them to be.

You'll likely wind up tweaking your architecture as you work through this initial set of data lake activities. Don't panic! If you've selected a particular streaming model that doesn't work the way you thought it would or how a vendor promised it would, then you want to find out early enough to make changes before you move ahead and continue with your data lake buildout.

Expanding Your Data Lake

Even before you start your kickoff activities, you should have a rough idea of what will come next. Figure 17-11 illustrates an example seven-phase, 27-month data lake road map.

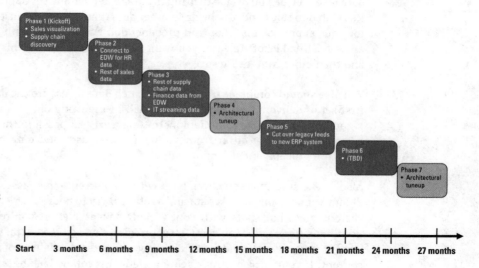

FIGURE 17-11: A multiphase, multiyear, high-level data lake road map.

You should note several key points about the example road map shown in Figure 17-11:

>> You need to have a high-level, single-picture view of your road map that will fit onto one slide or on a single page in a document. However, you definitely need to flesh out what you'll be doing in each of those phases. For example:

- What analytics will now be produced from newly ingested data?

- What sources will your data be coming from?

- What hot-spot current problems with your analytics and data are you solving in each phase?

- What day-in-the-life scenarios are you bringing to life with each phase's deliverables?

- What are your contingencies and fallbacks at each phase?

- What dependencies do you have?

- What risks do you face in each phase, and how will you mitigate them?

>> At approximately the 12-month point, after you've successfully completed three or four phases, you need to take a "pause for the cause" and do an "architectural tune-up" of your data lake. For two or three months, you won't bring in any new data or be adding any new functionality to your data lake. Instead, you'll do a deep dive on how well the data lake has been working (or not) during your first three phases. If you need to optimize your data flows or change around database tables or other storage, now is the time to do so, before moving ahead.

>> After your first architectural tune-up, you'll do another one every 12 to 15 months.

>> If your organization has other major systems initiatives underway or planned, they'll figure into your data lake road map. Notice that in Phase 5, you'll be cutting over existing data feeds from your legacy systems to those coming from an ERP implementation that is currently underway.

>> Notice how Phase 6 in your road map is labeled "TBD" for now. You may have an idea of exactly what you'll be doing at every phase for the next two or three years. Or, the view across the data lake may get foggier the farther out you look. (Now that's a perfect metaphor!) You may know right now that you'll be doing "something" at the two-year point, but you just don't know what exactly that "something" is right now. You can leave a placeholder because you'll constantly be updating your road map as time passes.

You definitely need to preview your road map with key stakeholders before you unveil it to the world, or at least to your executive leadership. Adjust the road map as necessary, and add any details that you may have overlooked. And then, you're on your way!

Chapter **18**

Booking Future Trips to the Data Lake

You need to have an eye toward the future, even as you juggle architectural patterns, enabling technologies, and everything else that goes into building your data lake. So, what's waiting over the horizon? You should take note of what's going on in the world of:

>> Data platforms

>> Artificial intelligence (AI)

>> Enhanced data governance

In this chapter, I let you know what to expect with data lakes in the future.

Searching for the All-in-One Data Lake

Suppose that your favorite lake resort has been in business for 20 years. During that entire stretch of time, the owners of the resort only allowed swimming and speedboats on the lake, with different sections set aside for each.

Now, the owners decide to start offering fishing, canoeing, waterskiing, and other activities to broaden their resort's offerings. So, what do they do? They buy 50 acres of land on the other side of the highway from the lake. They bring in the backhoes, bulldozers, and other heavy equipment and start digging and building. Then they construct an underground pipeline from the existing lake to this new giant hole in the ground. The water starts flowing from the existing lake into what will become the new one.

Soon enough, their second lake is filled up and in business. Next summer, when you go to the lake, you have some decisions to make. If you want to swim or zip around in your speedboat, you go to the original lake. If you decide that this summer you want to bring a canoe instead of your speedboat and also do a little fishing, you head to the new lake.

But what if you want to go swimming *and* do some fishing? You'll have to go back and forth across the highway, from one lake to the other. You'll swim in the original lake, and then go fishing in the new one. Back and forth, back and forth.

Sounds sort of silly, right? Why can't the resort owners just divide up their original lake into a bunch of different sections, each dedicated to a different sport or activity?

Your organization's operational systems and your data lake are sort of like the resort's two lakes. Your online and in-store applications, HR systems, supply chain management applications, systems for accounting and finance, and lots of other functions will all use relational databases or other data stores that are designed and optimized for transactional processing. You can certainly do simple querying and some light reporting against those transactional databases without adversely impacting database performance for your mission-critical applications. But if you try to run complex queries or sophisticated machine learning algorithms against extremely large volumes of data, you'll almost certainly slow down your overall database performance for your important applications and their transaction processing.

Ever since the earliest days of data warehousing in the late '80s and early '90s, you've had to copy data from your transactional databases into separate databases for your business intelligence functionality and complex analytics. At first, many technologists reacted to the idea of copying data from one group of databases into one or more others the same way you would react to building a brand-new lake just to allow fishing and canoeing: What a silly idea!

For years, the convergence of transactional and analytical data platforms has been one of the holy grails of enterprise data management, especially as big data technology began to take over from relational databases for complex analytics. "Big data is extremely powerful," the thinking went, "so, maybe we can take a fresh look at unifying transactional and analytical data platforms."

TECHNICAL STUFF

Alas, core big data technology lacks the *transaction semantics* necessary for a data environment to serve as an operational database. Think of how a data lake operates. Whether you're streaming or batch-loading data into your data lake, the data essentially becomes read-only after it's copied into your target data lake. If you need to update an employee's job status, or correct a sales transaction or update product specifications, you don't make any of those changes directly in the data lake. Instead, you make those changes back in your source applications, and then the changes — along with new data — flow into your data lake as copies of the original transaction data.

Wouldn't it be great if, once and for all time, you can stop copying data into data warehouses and data lakes for your analytical needs? Might the underlying data platforms for a data lake expand to be able to handle high-volume, high-throughput transactional applications, as well as complex analytics, all in a single environment? Figure 18-1 shows the difference between today's reality and tomorrow's promise.

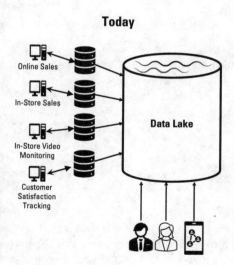
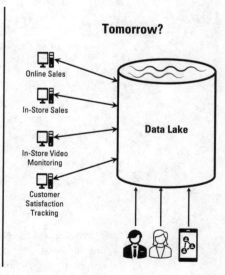

FIGURE 18-1:
Your data lake doing double-duty for transactional and analytical processing.

TECHNICAL STUFF

You can find some data services and products today that do support transaction semantics against an analytical data store. Delta Lake is an open-source storage environment that supports ACID (see the nearby sidebar) transactions to big data and Apache Spark workloads (see `https://delta.io`). Splice Machines (`https://splicemachine.com`) also combines online transaction processing (OLTP), online analytical processing (OLAP), and machine learning in a single platform.

TIP

As you build out your data lake, you should certainly experiment with transaction processing on top of data lake contents. Start small, with non-mission-critical applications. Maybe you decide to move a department-scale application to run on top of data lake content. Now, new data is written directly into your data lake, and updates occur directly in the data lake. If you have success, you expand into new applications. Remember that technology will continue to mature, and you can stay in lockstep with those changes.

Perhaps at some point, you'll have a single data lake infrastructure that fully and truly supports *all* your data management needs in a single platform. Product vendors large and small are certainly doing their best to turn your dream into a reality. So, keep watching!

ACID EATS AWAY AT YOUR DATA CHALLENGES

Back in the earliest days of relational databases, computer scientists needed to clearly delineate "real" relational databases from more simplistic sort-of-relational databases that were better suited for single-user personal applications. Those brainy computer scientists came up with the ACID properties. ACID properties have since transcended the world of relational databases and apply to data management in general. Here's what ACID stands for:

- **Atomicity:** Atomicity guarantees that any transaction against a database either fully succeeds or is determined to have failed and then fully rolled back. In other words, your database won't be corrupted by a transaction blowing up in the middle of a sequence of steps.

- **Consistency:** Consistency guarantees a higher level of correctness than simple atomicity. For example, if you're transferring money from one bank account to another, at the conclusion of the transaction the exact amount of money drawn out of one account is now included in the second account. The transaction begins with some form of a valid state and ends with another valid state.

- **Isolation:** Isolation means that even if you have hundreds or thousands of users concurrently reading from and writing to a given set of data — such as a relational database table — the end result will be as if those transactions all occurred sequentially rather than simultaneously.

- **Durability:** Durability ensures that after a transaction has completed and been *committed* into your database, the results of that transaction remain in effect even if a system later crashes or someone accidentally pulls a power plug from the wall.

As you consider whether to try to expand your data lake of the future into handling transactions, you'll be evaluating your data platform for its support of ACID properties along with overall query response time; data transfer times for extract, transform, load (ETL) or extract, load, transform (ELT); and so on.

Spreading Artificial Intelligence Smarts throughout Your Data Lake

Your data lake will serve up data for the most sophisticated and advanced analytics that you can come up with, including applications and systems that make use of AI techniques and technology. But what if you can pull some of that AI smart stuff back into the data lake itself?

Keep an eye on several areas where AI can really help you out:

>> Data lineage and cataloging

>> Explainable analytics

>> Building an analytics clearinghouse

Lining up your data

Data, data, everywhere! How can you possibly keep track of all the copies and permutations of every piece of data scattered across your data lake? You have tons of data in your bronze zone. Much of that data has cleaned-up versions sitting in your silver zone. And then you build numerous packages of data in your gold zone that will inevitably include much of the same data across multiple packages. And don't forget about your sandbox!

You use your data lake metadata to help you keep track of *data lineage* throughout your data lake. Where does some piece of data first come into your data lake?

Where does it go next? And next? What cleansing and transformation rules are applied at each stage? How many variants of some piece of data exist at any given point in time across your data lake components? Talk about a mind-numbing, tedious effort!

Vendors such as Informatica are applying AI to the data lineage problem. Informatica helps you build a "catalog of catalogs" that not only serves as a master inventory list, but also uses AI to help discover relationships among your data that would otherwise need to be traced manually.

Informatica and other vendors will continue to enhance their AI capabilities for data lineage. Even if your data lake is pretty far down the path and you've let data lineage slip as you've wrestled with other challenges, you can turn an AI-enabled data lineage engine loose on your data lake and let the AI do the heavy lifting.

Shining a light into your analytics innards

The answer is "5." Or the answer is "No." Or the answer is "Don't hesitate! Act now!"

Your data lake will support your organization's entire analytics continuum, from rudimentary descriptive analytics to the most sophisticated machine learning and AI. Users all over your enterprise will receive answers to questions they ask, as well as other insights that are "pushed" to them, even if they don't necessarily ask a particular analytical question.

But what does some answer or insight actually mean? Where did that number or decision or results set come from? How was a number calculated?

And most important of all: Can you really trust what you're being told or shown?

The concept of "lineage" doesn't apply only to data itself, as described in the preceding section. Beyond the fundamental data management mission of your data lake, you want to shine a light on how the data is used in analytical models of varying sophistication. In other words, you're after *explainable analytics*.

Over time, analytics will be equipped with increased lineage, tracing some end result all the way back to the original data and all the manipulation and calculation along the way — in the *analytics* side, not just in the data management side.

Because you're a good soldier in your organization, you're intensely interested in not only how you build your data lake, but also how your data lake will be used. After all, you began your data lake road map by "working backward," writing a hard-hitting press release and building numerous day-in-the-life diagrams to highlight how your data lake would be used. The last thing you want is for users to receive key data-driven insights but then hesitate or even freeze because they don't fully understand the ins and outs behind those insights.

Keep an eye out for emerging capabilities to equip the user-facing side of your data lake with an underlying "explanation engine" that will increase users' confidence in the insights they're being sent.

Playing traffic cop

After your data lake is steaming along at full speed, you'll be producing thousands, or even tens of thousands, of data-driven insights each day. Many of those insights will be explicitly requested by users in the form of Tableau or Power BI reports and visualizations, or as a result of analytical models that they build to satisfy well-known predictive needs.

REMEMBER

Beyond satisfying known analytics requirements, your data lake also needs to support *discovery analytics.* You'll be turning your sophisticated analytics loose on mountains of data with a somewhat open-ended mission of "go forth and find interesting and important patterns and insights out of all this data."

But after those interesting and important patterns and insights are produced, who should be alerted? Also, what about insights produced by one organization that will be of intense interest to someone in another organization? Who — or what — is responsible for routing those golden nuggets of wisdom to the place where they can be put to use?

Suppose you have a machine learning model dedicated to ferreting out important tidbits of information about your customers in each of your sales territories. Your account managers can use these insights as part of developing their account plans and sales strategies. Typical analytics, right?

But suppose that the machine learning model discovers something of importance about your latest line of products. Your product management and product marketing teams need to be alerted. However, you have no guarantee that a given account manager, or that person's boss, or anyone else in the sales organization will route the critical information over to the product team. Even if someone isn't being territorial or malicious, people have a tendency to focus primarily on findings of particular interest to them, and everything else is secondary.

You want your data lake to fight the problem of *insight leakage.* Your data lake can produce as many insights daily as you have fish swimming in your favorite lake. But if many of them fall through the cracks and don't reach those people who should be acting on those insights, you have a "tree falling in the forest next to the lake but everybody is on the lake partying so they don't hear it fall, so did it really fall?" problem.

You can use AI to build an *insights and analytics clearinghouse* as part of your overall data lake environment. Figure 18-2 shows how your clearinghouse can play "traffic cop" to:

>> Determine the nature of a particular data-driven insight

>> Decide which organization and which individuals within that organization need to be aware of what has been discovered

>> Route the insight along with supporting information to one or more people

>> Ensure that the insight is actually addressed and doesn't fall through the cracks

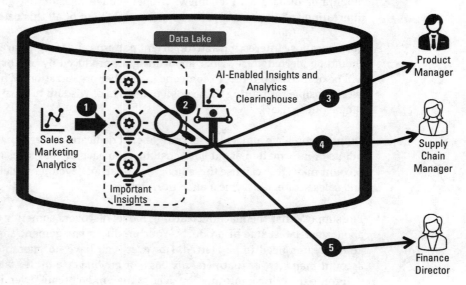

FIGURE 18-2: Equipping your data lake with an AI-enabled insights and analytics clearinghouse.

6

The Part of Tens

Chapter **19**

Top Ten Reasons to Invest in Building a Data Lake

O kay, you're convinced that your company or governmental agency absolutely, positively needs a data lake. How do you sell the idea to others in your organization?

You'll most likely need to build a financially oriented business case. But beyond the dollars and cents, you'll need to be well armed with a portfolio of solid, concise arguments to help convince the head honchos in your organization that they definitely need to pile into the car and take a trip to the data lake.

Supporting the Entire Analytics Continuum

Your organization probably has a few data warehouses and more than a few data marts in use. You'll probably be challenged with something along the lines of "Why do we also need a data lake?" or "Can't we just expand our enterprise data warehouse?"

Classic data warehouses and data marts are best suited to provide data-driven insights that fit the "tell me what happened" or "tell me what is happening" mold. They deal in cold, hard facts. Data lakes, on the other hand, broaden the flavors of data-driven insights into "tell me what is likely to happen" and "tell me something interesting and important from all of this data, without having to ask specific questions."

If you need more formal, techie-type names for these points along the analytics continuum, a data lake will provide not only descriptive analytics (as a data warehouse or data mart typically does) but also predictive analytics, diagnostic analytics, exploratory or discovery analytics, and prescriptive analytics.

In other words, your organization can finally achieve that elusive one-stop-shopping environment for all your analytical needs, rather than having those different classes of data-driven insights provided by many different noninte-grated components scattered around your enterprise.

Bringing Order to Your Analytical Data throughout Your Enterprise

If your organization has many different data warehouses and data marts scattered throughout your enterprise, you almost certainly have been dealing with uncon-trolled data duplication, conflicting definitions and business rules, and all the rest of the typical data chaos.

A well-architected, smartly built data lake helps you finally bring order to that chaos. Key data governance disciplines such as master data management, data quality management, and user metadata can finally be addressed in a holistic manner, rather than via a scattershot approach across numerous different components.

Retiring Aging Data Marts

As you head down the path toward a complete analytics continuum and addressing your data chaos, you can finally retire some of those aging standalone data marts. True, they've provided data-driven insights over the years, but they're expensive to maintain, and each one addresses only scattered pieces of your overall analytical needs. Most of those aging data marts are likely run out of your on-premises data center, and you've been itching to get out from under those legacy costs and move your analytical data management to the cloud, which is where you'll build your data lake.

As you steadfastly row toward your organization's analytics future along the data lake, you can toss out some of the baggage that's been weighing down your boat and slowing your overall journey. (How's that for a visual?)

Bringing Unfulfilled Analytics Ideas out of Dry Dock

Over the years, you've likely embarked on a number of analytics-oriented initiatives that began with lofty goals for the data-driven insights they were intended to deliver. If your organization is like most others, many of those analytical efforts wound up being scaled back during their development, even as they were successfully delivered.

Maybe you ran into data capacity limits. Perhaps you weren't able to capture and ingest data as quickly as you needed for the types of analytics you wanted to perform. Maybe you needed more computing power attached to your data than your data center servers were able to provide.

Guess what? The future has arrived, thanks to your data lake. It's time to take those unfulfilled analytics dreams out of dry dock and try to launch them once again. Chances are, the power and capacity of your data lake will help you finally set sail.

Laying a Foundation for Future Analytics

Imagine that one winter, your favorite lake somewhere up north freezes over and then gets a few inches of snow. You smash together a snowball and start it rolling along the lake. As the snowball rolls forward, it picks up additional snow along the way. If that snowball can somehow continue rolling for the entire length of the lake, it would be one giant ball of snow by the time it reaches the other side!

Enterprise analytics are much the same as that perpetual-motion snowball, rolling along and getting bigger and bigger during its journey. Analytical successes in one part of your overall company or governmental agency have a tendency to snowball into other parts of your organization. Before you know it, your overall organization has embraced analytics to an extent nobody would've thought possible!

By building and deploying a well-architected data lake, you can set your analytical snowballs in motion and reap the rewards.

Providing a Region for Experimentation

Imagine that you're out on your favorite lake, rowing or sailing or motoring your way along the water. Suddenly, off to your right, you see a side stream that you've never before noticed, heading into a notch in the cliffs. You turn your boat and head in that direction, intent on discovering exactly what's out there. You never know — maybe you'll find some long-lost pirate treasure!

Exploring new places can be a blast! The great news is that your data lake's sandbox will be there for you to explore over and over and over. It's like going out on your favorite lake and, almost every time, embarking on a new adventure, never knowing what you'll discover!

Improving Your Master Data Efforts

Tired of having a dozen different meanings and sets of business rules for what a *new customer* is? Maybe another dozen different — and conflicting — meanings for *active product* or *full-time employee* or *vendor in good standing*?

Master data management (MDM) is still a challenging proposition with a data lake, just as it has always been. But by consolidating your enterprise's analytical data into a single logical environment, you're off to a better start than trying to implement MDM across multiple independent data warehouses and data marts.

Opening Up New Business Possibilities

Your organization's new data lake isn't just for the techies. By consolidating trillions or even quadrillions of pieces of data and then triggering a new era of analytics and data-driven insights, you also open up new possibilities on the business side.

New products, new service lines, new markets . . . all can be thoroughly analyzed to a greater extent than with your legacy data warehouses, data marts, and business intelligence capabilities.

Keeping Up with the Competition

Even if you're a bit nervous about the journey from classic data warehousing to modern data lakes, guess what? Your competition is already on the road!

Think about the late adapters for personal computers and distributed computing in the 1980s, the Internet and e-commerce in the 1990s, mobile technology in the early 2000s, or social media in the 2010s. If you're late to the party, you're at a distinct disadvantage. So, in a way, you really have no choice other than to get your organization's fleet of boats out on the data lake. Even if you're not going to lead the boat parade, you absolutely don't want to be standing on the shore, watching all the boats go by and feeling left behind.

Getting Your Organization Ready for the Next Big Thing

Speaking of personal computers, e-commerce, mobile technology, and social media, the "next big things" in technology and business have a way of blowing up (in a good way) very quickly. The early adapters may make a few mistakes as they're blazing these new trails, but if they adjust quickly enough, they can reap the spoils of embracing these new technologies and the business opportunities that they provide.

By no means will data lakes be the last "next big thing." The tricky part of trying to play fortune-teller and predict the future of technology and business is that these mega-sized movements require bold thinking and action. A side benefit of embracing the data lake concept and then building and deploying a well-architected environment for your organization is that you can gain confidence from what you've accomplished. Then, when the "next big thing" — whatever it is — comes along, your organization can react quickly and charge forward.

Chapter **20**

Ten Places to Get Help for Your Data Lake

You don't need to go it alone! The constantly evolving nature of the entire world of data lakes means that you really need to stay up to date with the latest products and services, best practices, and (on the other side of the coin) incoming storms that can turn a beautiful afternoon at the data lake into new adventures in seasickness.

Fortunately, you have plenty of places to seek out help.

Cloud Provider Professional Services

If your data lake is built on Amazon Web Services (AWS) or Microsoft Azure, expert help in either of those platforms is right at your fingertips. Reach out to Amazon (https://aws.amazon.com/professional-services) or Microsoft (www.microsoft.com/en-us/professionalservices/overview) — or any other cloud service provider (CSP) you may be using — to get answers to the most puzzling questions or to make sure you're on top of the best practices for that platform.

Major Systems Integrators

The same big guys that have dominated enterprise-scale systems for a long time are all splashing around the data lake. Accenture (www.accenture.com/us-en), Deloitte (www2.deloitte.com/us/en.html), and IBM Services (www.ibm.com/services) are a few of the big-time systems integrators who can help you with your data lake. Maybe you need strategy and architecture work done, or perhaps you've already done the upfront work and need arms and legs to help build out the data lake. Either way, the big guys are an option.

Smaller Systems Integrators

You'll find hundreds of smaller-scale systems integrators who do data lake work. You definitely need to check them out — get client references, and make sure that they have the bandwidth to support your effort.

Individual Consultants

If you have your data lake effort well in hand, but you need very specialized assistance for a couple of tasks, you can always go the individual consultant route. Maybe you need help with the upfront planning and architecture, or maybe you need someone with Amazon Simple Storage Service (S3) or Amazon Redshift expertise. Whatever your needs, individual consultants are another option.

Training Your Internal Staff

You can always teach your folks to fish for themselves in the data lake. Even cloud-based implementations require some degree of expertise, especially when the cloud provider is primarily for the platform, which means that you'll still be doing the heavy lifting. If you have some sharp people in your organization who have a track record of successful implementation, why not train them in Amazon S3, Hadoop Distributed File System (HDFS), or even data lake architecture and component design?

Industry Analysts

You can't go wrong listening to what the pundits have to say. If your organization subscribes to analyst services from Forrester (https://go.forrester.com), Gartner (www.gartner.com), IDC (www.idc.com), or a similar organization, then you should definitely check out what reports about data lake vendors, best practices, and case studies are available to you.

Data Lake Bloggers

The good news is that anyone with a great "fishing at the data lake" story to tell can blog about their experiences. The bad news is that anyone can blog about data lakes, regardless of whether they know what they're talking about.

Still, you should spend some time checking out blogs related to data lakes. You'll soon know which ones are worth visiting on a regular basis and which you can just skip.

Data Lake Groups and Forums

Check out LinkedIn (www.linkedin.com) and other places where professionals gather for groups, forums, and boards related to data lakes. Just like the bloggers, you'll soon figure out which ones are worth spending time on.

Data-Oriented Associations

Most of the longtime data-oriented professional associations have evolved to include a strong representation of data lake topics among their conferences, papers, and courses. The Data Warehousing Institute (https://tdwi.org) and Data Management Association (DAMA) International (www.dama.org) are two of the most popular organizations you should check out.

Academic Resources

Even if you graduated from college a while back, you can still tap into the academic world for information about data lakes. Some of the most useful resources straddle the academic and professional worlds. The *Harvard Business Review* (https://hbr.org) or the *Stanford Business Magazine* (www.gsb.stanford.edu/magazine) are probably more for a data lake strategist and architect than a hands-on developer, but you can find some good "big picture" articles about data lake success stories and best practices. Other data-oriented academic journals, such as those from the Association for Computing Machinery (www.acm.org), present the results of academic research. The writing can be a little on the dry side (especially when compared to a *For Dummies* book!), but it's worth wading through some of the papers and articles about data lakes.

Chapter **21**

Ten Differences between a Data Warehouse and a Data Lake

In the beginning — say, around 1990 — data warehousing came onto the scene, promising previously unachievable levels of data integration. Data warehousing and its sibling discipline called *business intelligence* kicked off a new era of data-driven insights for companies and governmental agencies.

For all the power of data warehousing, organizations soon ran up against the limitations of what a data warehouse was able to support. In many ways, data lakes are the next-generation successors to data warehousing, overcoming many different technical and architectural barriers that capped what a data warehouse was able to do.

Data warehouses are still widely used and are often incorporated into an overall data lake environment. You should understand the distinction between the two disciplines to make the best architectural decisions for your organization.

Types of Data Supported

A data warehouse almost always contains *structured data* (numbers, fixed-length and relatively short strings of characters, and dates). You typically store this structured data in a relational database or maybe in some sort of multidimensional database that is commonly known as a *cube*.

A data lake will also contain structured data, but it will almost always contain *semi-structured data* (such as emails, blogs, full documents, or tweets and other social media posts). Even better, you'll also find *unstructured data* (such as images, audio, and video) in a data lake.

Because of the broader types of data in a data lake versus a data warehouse, the data lake needs to make use of big data technology for data storage. You may still find relational databases and cubes within an overall data lake environment, but they'll almost always sit alongside big data.

Data Volumes

Data warehouses have definitely been able to handle larger and larger data volumes over the years. In the early days of data warehousing, a single terabyte of data was considered to be ginormous and was a very difficult undertaking. The underlying relational databases grew far more powerful and were eventually able to store many terabytes of data, resulting in significantly larger data volumes.

But as the saying goes, "You ain't seen nothin' yet." Big data technology is capable of storing data volumes that data warehouse planners and architects can only dream of. And because data lakes are built on top of big data technology, a data lake can store significantly more data than you'll find in the typical data warehouse.

Sometimes you'll hear about super-super-supersize data warehouses that store petabytes of data, but remember that these data warehouses are built on top of highly specialized database platforms that may be better classified as big data. If Shakespeare were still around and happened to be in the data game, he might tell you, "Big data by any other name will still store phenomenally large amounts of data."

Different Internal Data Models

Data warehousing came onto the scene at the same time as business intelligence, and the two disciplines grew up together. The sizzle behind this combination was online analytical processing (OLAP), which is largely driven by analyzing data dimensionally. If you were using a business intelligence tool to access a data warehouse, you would ask questions along the lines of "What was our sales revenue last month, broken down by customer segment, by product line, and by territory?"

TECHNICAL STUFF

To support OLAP, you would organize the data in your data warehouse according to *measurements* (commonly known as *facts*) and the various dimensions that apply to each measurement. If you were using a relational database, you would build a star schema or maybe a snowflake schema.

In a data lake, you may still have some of your data organized dimensionally. But most of your data, especially semi-structured and unstructured data, will be stored using some other model.

For example, if your data lake uses Hadoop as a platform, most of your data will be stored in the Hadoop Distributed File System (HDFS). If you build your data lake in the Amazon Web Services (AWS) environment, much of your data will be in Amazon Simple Storage Service (S3) buckets, at least initially, before it finds its way into other data services.

Architecture and Topology

The original idea behind a data warehouse was "one-stop-shopping" for analytical data, and this concept was supported through a single centralized relational database. Over time, data warehousing evolved to more of a component-based approach, with multiple underlying data marts linked together and exchanging data in an architected manner.

Eventually, as relational databases grew more powerful, you would go "back to the future" and build a later-generation data warehouse in a centralized manner, using a single relational database rather than a series of integrated data marts.

Data lakes, however, are inherently decentralized and distributed. This decentralization is largely because of the underlying cloud platforms. Even components that may appear to be logically centralized have their data distributed across dozens or hundreds or even thousands of servers.

ETL versus ELT

You load and refresh a data warehouse through extraction, transformation, and loading (ETL). ETL requires significant upfront data analysis for you to fully understand the structures, business rules, and other nuances that come with the data you're going to store. You need to have your databases all set up to receive the incoming data, with all your fields set to the proper data types and sizes.

You load and refresh a data lake through extraction, loading, and transformation (ELT). With the ELT model, you blast as much data into the data lake as fast as you can, without having to worry about the upfront analysis and setting up your database fields. You'll still have to do that analysis eventually as part of the T (transformation) step, but you can wait until later and do so when the data is already staged in your data lake.

Data Latency

You typically execute your ETL for your data warehouse in some sort of batch mode — every day, every couple of hours, every 20 minutes, or on some other time interval. At each refresh point, you'll bring in new and changed data since the previous data warehouse refresh.

The ELT model of data lakes allows you to stream — or blast — data in as quickly as it's created in some source system. With data lakes, you typically have less *latency* (time delay) than you do with a data warehouse, meaning that data is available more rapidly for analytics, data-driven decision-making, and then taking data-driven actions.

Analytical Uses

You use a data warehouse to support "tell me what happened" data-driven insights. Essentially, a data warehouse serves as a rearview mirror into the past, telling its story through data. You deal in cold, hard facts, rather than hypotheses about what's likely to happen.

Even low-latency data warehouses still deal in the same types of cold, hard facts, though they're able to answer questions along the lines of "tell me what's happening right now."

A data lake can still answer "tell me what happened" and "tell me what's likely to happen" questions, but it also supports modern analytics that are largely predictive and exploratory in nature. You can answer questions that fit the mold of "tell me what's likely to happen" or "tell me something interesting and important out of all this data." You search for hidden patterns that may or may not be significant. You can even rewrite history by asking "tell me what likely would've happened if we had done something different."

Incorporating New Data Sources

The ELT model allows you to identify a new data source and quickly load the raw data into the bronze zone of the data lake. You don't need to profile and understand the data first; you can just stream or blast the data into the data lake, and it'll be all ready for you when you want to cleanse and refine it for your analytics.

With a data warehouse, you need to first understand the data that you want to add so you can set up the relational database tables where the data will be stored and accessed. Why? Because of the ETL model that the data warehouse uses. You can't just "load and go" with a data warehouse.

User Communities

Business users from all types of organizations around a company — finance, marketing, sales, human resources, supply chain, product management, you name it! — will access a data warehouse. For the most part, what they get will be finished products: ready-to-go reports or light analytics that they manipulate to drill into for more detail or abstract to less detail.

Who uses a data lake? Pretty much anybody! For the most part, anyone who would access a data warehouse for reports and other light analytics would also use a data lake. However, data scientists also spend lots of time working with a data lake, often grabbing gobs of data rather than predetermined reports and analytics. The practitioners of machine learning, artificial intelligence, and pretty much any form of advanced analytics will be right at home splashing around the data lake.

Hosting

You'll find some newer data warehouses hosted in the cloud, if that's the path that their organization's platform planners settled on for their overall hosting strategy. Older data warehouses are almost always hosted on-premises, in an organization's data center.

You would definitely be going against the grain if you were to build a data lake today that you host in your organization's data center rather than in the cloud. Some early-generation data lakes from the early 2010s that were largely built on the HDFS may be on-premises instead of in the cloud, but the overwhelming trend toward AWS and Microsoft Azure, in particular, has tightly linked data lakes with cloud platforms.

Index

Microsoft Azure SQL Database, 231–232

Microsoft Dynamics 365, 56

Microsoft SQL Server (MySQL), 53, 75, 161

MicroStrategy, 38

midrange systems, 190

migration paths, establishing for data warehouses, 37–39

minicomputers, 190

ML (machine learning), 221, 328

MongoDB, 208

monolithic bronze zone, 108–109

monolithic data lakes, 77

MSK (Amazon Managed Streaming for Apache Kafka), 100

Mueller, John Paul (author)
Machine Learning For Dummies, 2nd Edition, 230

multi-component bronze zone, 109–111

multiple-component data lake architecture, 11

MySQL (Microsoft SQL Server), 53, 75, 161

N

NextGen, 172

NoSQL databases, 53

O

object stores, 75–77, 142–143

object-extended relational databases, 14

ODBC (Open Database Connectivity), 164

ODS (operational data store), 213

OLAP (online analytical processing), 143, 164, 328, 347

OLTP (online transaction processing), 328

one-direction streaming, 229

one-off data feed, 171

one-stop shopping, with data lakes, 27

online analytical processing (OLAP), 143, 164, 328, 347

online transaction processing (OLTP), 328

on-premises hosting, 191–192

on-the-fly analytics, 138

Oozie, 234

Open Database Connectivity (ODBC), 164

open-source solutions
about, 70
for data streaming, 100, 103

operating data, 184

operational data, 14–16

operational data store (ODS), 213

Oracle, 198

Oracle's Exadata, 90

ORC, 209

ordering data, 336

P

PaaS (platform as a service), 197, 218

Parquet, 164, 209

passive analytics user, 162–163

patient administration data, 183

patient bedside care data, 183, 184

PCs (microcomputers), 190

Pentaho, 63

persistence
Azure Event Hubs and, 228
in data streaming, 113–115

persistence policies, 122

persistent streaming data, 144–145

personally identifiable information (PII), 158

pharmacy data, 183

PHM (population health management), 176

Pierson, Lillian (author)
Data Science For Dummies, 2nd Edition, 230

remediation strategy
  about, 259–260
  defining critical success factors, 279–282
  establishing timelines, 275–279
  gap analysis, 264–267
  identifying resolutions, 267–275
  setting key objectives, 260–264
  setting the stage for success, 284
Remember icon, 4
repairing data lakes, 270–274
resettling data warehouses, 39
resolutions, identifying, 267–275
resource clashes, 278–279
resources, Internet
  Accenture, 342
  Amazon, 341
  Apache Spark, 328
  AWS Data Exchange, 93
  Azure Databricks, 226
  Cheat Sheet, 4
  Computing Machinery, 344
  Data Management Association (DAMA)
    International, 343
  Data Warehousing Institute, 343
  databases, 214
  Deloitte, 342
  Delta Lake, 328
  Forrester, 343
  Gartner, 343
  Harvard Business Review, 344
  IBM Services, 342
  IDC, 343
  LinkedIn, 343
  Microsoft, 341
  Stanford Business Magazine, 344
retaining raw data, 129–133
retiring
  data marts, 32–33, 337

  data warehouses, 38
return on investment (ROI), 280
rideshares, 240–242
ROI (return on investment), 280
role-based data lake access, 160–161

S

S3 (Amazon Simple Storage Service)
  about, 10, 69, 75–77, 108, 112, 134–135,
    143, 154, 174, 200–203, 215
  Amazon Kinesis Data Firehose and,
    207–208
  buckets, 209
S3-IA (Amazon S3-Infrequent Access), 135
SaaS (software as a service), 192, 195, 197
Salesforce, 192
sandbox
  about, 18, 20–21, 151
  architectural options, 154–155
  data and, 155–158
  developing analytical models in, 152–153
  hospital example, 184–185
SAP S4/HANA, 56, 90, 198
scalability, 10
schema on read paradigm, 57
semi-structured data, 14, 305, 346
sequencing data lake repairs, 276–278
setting
  key objectives, 260–264
  timelines, 275–279
setup
  AWS Lake Formation blueprint, 205–206
  Microsoft Azure, 218–221
  role-based data lake access, 160–161
  usage-style data lake access, 161–162
shortfalls, identifying and prioritizing,
    266–267
Siebel, 192

silver zone
about, 18, 19, 91, 121–122
Amazon S3 and, 202
coordinating with bronze and gold zones, 111–113
coordinating with gold zone, 137–138
data in, 273
enhancing raw data, 122–124
enriching raw data, 125–126
impacting, 128–133
master data, 126–128
refining raw data, 124–125
storage options in, 134–137
simultaneous equations, 70
Slack, 248
slashes, in filenames, 201
snowflake schema, 38
software as a service (SaaS), 192, 195, 197
specialized data stores, 145–146
speed, of data streaming, 45–46, 57–58
speed layer, in lambda architecture, 106
split-streaming data, 87–89, 102
Splunk, 208
spreadmarts, 308–309
SQL Azure Analysis Services (SSAS), 233
SQL Server Integration Services (SSIS), 220, 232–233
SQL Server Reporting Services (SSRS), 233
Sqoop, 234
SSAS (SQL Azure Analysis Services), 233
SSIS (SQL Server Integration Services), 220, 232–233
SSRS (SQL Server Reporting Services), 233
staging layer, in data warehouses, 78, 84, 85–87

Stanford Business Magazine, 344
star schema, 38
Starburst, 69
storing
data, 74–82
data in bronze zone, 108–113
data in silver zone, 134–137
streaming data
about, 45–46, 99–103, 178–181
batch external data feeds *versus,* 91–92
how it works, 104–105
persistence in, 113–115
supplementing with batch data, 103–104
stream/streaming analytics, 115
strengthening analytics, 29–30
structured data, 12–13, 305, 346
subcategories, in gold zone, 141–147
success, setting the stage for, 284
support index, 247
surgery data, 183, 184
systems integrators, 342

T

Tableau, 38, 162, 164, 165, 317
TCO (total cost of ownership), 47
Technical Stuff icon, 4
technology, data lakes and, 62–64
tension index, 247–248
tiered storage, 136, 202, 224–225
timelines, establishing, 275–279
time-series database, 79
timesharing, 190
Tip icon, 3
topology, architecture and, 347

total cost of ownership (TCO), 47
training internal staff, 342
transaction semantics, 327
transmitting data, 82

U

unfulfilled analytics, 337
unstructured data, 13, 305, 346
upstream data, 119
usage-style data lake access, 161–162
user communities, 349
user layer, in data warehouses, 84

V

variety, of big data, 22
velocity
  as an assessment category, 265
  of big data, 22
  of data lakes, 253–255
vendor-enhanced open-source
  streaming, 100
vendor-supported solutions, 70, 100
volume, of big data, 22

W

warehouses, data
  about, 30
  data lakes compared with, 89–90, 345–350
  establishing migration paths for, 37–39
  flooding, 85
  resettling, 39
  retiring, 38
  split-streaming data, 87–89
  staging layer, 84, 85–87
  user layer, 84
Warning icon, 4

websites
  Accenture, 342
  Amazon, 341
  Apache Spark, 328
  AWS Data Exchange, 93
  Azure Databricks, 226
  Cheat Sheet, 4
  Computing Machinery, 344
  Data Management Association (DAMA)
    International, 343
  Data Warehousing Institute, 343
  databases, 214
  Deloitte, 342
  Delta Lake, 328
  Forrester, 343
  Gartner, 343
  Harvard Business Review, 344
  IBM Services, 342
  IDC, 343
  LinkedIn, 343
  Microsoft, 341
  Stanford Business Magazine, 344
wide-column database, 79
writing press releases, 312–314

Y

Yellowbrick Data Warehouse, 69

Z

zones
  bronze
    about, 18, 19, 91, 97–98
    Amazon S3 and, 202
    analytics and, 117–119
    coordinating with silver and gold zones,
      111–113
    cross-zone, 113–115

About the Author

Alan Simon is the managing principal of Thinking Helmet, Inc., a boutique consulting firm that specializes in enterprise data management, business intelligence, and analytics.

Alan began his technology career in 1979 while still in college, working on a prehistoric data warehouse that was hosted on an antiquated UNIVAC mainframe computer. From that moment, he was hooked on data management and data-driven insights. For more than 40 years, Alan has been at the forefront of disciplines such as data warehousing, business intelligence, big data and data lakes, and modern analytics.

In addition to working through his own firm, over the years, Alan has held global, national, and regional business intelligence and data warehousing practice leadership positions at leading consultancies and software firms. He has built both brand-new practices and turnaround situations into top-tier organizations, often working side by side with his consultants on critical client engagements.

Alan is especially known for being a "trusted adviser" to clients, helping them navigate through the hype and hidden traps when bringing emerging data technologies and architectures into their enterprises. His client work focuses on assessment, strategy, architecture, and road-map engagements for data lakes, data warehousing, business intelligence and analytics, and enterprise-scale systems, as well as rescuing and reviving problematic programs and projects.

Alan has also taught college and university courses since the early 1980s to both undergraduate and graduate students. He has authored more than 30 business and technology books dating back to the mid-1980s, including the first edition of *Data Warehousing For Dummies* (Wiley).

From 1982 to 1986, Alan was a United States Air Force officer, where he wrote software for the nation's nuclear missile attack alert system.

His "other other job" besides consulting and teaching is writing historical novels and contemporary fiction, including (so far) one title that appeared on the *USA Today* bestseller list.

Dedication

This book is dedicated to my wife, Erica Bianco Ellis, who has been my biggest supporter and inspiration since the day we met. Erica is my chief editor and adviser for everything that I write, as well as coauthor on several of my novels.

To put it bluntly: Everything that I've written in recent years (not to mention my life) is better than it would otherwise have been, all because of Erica!

Author's Acknowledgments

I would like to thank several people for their contributions to *Data Lakes For Dummies*.

Thanks to Steve Hayes, Elizabeth Kuball, and the great *For Dummies* team at John Wiley & Sons. I wrote two previous *For Dummies* titles way back in the '90s and was a behind-the-scenes uncredited coauthor of another *For Dummies* book in the early 2000s. Working on *Data Lakes For Dummies* has been the best experience of all of these *For Dummies* titles.

Thanks to Matt Wagner of Fresh Books, Inc., my literary agency. The first book that Matt sold for me was *Data Warehousing For Dummies* back in 1996, and he contacted me to let me know that the publisher was looking for someone to write that title. We've worked on many projects together since then. *Data Lakes For Dummies* makes the perfect bookend for where our professional association began a quarter-century ago.

And thanks to Amit Mudgal, a friend and former coworker, who served as the technical editor for this book. Amit is one of the most talented technologists with whom I've ever worked. When we worked together in the professional services organization of a business intelligence software company in the early 2010s, Amit was our go-to consultant for the toughest client situations. When he agreed to be the technical reviewer for this book — a perfect fit, given that he is now a senior vice president at a global company, leading their data lake effort — I knew this book was in good hands.

Publisher's Acknowledgments

Acquisitions Editor: Steven Hayes

Project Editor: Elizabeth Kuball

Copy Editor: Elizabeth Kuball

Technical Editor: Amit K. Mudgal

Production Editor: Tamilmani Varadharaj

Cover Image: © Who_I_am/iStock/ Getty Images Plus/Getty Images